ISLAM AND POLITICAL ECONOMIC SYSTEMS

EDITED BY
ABDUL KARIM BANGURA

cognella™
San Diego, CA

First published in the United States of America in 2011 by Cognella, a division of University Readers, Inc.

15 14 13 12 11 1 2 3 4 5

Printed in the United States of America

978-1-60927-858-8

Note: Some of the web addresses referenced at the ends of chapters may link to old, nonfunctional websites.

cognella™

www.cognella.com 800.200.3908

DEDICATION

To Humanity!

CONTENTS

ACKNOWLEDGMENTS

We, and hopefully many readers, owe gratitude to:

Allah/God (SWT), for all His blessings; without His guidance, nothing would be possible.

The numerous families to which we belong, for offering their encouragement and prayers.

CHAPTER 1

General Introduction

Abdul Karim Bangura

INTRODUCTION

This book is about how Islamic societies have fared under and dealt with the major political-economic systems that have operated throughout history. The political-economic systems examined include Mercantilism, Capitalism, Socialism, Social Democracy, Self-Reliance, and Contemporary Globalism. Each chapter begins with an introduction encompassing definitions of its major concept and their synthesis, including a brief statement about the essence of the chapter. Next, a thematic review of available literature on the system is presented. After that, three Islamic societies that have operated under the system are examined. In the end, a conclusion is drawn. Since the book is about various political-economic systems within which Islamic societies have operated, it makes sense to begin with synopses of the concept of political economy, the Islamic religion, and the Islamic doctrine of economics. These synopses may serve as background to the chapters that follow.

POLITICAL ECONOMY

What I present here is not new to political economists, from whom I have borrowed a great deal to write this chapter, and those who have read works in the field. It is targeted at the reader who is not familiar with this area of inquiry.

Over the past 30 years, Political Economy as a field of intellectual inquiry has witnessed a remarkable resurgence. Political Economy has emerged as one of the most popular fields of specialization for both undergraduate and graduate students, as well as the source of some of the most innovative and influential work by contemporary social scientists. The revival of Political Economy after nearly 50 years of neglect has enriched both public and social scientific debate. Given the increased interest and enthusiasm in the field, this trend is likely to continue into the future.

Political Economy is an area of inquiry that fuses postulates in the fields of economics and politics. The *economy* can generally be defined as the system of producing, distributing and utilizing wealth; *politics* can generally be defined as the set of institutions and rules that govern economic interactions. Thus, Political Economy has been ascribed two meanings. One group of scholars sees the subject as the study of the political basis of economic activities–i.e. the ways in which government policies affect market operations. The other group sees it as the economic basis of political action–i.e. the ways in which economic forces influence government policies. These two perspectives somehow complement each other, since markets and politics are in a constant state of mutual interaction.

People living in capitalist societies know that markets exist and are governed by certain principles that operate more or less independently of the will of individuals and firms. Any hot dog stand owner knows that an attempt to raise the price of a hot dog, for example, above that charged by nearby and competing hot dog stands will very quickly cause customers to stop buying hot dogs at the higher price. The hot dog stand owner would have learned a valuable lesson in what economists refer to as the market-clearing equilibrium point–i.e. the point at which supply and demand curves intersect; in other words, the point at which the number of goods demanded equals the number supplied. A central tenet in modern economic analysis is that, within carefully specified parameters, markets operate in and of themselves to maintain an equilibrium between demand and supply. *Ceteris paribus* (i.e. other things being equal), if the demand for a good far exceeds the quantity being supplied, the price for it will increase until the two are in balance. By the same token, if the supply of a good increases far beyond what is demanded, the price for it will decrease until the market-clearing equilibrium is restored.

If economies functioned like perfectly competitive markets, it would be relatively easy to describe and comprehend them. However, the freely functioning market is only a highly abstract model of what happens in the real world. A number of factors influence markets in ways that an observer can miss, if s/he focuses only on economic forces. Consumer tastes can change–how large is the market for out-door movie theaters today?–as can the technology needed to make products inexpensively (e.g., the photocopier), or even make entirely new goods that displace others (e.g., computers for typewriters). Producers, sellers, or buyers of goods can join forces to try to raise or lower prices. And governments can act, intentionally or unintentionally, to change patterns of supply, demand, consumption, prices, etc.

It is government's "intrusion" into economic matters that makes necessary to go beyond market-based, purely economic explanations of social behavior. Many market-oriented economists are continually surprised that government or interest groups have the ability to influence economic activities. Less dramatic are the everyday operations of governments, both at the local and national levels, that affect production, wages, prices, profits, etc. All of these aspects serve to shape modern economies and the functioning of the markets themselves. A thorough understanding of the suburbanization of the United States after World War II, for instance, will be impossible without examining government-financed highway construction, politically-driven patterns of local educational expenditures, and government tax incentives to home-mortgage holders. Not too many small or family-owned farms in the United States would continue to operate without government subsidies. Many Americans would be unable to attend college without public universities and government scholarships. And without tax incentives given to charitable donations, nonprofit organizations will not proliferate in the United States.

As a result, interest groups, politicians, and government bureaucrats have at least as much effect on the economy as do the fundamental laws of the marketplace. Over the years, social scientists, particularly political scientists, have sought to investigate how these political pressures shape governmental decisions and actions. Nonetheless, these social science models of political behavior are little more than didactic tools whose accuracy hinges upon many unpredictable factors such as underlying economic trends.

In essence, Political Economy as a field of inquiry is not new. As a matter of fact, until a century ago, virtually every thinker concerned about human society wrote about its political economy. Thinkers as diverse as Adam Smith, John Stuart Mill, and Karl Marx all believed that the economy was by nature political and politics was inevitably connected with economic phenomena. Not too many scholars before 1900 described and analyzed economics and politics separately.

It was not until the late 19th Century and the early 20th Century that the study of economics and politics became divorced. On the one hand, economists began to focus on the operation of specific markets and their interactions. By developing new quantitative techniques, economists were able to formalize certain laws of human behavior–for example, the law of demand and supply. On the other hand, political scientists began to concentrate on modern representative political institutions, mass political parties, more politically informed voters, and modern bureaucracies.

During the politically and economically troubled Depression years (1930s), the separation between the study of economics and politics increased significantly. As economists developed ever more elaborate and sophiticated models of *homo economicus*, political scientists developed even more complex models of *homo politicus*.

Since the 1970s, however, Political Economy as a field of study is continuously being rejuvenated. Two interrelated factors have been responsible for this resurgence. First, many academics became dissatisfied with the gap between abstract models of economic and political behavior on the one hand, and that between the actual behavior of economics and politics on the other. Consequently, these academics began to question the justification for a strict separation between the study of economics and politics. Second, as economic issues became highly politicized during the 1970s due to the disintegration of the stability and prosperity of the first 25 postwar years, political institutions became increasingly preoccupied with economic matters. While economic growth characterized the 1950s and 1960s, economic stagnation fed political strife and political conflict exacerbated economic uncertainty in the 1970s and 1980s.

It was only inevitable, for both practical and intellectual reasons, that social scientists decided to revisit the interaction between economics and politics in modern society. This rebirth prompted scholars to ask a series of fundamental questions and to propose a variety of contending approaches.

Indeed, contemporary political economists have not just simply reproduced the work of their predecessors. The separation and professionalization of the two fields did allow these scholars to provide new insights into earlier analyses. These new insights have spurred the construction of the new political economy, while at the same time paying attention to the earlier issues.

Scholars who would like to comprehend the political process must also take the economy into consideration and vice versa. This truism is a reflection of the real world in which politicians must pay close attention to economic development and economic actors must keep a close eye on political activities. A much clearer picture of social processes emerges when both economic and political affairs are examined together, instead of examining them as separate entities.

While this proposition is by now widely accepted, it is in application that agreement becomes problematic. Indeed, while government actions may affect economic trends, they can also reflect the pressures brought to bear by economic interest groups. And while economic interest groups may be key in determining government policy, it is the political system that may determine what the economic interests do. In order to get an integrated perspective of how politics and economics are intertwined, economic and political causes and effects must be discerned. In this effort, different schools of thought have emerged, suggesting different applications for the resulting view of society.

The Two Schools of Thought on Political Economy

Most studies in Political Economy can be categorized into one of two mutually exclusive schools of thought: (1) Classical and (2) Radical. Each of these schools possesses a unique set of simplifying assumptions employed to render society less complex and more readily comprehensible. The assumptions upon which each of the two schools is based lead political economists to perceive society in very different ways. Many Classical scholars regard direct investment in tax-free zones, for example, as a mutually rewarding exchange between entrepreneurs. Many Radical scholars, however, would see the entrepreneurs as exploiting the residents in those tax-free zones. Thus, a first step in studying Political Economy is to grasp the assumptions that undergird the two schools of thought.

The Classical School

While musings on the Classical perspective can be found in the works of early Greek thinkers such as Socrates (470–399 B.C.), Plato (né Aristocles) (428–348 B.C.) and Aristotle (384–322 B.C.), this school of thought is drawn primarily from the field of economics and can be traced to the works of Adam Smith and David Ricardo. These two scholars were reacting to the prevalent economic controls under mercantilism between the 16th and 19th Centuries. During this era, domestic and international economies were tightly regulated by governments in their efforts to expand their national power and wealth. Smith, Ricardo, and their followers argued that the philosophy that undergirded protectionist practice was faulty. Instead, these Classical scholars suggested that national wealth would be increased when free and unrestricted exchange is encouraged among individuals in both national and international economic spheres. As this view gained supporters in the early 19th century, many of the mercantilist protectionist policies were abandoned.

Three fundamental assumptions underlie the Classical school. The first assumption is that individuals are the principal actors within the political economy and, thus, are the appropriate unit of analysis. This assumption may appear quite obvious, since all social activities can ultimately be traced back to individuals.

The second assumption proffered by Classical scholars is that individuals are rational actors who seek to maximize utility. Rational action is generally defined as individuals making choices based upon cost-benefit calculations across a wide range of possible alternatives. And utility-maximizing is generally defined as individuals selecting the best alternative (i.e. the one that yields the highest level of subjective satisfaction) when given a calculated range of benefits.

The third assumption suggested by Classical scholars is that individuals make tradeoffs between goods in order to maximize utility. Consider the tradeoff between meat and potatoes. At high levels of meat and low levels of potatoes, some individuals–given their desire for the two products–might be willing to trade some of their meat for more potatoes. Likewise, if an individual has plenty potatoes but little meat, s/he might be willing to trade potatoes for meat. Therefore, according to Classical scholars, individuals increase their utility by exchanging goods with others. Those who desire meat more strongly than potatoes will trade the latter for the former. Others who desire potatoes more strongly than meat will make a similar trade. This process of exchange will continue until each individual, given the existing quantity of meat and potatoes, is as well off as possible without making someone else worse off. At this point, everyone will have maximized their uniquely defined utilities. Some will possess meat. Others will possess potatoes. And the majority will possess varying mixes of meat and potatoes.

The Classical perspective has traditionally been applied basically to the economy, in which it is assumed that there is no basis for conflict in the marketplace. Classical scholars opine that since market exchanges are voluntary, and if there are no barriers to trade among individuals, everyone can be made as well off as possible given existing supplies of goods and services. Classical economists believe firmly in the sanctity of the market as the allocator of scarce resources.

Thus, for Classical scholars, government should play only a minor role in the economy. They believe that many forms of government intervention in the economy would, intentionally or unintentionally, restrict the market and thereby impinge upon potentially rewarding trades.

Classical scholars do generally support the provision by government of certain "public goods": i.e. goods and services that are needed by society but would not be provided by private markets. For them, the government's proper role is to provide the necessary foundation for free and competitive market transactions: defend the country, protect property rights, prevent unfair collusion or monopoly, educate citizens, build infrastructure, and provide and regulate currency.

Of course, Classical scholars realize that governments often do far more than this, and they have utilized their theoretical techniques to analyze patterns of government activity. Expectedly, the principal Classical approach known as "public choice" or "rational choice" equates the political arena to a marketplace. For these scholars, politicians offer bundles of political goods when competing with one another in seeking political office; individuals and interest groups do likewise in seeking support for their preferred policies from office-holders.

The Radical School

The Radical school emerged with the writings of (Heinrich) Karl Marx, a 19th-Century political economist and capitalism's severest critic. The Classical school was given birth in response to the spread of Classical ideas in the 19th Century. Whereas Classical scholars saw the market as the mechanism that allows individuals to maximize their utility, Marx saw capitalism and the market as instruments used to foster the necessary conditions that create extreme wealth for capitalists (or bourgeoisie) and poverty for workers (or proletariat). While everyone may have been relatively better off than before, the capitalists were clearly expanding their wealth more rapidly compared to the workers. Marx rejected the claim that exchange between individuals necessarily maximizes the welfare of everyone in society. Thus, he saw capitalism as an inherently conflictual system that should be overthrown and replaced by a socialist system.

Like the Classical scholars, the Radical scholars also suggest three major assumptions. The first assumption is that classes are the dominant actors in the political economy and are, thus, the proper unit of analysis. Radical scholars identify two economically determined groups of individuals or classes: (1) capitalists who own the means of production and (2) workers who supply labor.

The second assumption suggested by Radical scholars is that classes act in their own economic interests. Similar to Classical scholars who assume that individuals act rationally to maximize their utility, Radical scholars assume that each class acts to maximize its own economic well-being.

The third assumption offered by Radical scholars is that capitalist economy hinges primarily on the exploitation of labor by capital. Marx began his analysis with the theory of labor value–the postulate that the value of any product is determined by the amount of past and present labor employed to produce it. Marx argued that under capitalism, the value of any product involves three interrelated components: (1) constant capital–past labor as embodied in plant and equipment or the new materials needed to produce the good; (2) variable capital–wages paid to present labor to produce the item; (3) surplus value–profits, rents, and interest expropriated by or paid to the capitalist. According to Marx, the capitalists' exploitation of surplus value denies workers the full return for their labor.

This third assumption leads Radical scholars to posit that since the relationship between capitalists and workers is essentially antagonistic, the political economy is inherently conflictual. For these scholars, surplus value is not the capitalist's "reward" for investment. Instead, they believe that it accrues from the exploitation of labor through the lower wages paid workers and the higher prices they are charged for goods and services they themselves produce. Since the means of production are controlled by the capitalists (a minority within society), labor does not receive its full return. This exploitative situation leads to conflict between the classes. According to Marx, the relationship is a zero-sum one: i.e. any gain by one class results in a loss by the other class.

Based on these three assumptions, Marx constructed a sophisticated theory of capitalist crisis. This crisis, suggested Marx, will ultimately lead to the overthrow of capitalism by labor. The capitalist system would then be replaced by a socialist system–a society in which the means of production are jointly owned by both classes, thereby eliminating the expropriation of surplus value.

Contemporary Radical scholars who study the political economy primarily focus on two sets of analytical and practical issues. The first of these issues has to do with the fate of labor in a global arena of increasingly internationalized capital. As multinational (firms owned by more than one nation) and transnational (firms that operate in more than one nation) corporations continue to grow and globally integrated financial markets continue to rise, the greater mobility of capital seems to have eroded labor's economic and political power. Should workers in a particular country demand higher wages or improved benefits, the corporations simply move their operations to other countries where workers are more compliant. Hence, Radical scholars believe that a more equitable division of surplus value is being significantly undermined as workers' ability to negotiate with capital continues to erode.

In essence, while Classical scholars see the political economy as inherently harmonious, Radical scholars perceive conflict to be endemic. Radical scholars adopt different assumptions and offer a very different understanding of the world. For Radical scholars, politics is determined by economics. Put differently, they believe that the nature of politics and the cleavages within and between societies have their roots in economics.

In sum, the two schools of thought lead to widely different explanations of specific events and general processes within a political economy. Their differences have spurred many debates in the field, some of which are contained in the following chapters.

THE ISLAMIC RELIGION

The name of the religion, *Islam*, comes from an Arabic root word meaning "peace" and "submission." Islam teaches that one can only find peace in her/his life by submitting to Almighty God (Allah–*Subuhaanahu Wa Ta'alaa*; henceforth, SWT: i.e. Glory be to The Most High) in heart, soul and deed. The same Arabic root word gives us *Salaam alaykum* ("Peace be with you"), the universal Muslim greeting.

Islam is a major world religion, with over one billion followers worldwide (approximately one-fifth of the world population). It is one of the Abrahamic, monotheistic faiths, the other two being Christianity and Judaism. Although Islam is usually associated with the Arabs of the Middle East, less than 10% of Muslims are in fact Arabs. Muslims are found all over the world, of every nation, and of every ethnicity or race. Muslim majorities are found throughout societies in the Middle East, in North Africa, in East Asia, and in the Pacific Islands. Large numbers are also found in societies in Western Europe, in Eurasia, and in North America.

Worship of Allah (SWT) is foremost in a Muslim's mind all the time. There are also five formal acts of worship which help strengthen a Muslim's faith and obedience. They are called the Five Pillars of Islam, which are discussed in the following paragraphs.

The first pillar is *Iman* or Faith. This is simply the declaration: "I bear witness that there is no deity but Allah, and I bear witness that Muhammad is His servant and messenger." A person becomes a Muslim when s/he declares this statement with purity of heart and conviction of faith. As mentioned earlier, Islam is based on faith in the Unity of God. When one declares the preceding statement, s/he testifies to the Unity of Allah (SWT) and to the message of the Prophet Muhammad (Peace Be Upon Him; henceforth, PBUH). When one bears witness that Muhammad (PBUH) is Allah's (SWT) messenger, s/he confirms that all of the prophets (PBUT) before him were also His messengers–Allah (SWT) is One, and His message is one.

The second pillar is S*alat* or Prayer. Formal prayer is the most important act of worship; it is humankind's connection to Allah (SWT) through which one gathers strength, guidance and peace of mind. Islam prescribes five formal prayers daily, through which Muslims manifest their belief, taking time out of their busy day to remember Allah (SWT) and renew the effort to follow His guidance. Five times each day (dawn or *Fajr*, noon or *Zuhr*, afternoon or *Asr*, sunset or *Maghrib*, and evening or *Isha*'a), Muslims rise, cleanse with water, and present themselves directly before Allah (SWT) for prayer. During the month of *Ramadan*, when Muslims fast (discussed later), a sixth prayer called *Taraveeh* is required at night to declare one's intention to fast the following day.

Far from being a ritualistic and mindless activity, prayer constantly reminds Muslims of the purpose of life itself and refreshes their faith in Allah (SWT). They go back to their wordly affairs conscious of their duties and strengthened against sin. Prayers said in congregation bond Muslims together in love and personhood. Prayer also symbolizes the equality of believers; there is no hierarchy, and all worshipers stand side-by-side in rows and bow only to Allah (SWT).

Aside from the five formal prayers each day, Muslims begin and complete every activity with Allah (SWT) being omnipresent in their minds. The word *Bismillah* ("In the name of Allah") precedes every action, and the word *Alhamdilillah* ("Thanks be to Allah") completes it. Muslims also make private supplications, and words in praise of Allah (SWT) fall constantly off their lips.

The third pillar is *Sawm* or Fasting. Muslims are reminded in the *Quar'an* that "O you who believe! Fasting is prescribed for you, as it was prescribed for those before you, that you may learn self-restraint. Fast for a fixed number of days. ...Ramadan is the month in which was sent down the *Qur'an*, as a guide to mankind, and clear signs for guidance and judgment between right and wrong. So every one of you who is present at home during that month should spend it in fasting. ...Allah intends every facility for you; He does not want to put you to difficulties. He wants you to complete the prescribed period and to glorify Him in that He has guided you; and perchance you shall be grateful" (*Qur'an* 2:183–185).

What the prayers seek to do five times a day, fasting in the month of Ramadan (ninth month of the lunar year) does once a year. During this month, Muslims do not eat anything nor sip even a drop of water during the daylight hours. Each and every moment during the fast, they suppress their desires and remember Allah (SWT) alone. This places in them a consciousness of duty and a spirit of patience that help to strengthen their faith in Allah (SWT). Discipline and hardship during this month bring Muslims face-to-face with the realities of life and the suffering of so many throughout the year. The whole month is filled with increased devotion, piety, and purity of mind, soul and body.

The fourth pillar is *Zakat* or Almsgiving. Every Muslim whose financial conditions are above a certain specified minimum must pay annually at least 2.5% of her/his savings to a deserving, needy person, a new convert to Islam, a traveler, or someone overwhelmed by debts. This fosters in a Muslim the quality of sacrifice and rids her/him of selfishness, greed and vanity. As all wealth is a gift from Allah (SWT), one has the duty to help his/her needy sisters and brethren when s/he is able.

The fifth pillar is *Hajj* or Pilgrimage. At least once in her/his lifetime, a Muslim who is financially and physically able must go on the pilgrimage to Mecca, Saudi Arabia, during the month of *Hajj* (twelfth month of the lunar year). Mecca is the spiritual center of the Muslim world. It was there that Abraham (PBUH) built the first house of worship (the *Kaaba*), towards which all Muslims everywhere in the world would face in unity in their daily prayers. "The first House of worship appointed for men was that at Bakka (Mecca), full of blessing and of guidance for all the worlds. Its Signs are manifest–the Station of Abraham–whoever enters it attains security. Pilgrimage thereto is a duty men owe to Allah, for those who can afford the journey …" (*Qur'an* 3:96–97). When this house was desecrated into a center of pagan worship, it was the Prophet Muhammad (PBUH) who cleansed it of its more than 300 idols and rededicated it to the worship of Allah (SWT) alone.

All pilgrims dress in pure white cloth and are required to suppress passion, refrain from any bloodshed, and be pure in word and deed. "For Hajj are the months well-known. If any one undertakes the journey therein, let there be no obscenity, nor wickedness, nor wrangling in the Hajj. And whatever good you do, be sure Allah knows it. And take a provision with you for the journey, but the best of provisions is right conduct …" (*Qur'an* 2:197).

The pilgrimage is a great international conference, wherein all people, kings or peasants, black or white, stand before Allah (SWT) as equals. During the ten days of the annual pilgrimage, several million Muslims from all over the world, of all nations, languages, and colors come together in the largest spiritual gathering of the world.

The teachings of Islam indicate a balance between the life of this and the world after. While often seen by some as a radical or extreme religion, Muslims consider it the middle road, as stated in the *Quar'an*: "Thus have We made of you a community justly balanced …" (*Qur'an* 2:143). Muslims do not live this life selfishly, with complete disregard for God. Nor do they neglect the world to devote themselves solely to worship. Muslims strike a balance by fulfilling the obligations of and enjoying this life, always mindful of their duties to Allah (SWT) and to others. Extremism in either direction is frowned upon.

God-fearing people should be the best in morals and manners. Islam forbids any action which infringes upon the rights of others or harms oneself. Forbidden to Muslims are dishonesty, theft, murder, suicide, bribery, forgery, interest and usury, gambling, lottery, consumption of alcohol or pork, backbiting, gossiping, slandering, hoarding, destruction of property, cruelty to animals, adultery, fornication, etc.

While forbidding these things, Islam enjoins upon humankind the use of all clean, healthy and useful things and asks that Muslims not deprive their bodies of clean food and healthy recreation. Islam also encourages marriage and stable family life, modesty, generosity, hospitality, respect for parents, honorable treatment of women, helping those in need, etc.

The law of Islam or *Sharia* forbids public nudity and orders Muslims to use decent and dignified dress. Muslims are called upon to practice moderation in this area as well. One of Prophet Muhammad's (PBUH) companions once said: "Eat what you wish and wear what you wish if you can avoid two things: extravagance and conceit." In dress and behavior, Muslims are to be modest. As urged in the *Quar'an*, "Say to the believing men that they should lower their gaze and guard their modesty; that will make for greater purity for them; and Allah is Well-Acquainted with all that they do. And say to the believing women that they should lower their gaze and guard their modesty; that they should not display their beauty and ornaments ..." (*Qur'an* 24:30–31).

According to the Prophet (PBUH), no man should expose his body from the navel to the knees, and no woman should expose any part of her body except her face and hands while in public. This is called "covering," and to keep these parts covered is the religious duty of every man and woman. Through this directive, Islam cultivates in its followers a deep sense of modesty, purity, and respect.

Islam enjoins humankind to control and regulate sexual desire and seek its fulfillment only within the bonds of matrimony. Marriage is a solemn contract and the basis of a stable family and society. The *Qur'an* describes husband and wife as comforts for and protectors of each other. Divorce, while frowned upon, is permitted in cases where the marriage is irrevocably damaged.

Throughout Muslims' lives, they must always be respectful of their parents because they suffer and make sacrifices for their children throughout their lives. The Prophet Muhammad (PBUH) once said that "Heaven lies under the feet of mothers." Muslims' duties to their parents come second only to their duties to Allah (SWT), and the majority of Muslim families have close, extended family ties. "Your Lord has decreed that you worship none but Him, and that you be kind to parents. Whether one or both of them attain old age in your life, say not to them a word of contempt, nor repel them, but address them in terms of honor. And, out of kindness, lower to them the wing of humility, and say, 'My Lord! Bestow on them Your Mercy, even as they cherished me in childhood'" (*Qur'an* 17:23–24).

There should be no place in a Muslim's heart for racial, national, gender, or other prejudices. The diversity of human life is one of the Signs of Allah (SWT), part of the beauty of His creation, and something to be admired and respected. As stated in the *Quar'an*, "And among His Signs is the creation of the heavens and the earth, and the variations in your languages and your colors; verily in that are Signs for those who know" (*Qur'an* 30:22). Righteousness is the only distinguishing factor among people. "O mankind! We have created you from a male and a female, and made you into nations and tribes so that you may know one another. Verily, the most honored among you in the sight of Allah is the one who is the most righteous. Indeed, Allah is All-Knowing, All-Aware" (*Qur'an* 49:13).

In dealing with non-Muslims, the believers are instructed not to be intolerant or narrow-minded. Muslims must neither abuse or speak ill of other religious leaders nor say anything insulting. "Invite all to the Way of thy Lord with wisdom and beautiful preaching; and argue with them in ways that are best and most gracious. For thy Lord knows best who have strayed from His path, and who receive guidance" (*Qur'an* 16:125). Muslims must not seek dissension unnecessarily; instead, they should live in peace and amity. Nor can a Muslim pass judgment on whether someone will go to Heaven or Hell; only Allah (SWT) is the Judge. "Those who believe in the *Qur'an,* and those who follow the Jewish scripture, and the Christians and the Sabians–any who believe in Allah and the Last Day, and work for righteousness–shall have their reward with their Lord. On them shall be no fear, nor shall they grieve" (*Qur'an* 2:62).

There should be a special place in a Muslim's heart for Christians and Jews, whom the *Qur'an* calls "People of the Book," meaning that people who have received previous scriptures. Muslims are encouraged to seek good relations especially with them, as they have more in common than with the pagans or atheists. When arguments or debates arise, Muslims are to treat them with kindness, try to find common ground, and if differences persist, to simply say: "Well, to you be your way, and to me mine" (*Qur'an* 5:82).

Muslims are absolutely forbidden from forcing their faith on others; this negates the very idea of free will and choice. The *Qur'an* says that "There is no compulsion in religion ..." (*Qur'an* 2:256). It is up to each individual to investigate religion and personally make a decision as to its validity and her/his faith in it. Muslims should not force Islam on anyone–the job of guidance belongs to Allah (SWT) alone. "If it had been your Lord's Will, they would all have believed, all who are on earth! Will you then compel mankind, against their will, to believe?! No soul can believe, except by the Will of Allah" (*Qur'an* 10:99). Indeed, it is this simplicity of its creed that has made Islam the fastest growing religion in the world today and also in the past.

Guided by the religion's precepts, the Islamic world has survived for many centuries; and its steadily incresing population has passed the billion mark (Said and Bangura 2004). It has been able to operate effectively throughout the ages and in all places, generating a splendid civilization in its early history. The savage wars of the Mongol hordes, the Crusades, European colonialism and neo-colonialism notwithsanding, the Islamic world has endured. According to late and renown Muslim theologian Muhhamad Abdul-Rauf, this survival bears witness to the existence of a working and adaptable concept of economy (1979:2).

As Abdul-Rauf also points out, Islamic precepts peameate all aspects of human life and divides all human behavior into five moral categories: (1) obligatory, (2) merely desirable, (3) forbidden, (4) merely undesirable, and (5) neutral. The judgment, he says, depends on how the activity bears on religion, human life, mind, descent, and property. His careful analysis of the precepts reveals the following principles (1979:2–4):

(a) Islam's goal is to guide man in his quest for salvation in the hereafter through fulfillment of the purpose of human existence on earth.

(b) The purpose of human existence is to serve God both inwardly and outwardly–by internal acknowledgment of God's magnificence and supremacy and by awareness of His presence, His munificence, and His call for human progress and righteousness, and by external compliance with God's teachings pertaining to ritual and non-ritual activities.

(c) The divine ritual guidance is to be accepted as given; it does not leave room for human choice or modification because it is the prescribed method in which the Creator wishes His human creatures to express their devotion to Him. The guidance covers the ritual declaration of God's uncompromisable unity and uniqueness and the validity of the mission of His Prophets and their scriptures. It also includes instructions pertaining to prayers, almsgiving, fasting, and pilgrimage to Mecca. Acknowledgment of these truths and compliance with these teachings inspires and reinforces correct orientation, certainty, a meaningful concept of life, and hope for the future. In short, Islamic guidance meets the spiritual and psychological needs of the individual and makes him a better social being.

(d) The non-ritual divine guidance covers the domestic, social, aesthetic, political, judicial, and economic arenas of human activities. It does not confine man to a single course with no choice, nor does it leave him a victim of uncontrolled greed, human vagaries, and stubborness. It grants man a wide range of choices and creativity, motivates him to satisfy his physical and psychological needs in progressive processes, but seeks to protect him from evil. In the particular area of economics, this is achieved in three ways: (1) A set of basic values–*hahud Allah* (the boundaries of God)–motivates and delineates the area or permissible economic action. These values should not be violated or transgressed, but within limits man is free, indeed urged, to use his intellectual and physical endowments for betterment of his life and his society. (2) Along with this value system Islam provides general guidelines that serve as a chart or a compass for steering man through the large area of human freedom in the sphere of the economic activities. (3) Man is also given a set of divine ordinances, some urging specific actions to promote the well-being of humanity and others warning against certain damaging factors. These specific injunctions are the foundations on which the Islamic framework of economics rests.

Given the preceding analysis, Abdul-Rauf defines the Islamic concept of economics as "a framework for motivated but free human action within the Islamic value system. That action must respect specific ordinances pertaining to economic life and take into account the spiritual and material needs of the individual and his society in a balanced and harmonized way" (1979:4).

THE ISLAMIC DOCTRINE OF ECONOMICS

Islamic economic doctrine is closely intertwined with the religion's concept of life, which is based on a network of interrelated notions of God, humanity, the relationship between humans and God, the position of humans in the universe, and the relationship between humans. At a time when the world of business and industry is desperately in need of ethical safeguards against large-scale corruption and widespread pollution and shortage of energy pose a threat to humanity, Islam's moral precepts are an excellent source not only for developing ethical guidelines for effective control of economic behavior but also compelling motivation for global cooperation in the efforts toward the salvation of humanity (Abdul-Rauf 1979:1).

As Abdul-Rauf correctly argues, economics is not a value-free, pure science; it is a division of the social sciences. Economic behavior is human action that seeks to satisfy human needs; therefore, it is bound to generate emotional vibrations. Consequently, economic behavior can be measured and assessed in moral terms. The belief that economic behavior is neutral has generated undue emphasis on material success, controlled only by the so-called invisible hand and resulting in the rise of ruthless entrepreneurs and the merciless exploitation of the weak (Abdul-Rauf 1979:1).

Included in the relevant values that delineate the economic framework prescribed in Islam is complete commitment to God, the Creator and Provider of all ecological resources, and the constant awareness of His presence even in the depth of material engagement. From the *Qur'an*, we read: "O you who have believed, let not [your preoccupation with] your wealth nor your children distract you from the remembrance of God. Whosoever can be so distracted are indeed losers" (63:9). And also from the *Hadith*, we read: "Serve God as if you see Him; for if you do not see Him, He sees you" (quoted in Abdul-Rauf 1979:4).

Appreciation of the wealth and all the ecological resources provided by God for the satisfaction of human needs is another Islamic value. As a favor from God, wealth should be sensibly treated, not to be abused, destroyed, wasted, or laid idle. God has provided humans with abundant resources, albeit scarcity is caused by human limitation. Humans must develop greater knowledge and skills and should strive to explore, to discover, and to exploit these resources in moderation for their own best interests. God could have made all of the needs of humans to be easily met; but without the economic challenges, humans would be idle, dull, and given to criminality (Abdul-Rauf 1979:4). As the *Qur'an* states, "If God were to enlarge the Provision for His servants they would surely rebel in the earth, but He sends down by measure as He wills. Surely, He is Knowing and Aware of His bondsmen" (42:27).

Wealth is to be regarded not as an end in itself, but as a means to satisfy needs, to provide sustenance–in moderation–for survival, for a limited term of life on earth, in preparation for a more meaningful and lasting life hereafter. To treat wealth otherwise, humans become materialistic, selfish, ruthless, and greedy and yet can never be satisfied.

As the *Hadith* state, "Whosoever makes material success his uppermost goal, God will make [the threat of] poverty ever present under his eyes" (quoted in Abdul-Rauf 1979:5).

In essence, real ownership of wealth, consumable or productive, belongs to God. Humans' temporal possession of wealth is limited and is granted by God: i.e. humans are merely "trustees" for a term. Realization of this dual ownership guards against dishonest and selfish tendencies that are often the outcome of the deceitful notion of absolute ownership (Abdul-Rauf 1979:5).

Despite the fact that humans are created equal, and no one may claim inherent merit over another, they are also created with different talents and are bound to attain different degrees of success. It is a duty of humans to accept their fortune, not to despair or to be resentful, although they are to struggle as hard as the can for their best interest. From the *Qur'an*, one reads: "And He (God), has made you the viceroys in the earth, and raised some of you over the other [in fortune] in order to test you in the gifts He has given you" (6:165). The *Qur'an* also states: "If God has so willed, He would have made you one nation, but [His plan is] to test you in what He has given you. So strive for good things as in a race. To God is your turn, all of you; when He will show you the truth concerning your diversity" (11:118).

The idea that material superiority does not entail higher merit is implicit in the notion of "trusteeship" and testing through wealth and worldly success. Since all people are created equal, righteousness is the only criterion by which a person's rank is raised with God. As a corollary of human equality, points out Abdul-Rauf, all people are equally entitled to the following human rights (1979:5–6):

(a) *Haqq al-Hayah* (the right to live): Encroachment on this right is a grave sin, next to disbelief in God, and entitled the family of the victim to claim capital punishment.

(b) *Haqq al-Hurriyyah* (the right of liberty): Encroachment on this birthright is dehumanizing to its victim.

(c) *Haqq al-Tamalluk* (the right of ownership): This right can be legitimately earned through labor or it can be received as a gift or as a share in inheritance. It is subject to certain restraints including payment of alms and charitable obligations.

(d) *Haqq al-Karamah* (the right to dignity): This is another birthright that entitles each individual to respectful treatment.

(e) *Haqq al-'Ilm* (the right, even obligation, of education): This right leads to invention and greater production.

It is only in accordance with the will of God that everything, including the outcome of the planning and efforts of humans, happens. This Islamic precept, known as *qadar* or *qismah*, urges humans to plan the course of their activities carefully and exert enough effort and energy to achieve their goals. Yet, the desired ends hinge upon the blessing of God. The planning and effort of humans are not the sole factors that count.

From this doctrine, two things emerge. First, since achievement of goals requires planning and effort as well as God's blessing, Muslims should not neglect their duty to work hard to earn a living. Heaven, it is stated, does not rain gold or silver; it must be earned the hard way. Negligence, on the pretext that whatever has been predestined for Muslims shall come no matter what they do, is condemned as lazy *tawakul*, "forsaking one's duty." When hard work is accompanied by the belief in the role of the divine hand, it is called sensible *tawakkul*, "pursuing ends through regular measures while conscious of the need of God's blessings" (Abdul-Rauf 1979:6).

Second, should Muslims occasionally fail to reach their goals, they can surrender and resign themselves to their fortunes and accept it as an act of God without resentment or despair. Muslims must renew their efforts in hope and faith in God. This belief spurs Muslims to exert their efforts toward worldly success and sustains them at times of difficulty and hardship. It inspires them with a sense of satisfaction and contentedness, a virtue of significant merit in Islam (Abdul-Rauf 1979:6).

In addition to the preceding value system demarcating the area of free economic action, the Islamic economic framework calls on Muslims to uphold the Islamic virtues of truth, honesty in dealings, respect for the rights of others, pursuit of moderation, sacrifice, and hard work. These virtues must guide Muslims in their economic struggle through the process of acquisition, production, distribution, and consumption. Muslims must legitimately acquire the means to live through their labor and hard work. They must know that idleness and apathy are discouraged in their religion, which leaves nothing unexplained, even the manner of eating and dressing. They must scrupulously avoid all suspicious sources of income and never attempt to thwart the efforts of others. Moderation would guide Muslims in all situations. They are advised by Prophet Muhammad (PBUH) in the *Hadith* as follows: "Eat and drink. Dress yourself well and give away in charity. But there should be no extravagance or arrogance" (cited in Abdul-Rauf 1979:7).

Muslims' possessiveness and their concern to satisfy their personal needs must harmonize with their obligations to their society–their families, their ethnic groups, their neighbors, and the state of which they are citizens. The needs of an individual Muslim and those of society are intrinsically interdependent. Apart from their obligations to their families, Muslims should neither let their neighbors smell their cooking without letting them share it, nor should they let their children play outside with new toys unless they have presented their neighbors' children with similar toys. In addition to the *zakat*, Muslims must hand over to the state whatever it may demand from them and must respect its policy, which must be in the interest of all citizens. Reciprocally, society must offer its Muslim citizens security, protect their lives and property, and respect their dignity–alive and dead [a dead person is entitled to a decent funeral service, which includes a mandatory full washing, shrouding, prayer service, and respectable burial] (Abdul-Rauf 1979:7).

Welfare economy in Islam does not hinge upon increasing the aggregate welfare of the community by encouraging an individual Muslim to maximize his/her own interest and be indifferent to the interests of others. It is based upon the bond of universal familyhood in which the individual Muslim, in seeking to benefit himself/herself, avoids malevolence to others. In the *Hadith*, Prophet Muhammad (PBUH) says: "No person may become a perfectly true believer unless he loves for others what he loves for himself." He also says that "A Muslim is he who causes no harm to another, neither by hand nor by tongue" (quoted in Abdul-Rauf 1979:7).

The individual Muslim's spiritual aspirations and material endeavors must be harmonized. While a Muslim is admittedly a biological organism and social entity with sets of basic needs, s/he is also a psychological being with a divine heart. Thus, although s/he is compelled to meet his/her biological and social urges, s/he is also moved by his/her divine element and years to reach a state of spiritual elevation (Abdul-Rauf 1979:7).

The word for religion in the *Qur'anic* tongue, *din*, connotes a whole way of life. Religion is neither merely private matter, nor does it touch only the periphery of individual lives; it is both private and public, and permeates the entire fabric of society. Economic pursuits are meritorious, leading to both material sustenance and God's pleasure. Consequently, economic pursuits can neither be divorced from the spiritual objective–let alone be elevated over it–nor be separated from the religious content and become purely materialistic. In their economic pursuits, Muslims should strive to meet not only their material needs but also their social obligations, whereby they hope to improve their position with God (Abdul-Rauf 1979:8).

Islam discourages monastic indifference to physical needs and indulgence in sensual pleasure and the maximum satisfaction of human wants. It preaches moderation–not for either extreme. A want can be painful and disquieting; its satisfaction can bring relief and lead to peaceful equilibrium. Relief can be brought about through reasonable moderate satisfaction. Maximizing satisfaction–e.g., overeating and luxurious living–can result in complications and trigger other wants. Hence, the *Qur'an* and the Prophet (PUBH) abhor extravagance and laud moderation (Abdul-Rauf 1979:8). We read the following from the *Qur'an*:

"And the sky, He has raised,
And the balance He has placed
That you may not transgress the balance.
And establish the balance equitably and do not fall short in balancing" (55:7–9).

And the Prophet (PBUH) says in the *Hadith*: "The child of Adam never fills a container more harmful for him than his own stomach. If he must fill it, let him fill only one third with food, leaving one third for water and one third for breathing" (quoted in Abdul-Rauf 1979:8).

Observing the principle of justice and fair dealing is the overall absorbing tenet of Islam dominating human interactions. We read from the *Qur'an*: "And if you judge between mankind, do so with justice" (4:58), and "whose among you commits injustice, We shall let him taste a great punishment" (25:19). In the *Hadith*, the Prophet (PBUH) says that "Injustice is darkness on the Day of Resurrection" (cited in Abdul-Rauf 1979:8).

As the individual Muslim must be just and fair in his/her economic dealings with others, so must the state also be just and fair in dealing with citizens. Except for compelling reasons, state interference must be minimal. Unnecessary repressive measures should be avoided. Ideally, the state's functions should be restricted to the administration of public goods, the conduct of national economic affairs that are beyond the jurisdiction of the citizenry, and the general supervision of the market to protect against malpractice such as hoarding of food, inflated prices and deceit. An example of such supervision is the traditional post of *muhtasib*, who checked the weights and measures employed in the marketplaces and looked into cases of fraudulent practices (Abdul-Rauf 1979:9).

In addition to the preceding set of values that demarcate the large area of freedom of economic action and the tenets that serve as guiding posts, Islam also provides specific ordinances. Some of these ordinances are positive injunctions that serve as sources of energy or fuel for economic activity, and others are prohibitions that point out trouble spots that may wreck economic activity. Abdul-Rauf calls these ordinances the "Ten Commandments" of the Islamic economic system and describes them as follows (1979:9–12):

1. The first is the payment of the *zakat*, an almsgiving duty, amounting to 2.5 percent annually on income and saving. Ten percent is due on an agricultural harvest if irrigation was not at cost and no effort to the farmer; otherwise, only five percent is due. *Zaka*t also applies to commercial goods, some categories of livestock, excavated treasures, and mined wealth. *Zakat* ideally would be collected by the state treasury. Otherwise, the individuals responsible have to distribute it themselves, as is the case today in most Muslim territories. In either case, *zakat* has to be given to the destitute, to *zakat* collectors, to those who fall in debt to make peace, and to wayfarers or to assist in preaching the faith, in freeing slaves, and in the struggle for Islam. Unlike modern taxation, *zakat* is a flat rate and does not rise exuberantly on an ascending scale. Thus, it does not discourage working for greater gain, nor is it exposed to evasive or dishonest measures. Equity is achieved by encouraging voluntary charities, *sadaqat*, which assure seven hundredfold rewards with God. Moreover, in case of need, the state may levy some taxes on the richer.

2. The maintenance costs for certain categories of relatives must be paid–particularly for one's wife, needy parent, female children till they marry, and male children till the age of puberty. The wife's right to maintenance is due whether or not she has financial resources of her own.

3. The obligation of charitable assistance to one's kin, to one's neighbors, to orphans, and to the needy is denoted by the term *haqq*, which is an emphatic word meaning "an inalienable right." Charity is better paid in a concealed manner, however, so as not to embarrass the receiver. He is also to be treated politely.

4. Working hard to earn one's own living and the living of dependents is highly praised. Food so earned is the most blessed, and the hand that toils will never burn in hellfire. Struggle for living is believed to be as meritorious as the struggle for the faith; and the hand that gives is better in the sight of God than the hand that takes. For Muslims, however, "labor" and "work," which are praised in the *Qur'an* hundreds of times, are identical. Thus, we are all workers and laborers, even though one may be employed or an employer, one deriving wages and another a profit.

5. A worker, manufacturer, administrator, or whoever should exert the utmost effort to make his product as perfect as possible. It is related that the Prophet (PBUH) said: "God verily likes to see any one of you, when he does something, to make it as perfect as he possibly can" (*Hadith* no. 1876).

6. The conditions laid down in the *Shari'a* law for the validity of business and financial transactions must be fulfilled. These laws make the transfer of goods safe and easy and facilitate the conclusion of economic transactions between the contracting parties. They also ensure the absence of vagueness or misunderstanding–whether the transaction is a contract of sale, partnership, employment, cooperative agriculture or irrigation, or anything else. In the final analysis, the goal is to reduce the causes of social tension or litigations and promote an optimal climate of peace. Writing down the terms of financial agreements is strongly recommended. The legal requirements as stipulated by the jurists pertain to the contracting parties the commodity being transacted, the price involved, and the terms of the contract conveying the acceptance by both parties, the wording of which should be categorical and unambiguous. The parties should be responsible free agents of sound mind; the commodity should be clearly specified, truly owned by the seller, and accessible and deliverable; and the price also has to be made specific. Goods so transacted have to be of economic value Islamically; therefore, contracts involving legally unconsumable material such as wine, pork, or polluting matter are not valid.

7. Pledges, trusts, and terms concluded with other parties must be kept. The *Qur'an* reads: "O you who believe, violate not [your covenant with] God and His Messenger, or the pledges amongst you" (8:27). "Let him who has been trusted [with anything] be true to his trust" (2:283). "Verily God commands you to return the trusts to their owners" (4:58).

8. The ordinances pertaining to the distribution of the estate of a deceased person among his heirs must be respected as laid down in the *Qur'an* (4:11–12, 176). The heirs include the deceased person's surviving spouse, surviving parent or parents, and all surviving children. In the absence of a father or a male child, brothers and sisters (of the deceased) may share the estate. In some cases, paternal uncles and cousins may also have a share. A person may not make a will which deprives one of his heirs or which favors one heir over another, nor may he make a will involving more than a third of his estate.

9. Usury is among the serious sins, and all usurious practices should be avoided. Debate over the question of earning a fixed interest on deposits in financial houses has subsided with the availability of undebatable alternatives with no fixed interest, such as investment in the newly formulated Islamic Banks (to be discussed later). Arguments that interest encourages the practice of saving or that interest is a compensation or reward for voluntary restraint from overspending have been exploded. The individual is impelled to save by a deep desire for financial security, and Islam itself encourages saving. "To leave your heirs self-sufficient is better than letting them be a social liability–stretching their hands begging" (*Sunan*). There are also those who save but do not invest in interest-bearing saving accounts. Moreover, although interest is claimed to be a reward for abstention, a rich man who saves cannot be described as sacrificing to the same degree as a low-income saver. Nor does this theory explain why wealthy persons charge exuberant rates of interest on loans.

   Prohibition of usury has to be understood in the light of the Islamic philosophy of wealth and the legitimate ways of acquiring it. Earning should not involve the exploitation or the hardship of others and should be in keeping with the spirit of brotherhood and cooperation. Condemnation of usury is in keeping with the Islamic prohibition of earning without effort or risk and with the cooperative spirit it promotes. Usury is a form of hoarding because it may impede the function of money as a tool in the exchange of goods, and it is inconsistent with the principle of human equality. The *Qur'an* reads: "And whatever you give to invest and increase your wealth through usury is not an increase with Allah. But what you give in charity for the sake of God, such givers are those who receive multiple blessings and rewards" (30:39).

10. Last but not least, there must be respect for other peoples' property and abstention from unproductive malpractice, profiteering activities, and disruptive transgressions, such as robbery, extortion, deceiving, gambling, hoarding, monopoly, and distributing harmful drugs or pornographic material. Earning through expediency and manipulation of the law–now common in our daily lives–is not legitimate. The Prophet (PBUH) once said: "It may happen that one of disputing parties is more effective in presenting his case than the other, If I should judge in his favor [under the effect of his descriptive presentation], let him know that what he gets is a place in Hellfire" (*Sunan*). Even when the judgment is made by the Prophet (PBUH) himself on the basis of deceptive evidence, it does not justify the resulting earning. Control emanates from the Muslim's inner conscience and his awareness of the watchful eye of God, not the fear of the court and its agencies from which one can easily escape.

These "Ten Commandments," asserts Abdul-Rauf, give the Islamic system of economics its distinctive character. The underlying concept is that the economic community is akin to an organic body, within which each cell grows and contributes to the well-being of the other cells. As the Prophet (PBUH) is quoted to have stated, "The believers in their mutual love and concern are like one body; if a part of it complains the other parts call each other to come to its assistance, sharing its pain and sleeplessness" (quoted in Abdul-Rauf 1979:12).

The preceding ideal Islamic concept of economics was fully implemented in early Islam under the guidance and leadership of Prophet Muhammad (PBUH) in Medina. It successfully survived the severe test it faced shortly after the passing of the Prophet (PBUH), as nations with different cultures and backgrounds came within the fold of the state. Drawing upon the wisdom of the early caliphs and their advisers and their long experience with the Prophet (PBUH), the guardians of the state were able to effectively meet the challenge. While they employed their judgment and the tool of analogy, they also relied heavily on the Holy *Qur'an* (Abdul-Rauf 1979:12–13).

Succeeding Muslim generations, particularly at the grass-roots level of Muslim society, continued to rely upon the Islamic values and injunctions pertaining to economic behavior. These Islamic tenets were inculcated and internalized by the recitation of relevant in the *Qur'an* and the repetition of popular phrases that praise the virtue of relying on God and emphasizing God's possession of all that is in heaven and the earth and the return of everything unto Him (Abdul-Rauf 1979:13).

Employing this system as a guide, Muslims held together the political reins of a vast empire, started an efficient postal service, struck coins (the golden *dinar* and silver *dirham*), built roads, canals, palaces, castles, and cities, and left behind magnificent landmarks. Muslims set up professional and trade guilds which cooperated in various parts of the Islamic *umma* and organized and developed their various skills in each locality. Their artifacts can be found in Islamic museums in the Muslim capitals, and their international trade left some traces in European culture, including the terms "traffic" and "tariff" (Abdul-Rauf 1979:13). That numerous languages all around the world have been impregnated with Arabic words via Islam is hardly a matter of dispute.

A number of factors forced Muslims to move away from the model set by the Prophet (PBUH) and the early caliphate, leading to the progressive erosion of the spirit of sacrifice and generosity. These values and injunctions have been progressively conquered by the powerful corruptive forces of greed and love for wealth, especially among the ruling and influential classes. According to Abdul-Rauf, the following major factors have crippled the Islamic economic system and led to the current confusion (1979:13):

(a) Political upheavals, starting with the introduction of the dynastic concept in Islam, concentrating power and corruptive influences among certain families and their entourages, and this was inherited by succeeding generations.

(b) The widespread devastations of the Mongol wars and the Crusades erased cities, demolished libraries and schools, and eliminated scholars.

(c) Ascetic tendencies arose, fed by the oppressive climate and reinforced by some misguided Sufi doctrines.

(d) European colonialism in recent centuries caused the fragmentation of the Muslim world and the loss of Islamic identity. Muslims were compelled to abandon their heritage in favor of European institutions and were gradually imbued with divisive nationalistic tendencies.

By the time the Islamic world regained its sovereignty, it had been fragmented into separate nations laboring under the heavy burdens of inequity. These entities are now struggling for their economic survival and responding in one way or another to the pressure of two competing systems: capitalism and socialism. Modified varieties of socialism have made inroads in most Muslim countries because of the ideology's attractive claim of egalitarianism and the discouraging association of capitalism with Western imperialism. The process of pressure and responses led to debates over the question of which of the two systems is more compatible with Islam. The Islamic economic doctrine permits degrees of individual freedom and state intervention but leaves the determination of these degrees to the wisdom and consciences of those involved, who must consider current conditions. This flexibility opens up Islamic economics to alternative options (Abdul-Rauf 1979:14).

In order to deal with the external pressures and the intricately entangled economies that have been imposed on them for centuries and that are based on alien values, the Islamic people have responded by employing three major approaches. The first approach is that of the centralists or traditionalists who believe that Islam can meet the challenge intact. The second approach is that of those who turned to the East in the belief that the Islamic principle of social justice is socialistic. The third approach is that of those who turned to the West and advocate capitalism on the ground that it permits ownership–a sacred right in Islam–and promotes free private enterprise, which is more compatible with the Islamic doctrine of individual responsibility (Abdul-Rauf 1979:14).

The story of Abu Dharr, a notable Companion of Prophet Muhammad (PBUH), attracted the attention of the advocates of socialism and even of its radical form, Marxism. In Syria, during the reign of the third caliph, Abu Dharr became quite alarmed by the misuse of the treasury and the luxurious lifestyle of the Umayyad ruler in Damascus. Abu Dharr advocated that any surplus of income over needs be given immediately to charity, and he substantiated his position by citing several *Hadith* he attributed to the Prophet (PBUH). According to one of these *Hadith*, while walking in the outskirts of Medina, the Prophet (PBUH) told Abu Dharr that "Should this mountain of 'Uhud be turned into gold for me, I would not wish that the nightfall comes before I have disposed of it all in charity except two carats" (cited in Abdul-Rauf 1979:15).

Fearful that Abu Dharr's vigorous criticism might lead to unrest, the Umayyad governor of Syria complained to the caliph. The caliph summoned Abu Dharr to Medina but was unable to dissuade him; the caliph then banished Abu Dharr to a lonely hamlet where he soon passed away. A *fatwa* (religious ruling), issued in the early 1950s by Egypt's al-Azhar University, the leading theological school, supported the caliph's opinion over Abu Dharr's (Abdul-Rauf 1979:15).

Aspiring to restore Islam to its original purity and escape from alien influences, the centralists or traditionalists have attempted to prove the compatibility and adaptability of the Islamic economic doctrine to the necessities of modern times. They developed the concept of interest-free Islamic Banks, modeled on the successful experiment in Mit-Ghamr, an Egyptian Delta town, in the mid-1960s. After long study and investigation, the first major project of this type was launched in Dubai in March of 1975. The immediate success of the Dubai experiment has led to a series of these banks in many Muslim societies (Abdul-Rauf 1979:15).

For the sponsors of Islamic Banks, these financial institutions are not much different from the familiar Western banks that operate in all Muslim countries. The only difference is that the Islamic Banks are not based on fixed rates of interest on loans or on deposits which, from their point of view, are usurious under *Shari'a* law. The Western banks, they point out, not only deal in money but also invest in agricultural, industrial, commercial, and human projects. Thus, Islamic Banks can deal and invest in such projects but without the use of usurious interest rates (Abdul-Rauf 1979:15).

Islamic Banks generally maintain three types of account: (1) non-profit accounts with very small minimum deposit from which withdrawal can be made at any time; (2) profit-sharing deposit accounts, with a modest minimum balance, from which withdrawal can be made annually or at shorter intervals; and (3) social service funds, consisting of gifts, from which payments are made in emergencies such as accidents involving members (Abdul-Rauf 1979:16).

Another relatively new financial institution is the Islamic Development Bank, which was launched in 1976 under the auspices of the Permanent Islamic Secretariat of the Foreign Ministers' Conference with headquarters in Jedda, Saudi Arabia. It is an intergovernmental institution designed to promote economic cooperation among Muslim countries in accordance with the *Shari'a* law. Abdul-Rauf delineates the following as being among the activities of the Islamic Development Bank (1979:16):

(a) participating in capital for projects;

(b) extending loans to institutions and productive projects in member countries;

(c) extending financial assistance in various forms for economic growth and social progress;

(d) helping in international trade between member countries and in the production of commodities; and

(e) extending technical assistance, particularly in training personnel, in economic development, research, banking, and other economic activities in accordance with *Shari'a*.

A related effort in international economic cooperation among Muslim societies is the creation of an Islamic Common Market that has been very slow to come into fruition. Under the auspices of the Permanent Islamic Secretariat, a memorandum on the subject was submitted at the ninth session of the Islamic Conference of Foreign Ministers held in Dakar, Senegal, in Jumada of 1398 A.H.–i.e. April of 1978 (Abdul-Rauf 1979:16). On September 28 and 29, 2004, a meeting held in Tehran, Iran to discuss the acceleration of the creation of the common market was attended by representatives of 50 Islamic countries.

ORGANIZATION OF THE REST OF THE BOOK

The rest of this book is divided into six chapters, each one dealing with Islam and a particular political-economic system. Chapter 2 by Ava Aprin and Matt Jacobs is on Mercantilism. Chapter 3 by Lisa Livingood deals with Capitalism. Chapter 4 by Arshi Saleem Hashmi and Jacques Goudeau is about Socialism. Chapter 5 by Ava Aprin and Meaghan Ehni examines Social Democracy. Chapter 6 by Mubarka Haq and Nicole Rowsell discusses Self-reliance. And Chapter 7 by Yoseph Nasser is on Contemporary Globalism. To insure coherence and cohesion, each chapter is divided into four sections: (1) an introduction encompassing what the chapter is about, a definition of the political-economic system and its essence; (2) a review of existing works on the system stating their similarities, differences, strengths and weaknesses, and how the chapter adds to them; (3) an analysis of findings on the use of the system in at least three Islamic countries and an assessment of the successes and limitations of the system; (4) a conclusion summarizing the main points in the chapter and how the system can be useful in promoting peace in today's world and in the future.

Together, these chapters demonstrate that Islam recognizes the existence of an economic problem which lies not in the scarcity of consumable goods but in the shortcomings of humans, who are so created that they must fulfill the needs of their animal nature. These needs impel humans' economic activities and creativity. The goal of the moral concept of economics is to balance humans' needs as animals with their needs as spiritual beings. In the harmony between these two aspects lies humans' true and perpetual happiness–no matter what the degree of their material successes might be. Thus, Islamic economics is a framework of a value system which defines the boundaries of the free area of, and provides a sensible motivation for, economic action. Within these limits, economic action is steered by the concept of a fair balance between human and spiritual needs and between individual and social obligations.

At no time did the dynamics of the Islamic economic doctrine lose its vitality, albeit it may have appeared to do so because of colonial domination. Despite the severe challenges, the revival of Islamic dynamics is manifesting itself in the development of the Islamic Banks and the effort to create an Islamic Common Market.

CHAPTER 2

Islam and Mercantilism

Ava Aprin

Matt Jacobs

INTRODUCTION

Arab cultures have had a long history of merchant driven commerce, living as they did on the trade routes between three great empires: Egypt, Persia, and later Byzantium. As Islam from the 7th Century C.E. onwards spread rapidly across northern Africa, Spain, the Middle East and Asia, Arab trade assumed an unprecedented global character. The principal force that shaped Islamic society was, of course, the religion itself. However, as early as the period of the caliphates, the simplicity of the Arab way of life was enriched by contact with the people with whom they traded. The geographic spread of Islam allowed for great social and economic mobility through trade, land speculation, and Islamic teaching. Thus, Islam, a civilization with no centralized rule, forged itself a period of almost unprecedented economic prosperity and influence. The merchants of Baghdad and other major cities bought and sold commodities from India, Russia, Spain, and Sweden. Carpets and textiles were exchanged for gold from Central Africa or furs from the Baltic. Maritime traders moved eastward while caravans moved west by land. Local rulers and Muslim governors worked to maintain an efficient road network to promote trade. Early Islamic trade provided the foundation for the European dominated future of global economics, including the system that would later become known as mercantilism.

Islam establishes guidelines and values that form the basis of the entire political, social and economic spheres of the state. Its teaching is regarded as a social structure, a philosophy of life, a system of economic principles, and a ruling order to which the

Muslim believer must conform. All Muslims believe that religion cannot be separated from political life, and a Muslim's life should be governed by the law of Allah as revealed to the Prophet Muhammad. It is the affirmed right of Muslims to be governed by the *Shari'a* and voluntarily subject themselves to its rulings. It is also believed that the prime reference for their conduct should be the *Sunnah* of the Holy Prophet.

All of these primary texts of Islam speak favorably of trade and private enterprise. For example, Prophet Muhammad urged pious Muslims to trade during their pilgrimage to Mecca. The Prophet himself was a merchant, as was his first wife, Khadija. Islam portrays trade as an independent endeavor and does not glorify the role of the state in commerce. While in concept Islam is compatible with modern ideas of a limited state role in the economy, it has regularly opposed the introduction of socialist measures in the Muslim world and expresses its preference for market principles, as long as they are consistent with "social justice."

The medieval Europeans essentially learned international trading from their Islamic neighbors, evidenced in part by the number of economic terms in European languages that are derived from Arabic, such as tariff and traffic. From the 1300s, Europeans began expanding their mercantile practices, resulting in a social mobility hitherto unobserved in European culture as well as pushing Europeans, as it did the Muslims, to explore distant parts of the globe. The voyages of discovery were entirely driven by mercantile ambitions.

The term mercantilism was coined by the economist Adam Smith in 1776, from the Latin word *mercari*, which means "to run a trade," from *merx*, meaning "commodity"" (Smith 1776:15). It was initially used solely by critics such as Smith. Soon, it developed into a theory that would spark many other changes to international trade and relations. "Mercantilism as an economic theory originated in the 17th Century when trading states were striving to accumulate economic wealth and, thus, gaining power by expanding exports and limiting imports. It acknowledges that economic forces and conditions play an important role in the international relations of each country with others" (Viotti and Kauppi 1997:356). It is defined as an "economic nationalist theory that maintains that world political relations are heavily influenced by competition among countries for resources, wealth and thus power" (Rourke & Boyer 1998:254). A nation's wealth was related to the amount of gold it could accumulate. Running trade surpluses while accepting gold as payments for the exports and services became national economic policy. Governments would play a role in the economy by encouraging exports and discouraging imports, especially through tariffs. In contrast to the laissez-faire approach of the 19th and early 20th Centuries, the mercantile system served the interests of merchants and producers. The goal of these policies was, supposedly, to achieve a favorable balance of trade that would bring gold and silver into the country.

Mercantilism is viewed as a time period when "rulers were hard pressed for money and needed more of it as it fell in value. The desire of kings and their advisers to force gold and silver to flow into their own kingdoms was one of the first impulses leading to mercantilist regulation" (Palmer 1984:117). Mercantilist society was one under which governmental control was exercised over industry and trade in accordance with the theory that national strength is increased by a preponderance of exports over imports.

> Mercantilism was characterized not so much by a consistent or formal doctrine as by a set of generally held beliefs. These beliefs included the ideas that exports to foreign countries are preferable both to trade within a country and to imports; that the wealth of a nation depends primarily on the possession of gold and silver; and that governmental interference in the national economy is justified if it tends to implement the attainment of these objectives. The mercantilist approach in economic policy first developed during the growth of national states (Lipson 1959:5).

The Peace of Westphalia in 1648 marked the emergence of the territorial state. This treaty gave power to the modern state at the expense of other political forms and soon became the primary political unit in Europe. This solidification of borders meant that the network of localized trading hubs that once existed across the discovered world were only accessible to those who centrally controlled them. As there was a rise in the powerful nation-state, there also grew the necessity to preserve the integrity of the state with a strong military. Money, or gold, was needed to strengthen the navies and the armies. There was also the belief that wealth was finite. The financial growth and development of one state was inversely related to the loss of wealth of another. "The precepts of mercantilism were the economic component of state building, providing much of the rationale and suggesting some of the procedures of national unification, seen especially in England, France and Spain" (Eatwell 1987:446).

"The government sought the material means of acquiring and consolidating domestic administrative authority and military strength for foreign excursions and colonization" (Eatwall 1987:446). Mercantilism fueled colonialism under the belief that a large empire was the key to wealth and that, in turn, the more territory a state governed, the more wealth would directly enter the colonizing state. Colonized territory would provide much of the imports of the state, thereby allowing states to focus on exporting the growing amount of resources through colonization.

The spread of Islam is what provoked the European resurgence through mercantilism. The threat that the Islamic world represented, both religiously and economically, placed European nations at a negative global advantage. From the 1300s on, Europeans began expanding their mercantile practices, resulting in a social mobility hitherto unseen in European culture as well as pushing Europeans, as it did the Muslims, to explore distant parts of the globe. The voyages of discovery were entirely driven by mercantile ambitions.

While many institutions of early Islamic trade practice carried over into the mercantilist era, there were notable differences in the overall philosophies of the two. By looking at the cases of countries that shifted from an Islamic trade system to a form of European mercantilism, the inherent differences and problems become apparent. Islamic commerce was fundamentally liberal in character, based on the concept of the universal enrichment of all trading parties. Mercantilism is based on a power philosophy, seeking the benefit of one party at the expense of the other.

In order to understand the implications of a mercantilist economic approach, three main questions must be examined: (1) What institutions carried over from an Islamic economic style into mercantilism? (2) How did religious practice change on the individual level, as the local trading system shifted from an Islamic economic style into mercantilism? (3) Is Islamic practice compatible with mercantilism and other forms of power economics?

The answers to these questions are critical for understanding both the past and present. Many of the deeply dividing issues between the West and the Islamic world that still exist today are rooted within the damage done during the Mercantilist colonial era. Likewise, in order to create a better functioning and more peaceful world, it is necessary to understand whether the West's present state of power politics can co-exist with an Islamic worldview.

REVIEW OF RELEVANT LITERATURE

Historical and modern surveys of trade practice in the mercantilist era have yielded broadly differing conclusions about its effectiveness and long-term consequences. Critics past and present have assailed both its regulation-heavy style of governance and the fundamental notion that economic prosperity is the sole measure of a nation's success. What is clear is that the practice of mercantilism left a permanent mark upon the face of the world. Even today, there is a clear distinction between the rapidly developing Western nations that chose to pursue an aggressive economic policy based on monetary accumulation and those elsewhere that were left to face the consequences of their legacy of economic imperialism.

Previous works on the mercantilist theory have revealed several themes that have been particularly contentious in the debate over the practical advantage and consequence of a "bullionist" economy. The most notable of these are the strict control of industry by the government, the maintenance of a favorable balance of trade, and colonization. By examining different perspectives on these base institutions, the role of Islam within their context becomes more accessible. This helps to reveal successful and failed paradigms of thought within the Muslim world and, in turn, indicates newer and more progressive ones.

In order to gain proper insight into the world in which Muslims lived from the 16th to 18th Centuries, it is necessary to look at the works of both historical and current economic theorists. Each of the aforementioned themes has fluctuated in its pertinence to the present throughout time. Whereas the implications of an aspect of mercantilism such as colonization was simply an ethical and practical side note in the times of Adam Smith and Jean Baptiste Colbert, its legacy has shaped the opportunities and livelihoods of billions of the world's 21st Century inhabitants. In that respect, the input of modern day commentators on mercantilism is far more valuable and accurate. This chapter seeks to approach the topic thematically and examine each of its facets in the context of thinkers from different eras.

"Accumulated wealth was vital to as well as a result of power. Wealth was intimately associated with specie, and the rising accumulation of gold and silver was taken as a reflection of increasing wealth" (Eatwell 1987:445). More bullion could provide a convenient state reserve. During the mercantilist era, there was extreme competition amongst states. States were at a zero-sum balance, "a concept in game theory that one side's gain amounts to the other side's loss" (Viotti and Kauppi 1997:366). The economic and political strength of a country was directly related to the amount of its gold reserve. There was this global race to attain all the gold the earth had to offer while still maintaining its security.

Commercial protectionism was one of the hallmarks of mercantilist policy. Strict state economic control had been exerted from the imposition of the modern nation-state system, which is considered to have taken place at the Peace of Westphalia in 1648. State control was manifested in a number of ways; most notably, there was strict control of imports and a very high tariff rate aimed at disrupting foreign trade that decreased the amount of wealth flowing out of the country. D. C. Coleman sums up this premise with Daniel Defoe's statement in 1713 that "nothing that is consumed at home is an advantage to national wealth" in his work (Coleman 1980:781).

The role of a central government was essential to the regulation of all the trade that was occurring during this period. The government played a tremendous role in both motivating the people as well as regulating them. Now that there were territorial divisions, there was also a strong sense of nationalism amongst the nations. With the cue of the governments, the people in many European countries were called together to unite as one. The government was using any tactic to promote activity amongst merchants and the overall population. It was a very competitive time period. "Under mercantilism, governments fought to steal skilled workers from each other while prohibiting or discouraging the emigration of their own skilled workers, who might take their trade secrets and mysteries to foreign parts" (Palmer 1984:115). The government support of the merchant class is what allowed so much prosperity in many textile fields of the countries. "A merchant backed by a national monarchy was in a stronger position than one backed merely by a city. This backing on a national scale was given when national governments subsidized exports, paying bounties for goods whose production they wished to encourage, or when they erected tariff barriers against imports to protect their own producers from competition" (Palmer 1984:117).

The relationship between imports and exports is referred to in mercantilist discourse as the balance of trade. "A favorable balance of trade, a surplus of exports over imports, brought money back into the country. The balance of trade became the barometer which registered the economic condition of a nation. The theory of balance of trade became the corner stone of the mercantilist theory of foreign commerce" (Lipson 1959:86). Jean Baptiste Colbert was France's foremost economist in the mid-17th Century and a proponent of using heavy government regulation to maintain this balance at a favorable level. He pursued an approach of strict protectionism, and it was due to the success of his strategy that England began to enact similar policies (Packard 1923:423). In 1651, the British Acts of Trade, better known as the Navigation Acts, were passed. "Navigation acts prohibited vessels of bringing in goods other than those produced in their own country" (Durant 1935:258). These laws restricted the transport of any goods or materials except on English ships and required the routing of all products through Britain (Sawyers 1992:263). This led to various areas being devoted to individual European hegemonies. Later, frequent skirmishing was common throughout Asia and along trade routes between Dutch merchants and their English counterparts in an effort to take over areas with valuable resources and luxuries (Irwin 1991:1296).

These confrontations highlight another characteristic of mercantilist policy, which is the expansion of both the merchant marine and navy. In response to the much more aggressive economic policies of European nations, the lines between trading vessel and military ship became blurred so that precious onboard cargo could be adequately defended. There was a need for ships, for exploration, as well as defense. The ship was the connection to the outside world as was a means for protection from the outside world. It was government policy throughout Europe to compel the arming of all ships engaging in long distance commerce due to the perils of piracy brought on by resource hording (Barbour 1930:290). There also was a need for men on the ships for both exploration and in a military capacity. For Example, "England used many incentives to the lower class to persuade them to assist in the exploration and defense of the country" (Durant 1935:172). There were bribes of nobility by the government, giving many Englishmen a false sense of wealth and nationalism.

Another critical foundation of mercantilist economy is its strict reliance on domestic agriculture. This was necessary in order to create a stable base upon which to support the poor within society. As the major dividends did not effectively filter down past the merchant class and aristocracy, it was necessary to create a self-sufficient peasantry. Mercantilists believed that "in order for the exports to exceed the imports, the country must provide for itself. Equally, if the country were to export goods, it had to make enough to provide in terms of trade as well as for domestic use" (Durant 1935:185). The protection of agricultural interests was carried out by enforcing strict measures protecting domestic producers from foreign competition. Not only was agriculture the largest employer during the mercantile era, it was also the largest domestic industry as well (Cain 1980:467). The most notable legislation enacted to defend the local agrarian economy was England's Corn Laws of 1815. In the aftermath of a terrible harvest that year, these laws were passed in order to prevent the collapse of the English agricultural economy because of foreign competition. The Laws succeeded, and they remained one of the most powerful trade barriers until they were repealed later in the century.

While these concepts were all controversial from the time of mercantilism until the present, the institution that had the most far-reaching and long-lasting consequences was certainly colonialism. "The foundation of colonies provided the means by which foreign commodities could become native to the mother country. It opened up the vision of an empire knit together by economic ties, in which each part sustained and nourished the whole, and the mother country and the colonies were made complementary to one another" (Lipson 1959:154). It is argued that the relationship was not complimentary; rather, it was exploitative on the part of the mother country. This is especially prominent when considering mercantilism not from the perspective of a Western economist, but from that of colonized people in the past as well as their descendants living today. One rationale for colonization in the case of England is the fact that it was not a gold rich country. "There was not a more effective way of compensation from a mercantilist perspective. The mother country can just oversee vast areas and watch gold and other precious metals flow into her country" (Eatwell 1987:446). Throughout the era, huge swaths of an area ranging from the Americas to Asia were carved out as sources of raw materials for the increasingly imperial powers of Europe.

It is a testament to mercantilism's simplistic concept of accumulation and export that its existence as an actual theory was not suggested until Adam Smith sought to refute it in his *Wealth of Nations* in 1776. He pointed out that practically, regulation within the economic sphere was against the interest of the common working class because of the collusion that it implied between the upper class that controlled production and the government. Further, he pointed out that international trade was a positive-sum situation, as mutual benefits could be achieved for both parties in an economic relationship (LaHaye 2004). This discredited the prevailing belief that a nation-state must succeed by accumulating wealth at the expense of its competitor.

Sir Robert Peel represented the crumbling system of mercantilism in the aftermath of Smith. He was initially a great advocate of the mercantilist school, being particularly interested in its quantitative nature and simplified philosophy of human behavior (Hilton 1979:591). Despite his rise to prominence espousing his belief in bullionism, he made a rapid political transition late in his career. This change became particularly evident during his stint as Prime Minister in which he overturned the Corn Laws.

Indeed, many scholars throughout the 20th Century followed Smith's lead in asserting that mercantilism was less effective as a method of trade than successive policies. Cain and Hopkins note the inherent inefficiency of a market of nation-states with export-reliant economic policies. If all parties disrupt imports with protective tariffs and embargos, it is impossible for any one economy to greatly expand. The colonized regions throughout Asia and the Middle East were not lucrative for Europeans as they already had their own established industries. It was not until the American colonies began to expand at a rate faster than their production capabilities could support that a market with heavy reliance on European exports was found (Cain and Hopkins 1980:471).

In her assessment of Dutch and English shipping patterns during the mercantilist era, Violet Barbour supports the proposition that the intrinsic cost of neglecting key markets for exports is far too great. She also points out that the expenses in creating an armed merchant marine were greater than building a peaceable framework for trade (Barbour 1930:287). Ralph Davis supported this latter conclusion in his assessment of English trade policy in the 17th Century, writing that "in these circumstances, the shipping industry had to grow much faster than did the value of trade; and by 1700 it was making very heavy calls on the nation's resources of capital and manpower." He also cites the fact that bulk cargos of raw goods such as coal and timber were often far more expensive to transport (because of their tonnage) than they were worth (Davis 1956:60).

There are, however, also those who acknowledge many of the concepts and base assumptions of mercantilism. In a consideration of European trade supremacy over the Ottoman Empire, Charles Issawi notes the nature of Westerners during the era as being characterized by "restlessness, individualism, skepticism, [and arrogance] towards nature." Despite this chilly appraisal of Western values, he points out that it was neither military strength nor technology that propelled the West above the Islamic world, but the aggressive trade policy characteristic of the mercantilist era (Issawi 1980:503).

Regardless of one's opinion of mercantilism's effectiveness, it is indisputable that the most devastating effects of these policies manifested themselves not in Europe, but in those countries upon which it relied for sustenance. Robert Schuyler quotes Josiah Tucker, a contemporary theorist and politician of Adam Smith, as describing the unnecessary militaristic infrastructure being set up at mercantile trading posts throughout East Asia. He cites large garrisoned forts springing up throughout the region, despite their inability to prevent local trade with the French or to even stem an invasion bent on seizing the resources of the colony (Schuyler 1922). This is an especially interesting revelation because Tucker was a staunch mercantilist. This indicates that while the establishment of trading posts in pursuit of resources was natural, the militaristic, colonizing character was not. This is further supported by Tucker's clear distinction of the posts as inconsequential to any mercantile aspirations.

In a general study of mercantilism and its underlying structures, Eli Heckscher comes to the similar conclusion that many of the negative aspects of mercantilism, especially in regards to its generally war-like posturing and ill treatment of colonies, continued to exist under the *laissez-faire* policies initiated by Smith (Heckscher 1936:53). He attributes this to the fact that both were rooted in the same philosophy of natural law. In a more recent study that draws heavily from Heckscher, Paul Rich echoes his conclusion that the behavior of Europeans under both systems was characterized by "amorality, ruthlessness, and a lack of humanitarianism" (Rich 2003:131)

This is a critical point to consider in understanding the role of Islam within the mercantilist world of the 16th to 18th Centuries. Clearly, the seeds sown by the aggressive mercantilist policies of this time led to both direct and indirect frictions between Muslims and the West that have continued today. Regardless, it is crucial to discern whether this European antagonism is rooted within the policies of that era, or whether there was something inherently incompatible between European values and those of Muslims.

The study of the mercantile socio-economic system is one that is focused purely on Europe. With the strong roots that Islamic countries had in trade, it is a wonder why there is no insight into how mercantilism existed in or affected the Islamic countries surrounding Europe. Much like the European countries, Muslim countries faced two coexisting needs. There was the importance of attaining economic stability and growth, as well as providing a religious balance throughout the race for power that existed in the mercantile era.

This chapter will, hopefully, give a broader perspective to the study of mercantilism. It will not only add geographic depth, it will also add a religious one. The growth of Islam was in many ways fought by the mercantile efforts of the Europeans. Islam, being the more recent of religions, although covering the past as other religions had, was facing the troubles of being such a vast society transcending new borders while trying to adjust to them. Islam spread through its pre-mercantile merchant endeavors. It made its way all the way to the far east and as far west as Spain. However, nation-states divided this vast entity into smaller entities that were caught up in the competition that was at the center of the mercantilist period.

Furthermore, this chapter draws upon three Islamic countries that were involved in the mercantile society. Each case study reflects the applications and implications of a mercantilist society in a country that is categorized as Islamic. The in-depth look at all the themes of mercantilism as they pertain to each country assists in attaining a more global perspective on the definition of mercantilism as a whole. Confidently, after this chapter, the definition of mercantilism will be augmented to incorporate a civilization that was in many ways founded on a mercantile routine.

ANALYSIS OF FINDINGS

As the trade policies of the mercantilist era were implemented, contact between European and Eastern traders increased to a level previously unseen. As Europeans relied on ever more aggressive means to accumulate resources, they found themselves commercially interacting with foreign peoples with incredibly different worldviews and economic philosophies. Oceanic exploration and commerce brought Europeans into contact with Africans, Native Americans, Chinese, Arabs, and numerous other cultures that had no concept of bullionism. While Islamic cultures ranging from Morocco to South East Asia had their own differences, they were collectively forced to adapt to the practices of Western traders over the period of time ranging from the 16th to 18th Centuries.

It is quite possible that mercantilism is the most fundamentally difficult economic system to which an Islamic society could hope to adapt, based on its inherent free trade policy. From Islam's origin, merchants moved freely from across the Middle East and Asia, relying on both imports and exports to acquire wealth and goods such as garments (silk and linen), spices, and grain. Prominent figures in Islam were merchants, including the Caliph Abu Bakr and even the Prophet Muhammad (PBUH) himself (Labib 1969:86). In the period running up to the age of mercantilism, the intercontinental network of trade was not something utilized primarily for centralized national gains, but it was centrally focused on providing goods and services only available in certain regions elsewhere and enriching personal wealth. To varying degrees in different regions, individuals acted with economic independence, both for personal enrichment and to fulfill the consumer-like needs of their countrymen.

The pre-mercantilist Islamic economic system that was prevalent to the east of Europe was based on a complex perception of trade that Sanjay Subrahmanyam characterizes as a "commercial nexus" (1995:754). In contrast to the Mercantilist tendency to greatly simplify all of economic theory into the rigid confines of bullionism, Muslims recognized the complexity of trade and the necessity of interaction with others. While it could be argued that the notion of commerce as confrontation that prevailed in Europe was a response to the Catholic-Protestant division there, it is a fact that there were religious and cultural tensions between members of distant Islamic cultures on par with that of any sectarian division in the European Christian community. The 15th Century Arab navigator, Ahmad ibn Majid, commented on the Malay Muslims that he met upon his journeys as follows:

> These are bad people, who do not know any rule; the Infidel marries the Muslim, and the Muslim the Infidel woman; and when you call them 'Infidels', are you really sure that they are Infidels? And the Muslims of whom you speak, are they really Muslims? They drink wine in public, and do not pray when they set out on a voyage (quoted in Subrahmanyam 1995:756).

Clearly, this echoes similar assertions made by Catholics and Protestants about the legitimacy of the other's religious beliefs and practices. Conflict in Europe ensued after its division into violently partisan societies that defined economic gain as the expression of dominance over the *other*, instead of personal enrichment. Islamic cultures in the East, on the other hand, recognized the gains offered by interactive and peaceable trade, as opposed to war and state-sanctioned piracy. Muslims did not consider competition to equate to resource limitation but, indeed, a means of enrichment through the trade of goods and raw resources such as sugarcane, cotton, rice, silk, and paper. It also led to the innovation and spread of new technologies upon which the foundation of the modern world were built, such as increasingly complex mathematic principles (including the introduction of Arabic numerals) and navigation by compass (Labib 1969:80).

As Europeans began to take an increasingly assertive economic posture throughout the first half of the 16th Century, Muslim communities coped and adapted in ways as diverse as their religious practices. These responses have had a definite outcome affecting both their current economic status, as well as the nature of their relationship with the West today. While the modern states that exist within the former boundaries of the Ottoman Empire, Mughal India, and Indonesia are in greatly differing situations today, it is undeniable that their interactions with European merchants between the 16th and 18th Centuries did as much to shape the lives of Muslims as any other circumstance since the times of Prophet Muhammad. Despite the fact that the Islamic experience varied, depending on geographic location, there are many critical aspects of Islam that can be discerned from the differing responses to the radically new perceptions of economy and sovereignty that Europeans brought with them. By comparing the reactions of three completely different Islamic societies during the Mercantilist era, many common patterns emerge, despite the radically differing outcomes that are now visible at the beginning of the 21st Century.

Ottoman Empire

The Ottoman economy and its experience throughout the mercantilist era comprise a particularly interesting example of how Islamic trade philosophy clashed with that of the Europeans. While many of the institutions of the empire were similar to those of its European competitors, the philosophy of governance was starkly different and eventually led to its domination. The Turks utilized tariffs, regulated manpower allotment, controlled land, and set industry quotas (particularly in agriculture) to a degree very similar to their Western counterparts. The use of these controls fulfilled purposes that were completely different, however, and proved inefficient at sustaining economic success after the rise of mercantilist policy.

Whereas European tariffs were oriented towards blocking any imports and maximizing exports, the Ottomans enforced an import rate of three percent, while taxing exports at 12 percent (Mardin 1969:262). The primary purpose of this was not for revenue, but for maintaining a high rate of consumption among all the classes. And unlike in Europe where economic pressure was placed on the peasantry by the governments' tendency to invest only in the merchant and artisan classes, the Turkish producer class found itself pressured to both meet quotas and maintain fixed prices for the benefit of military sustainability and as a means of provision for the masses. While this was effective in maintaining state control of the economy, it failed to consider the increase in agricultural production and innovation that privatization tends to promote.

Overall, to a far greater degree than sovereigns in Europe, the Sultan sought to sustain and enrich the lives of his poorer subjects. The lower of the two Ottoman castes, the *reaya* (non-military, non-governmental subjects), were privy to an honest concern for their well-being by the monarch, although this declined considerably under the increased pressure of European mercantilist policy. This concern was motivated by the Sultan's desire to act as a "father to his subjects" as a part of the Islamic practice of *hisba* (Mardin 1969:260). The use of trade to preserve a vibrant consumer economy for the *reaya* was not, however, just a compassionate government policy, but a tool for maintaining a stable balance of power in Ottoman society. Economic progress was not determined by accumulated bullion but continuity of the status quo.

Another key difference between the mercantilist and Ottoman centralization policies can be seen in the latter's use of *commenda* contracts. Whereas European trade tended to be government funded and oftentimes monopolized, the *commenda* system involved an often lifelong business partnership between a private investor and a merchant. In this relationship, the *commendator* (the patron) would give a certain amount of funds to a *tracator*, who would effectively become a manager and decision maker seeking mutual success. *Commendas* were the most prominent source of funding for Ottoman business ventures, especially in long distance trade. This arrangement did not come to exist merely as a convenient way of yielding competition and innovation, it was also deeply rooted in Islamic tenets of trade. The Prophet Muhammad was himself bound within a *commenda* contract with his wife Khadija (Labib 1969:91).

The differences and similarities of the Ottoman and mercantilist systems are very overt. Even in their similar maintenance of macroeconomic policy, the former lacked the level of micromanagement that made European policy what it was. Further, the Turks' more equitable reinvestment is contrasted by the West's constant financial reinvestment into the merchant and artisan classes. This was manifested on both the macro and micro economic levels. Halil Inalcik writes that although Ottoman subjects "did not entirely abandon the method of burying their wealth in the ground, the hints provided by [numerous] sources reveal that money should be 'set to work' and not left idle are the expressions of a real general tendency" (Inalcik 1969:97). This was echoed by the socially compassionate (and politically pragmatic) policies of the Ottomans.

By allowing the operation of privatized and competitive industry, the Ottoman Empire succeeded by creating the most consumer opportunity for its people and maintaining the balance of power for over 500 years. Unfortunately, it also created an economic system that could in no way compete with Europeans. By utilizing a tariff system that discouraged exports, the Ottomans eventually lost the financial resources that were necessary to maintain the social hierarchy that was critical to the empire's survival. In response, revenue was gained by placing increasingly heavy taxes on the general population, such as the annually increasing *avariz* tax which was previously only implemented in times of war. The process of economic collapse took place over the entire mercantilist era; however, foreboding signs were present from very early on. The first open revolt in Ottoman history took place in 1590 in response to financial hardships and the corruption that rapidly manifested itself as the Ottoman grip on government owned land collapsed, depriving it of its primary mode of maintaining the status of its military upper class, the *askeri* (Goldstone 1988:112). Over the next 200 years, Ottoman strength would diminish rapidly, as this class withdrew support and oftentimes defected to mercenary forces due to lack of appeasement.

During the mercantilist era, the Portuguese were first to arrive in India. From the beginning and throughout the 1500s, "the crusade against Islam and the winning of the souls for the Catholic church had been Portuguese goals equal to trade in importance" (Greaves 1990:411). In India, they competed with Indian and Arab traders and after the end of the 16th Century with Dutch and English merchants and their ships. "The Portuguese arrived well before the establishment of the Mughal Empire in 1526, they were a tiny handful with no effective means of confronting any of the Indian states of the south let alone the soon triumphant Mughals" (Greaves 1990:650).

India's experience throughout the mercantilist era was shaped by many of the same European influences as the Ottomans'; however, their pre-European economic structure was completely different, as was their outcome at the close of the mercantilist era. Like that of the Turks, the economic structure of early 16th Century Mughal India was agrarian and locally based. While the industrial infrastructure of the empire was extremely limited in comparison to Europe's, India had a similar agricultural production per capita, more land, and more fertile soil. It also featured one of the world's most advanced systems of irrigation. The primary crops harvested for both sustenance and trade were maize, coffee, and tea; and while the output may not have been as large as Europe with its more advanced technology, Mughal agricultural surpluses were actually greater due to a much lower cost of living for the average Indian (Habib 1969:35).

Long distance trade played a large part in the Mughal economy as well, with Indian merchants engaging in overseas business in Arabia, Africa, Persia, and even China. While there was government funded merchant activity, there were no monopolized Indian companies or firms invested with local political sovereignty in the sense of European mercantilist entities such as the English East India Company. The majority of trade was run by the traditional Muslim merchant classes that were primarily found along the Indian coast.

Mughal India

Just as the Ottomans sought out trading partners of diverse religious, ethnic, and geographical backgrounds, Islamic merchants of the Mughal Empire also embraced trade with others. While European nations shunned even transportation outsourcing to foreign firms, members of the Hindu and Jain commercial classes played a critical role in trade, notably as fiscal officers and agents (Richards 1981:292). Women from the Mughal nobility also were known to play a critical role in financing and managing trading expeditions by Indian merchants.

One of these noblewomen merchants played a signficant role in an economic and political clash that embodied many of the differences between Mughal and Western mercantilist economic behavior. In 1613, Portuguese privateers seized India's largest trading vessel on the Red Sea despite the fact that it carried documents assuring its protection by the crown of Portugal and was owned by the mother of the Emperor, Maryam-uz-Zamani.

A Hindu convert to Islam, she was one of the wealthiest individuals in the entire empire and was known for her investment in the construction of mosques, wells, and other forms of religious and social infrastructure. The Mughal emperor, Jahangir, dealt with the act of piracy in an unusually harsh manner by ending missionary activities in Agra, blocking trade into Surat (the largest Indian port), seizing the Portuguese trading post of Daman, and suspending all allowances to Portuguese priests in all of India. This response occurred firstly because it contradicted the policies of free trade and fair competition, and secondly because of the violation of Maryam-uz-Zamani's honor as a Muslim woman (Findly 1988:233).

Whereas mercantilist policies played the central role in the collapse of the Ottoman Empire, the arrival of colonialism in Southeast Asia at the beginning of the 18th Century and the subsequent fall of the Mughal Empire into British colonial dominion are more closely related to internal factors. Aziz Ahmad attributes this collapse to ineffective policy towards the Empire's Hindu population (Ahmad 1976:148). Due to the domestic roots of Mughal failure, analysis of the relationship between mercantilism and Indian trade policy is most useful not in discerning clues to the end of self-determination in that part of the world, but instead locating where the fundamental friction between Islamic values and aggressive Western trade policy lie. The case of Maryam-uz Zamani shows that taking unfair and antagonistic economic actions (in this case, state-condoned piracy) will not be met with infinite tolerance by sovereign Islamic entities such as the Mughal Empire.

At the fall of the Mughal Empire in 1717, the government that the British East India Company created was one that was initiated by the need for the company to protect its interests. The company survived due to the security created for trade goods in storage and in transit and could offer its Indian partners the same security (Greaves 1990:655). Because the fall of the mighty Mughal Empire had devastating administrative and security consequences, the military support provided by Britain attracted many merchants. Proving the critical nature of economic policy and other more peaceful processes of government, it has been said that "Mughal attention was concentrated on military conquest, which meant mounting demands for revenue but also decreasing attention to normal administration or its supervision" (Greaves 1990:475). Although the Mughal Empire was at one time as wealthy and as large as all of Europe combined, it concentrated entirely on obtaining revenue and spent far too little time organizing a system to generate production. India's attempt to compete in a mercantilist society was stifled by the lack of understanding and structuring that was necessary to benefit in every aspect that mercantilism benefit Europeans who invented the system.

Following the Muslim conquest of northern India, Islam was also carried into insular Southeast Asia by converts among Indian traders. Arab traders had been active in inter-Asian trade well before India had extended its commercial networks through most of maritime Southeast Asia. However, "Indian converts to Islam were primarily responsible for carrying the new religion to insular Southeast Asia, following long established trade routes by sea" (Greaves 1990:232). As many traders and rulers were coming into contact with Indian merchants, conversion became common among many islanders in the archipelago. Local merchants in many of the Southeast Asian kingdoms adopted Islam as an advantage in dealing with Muslim traders from India.

Indonesia

A number of scholars have speculated about why Islam seemed to receive more converts after the 13th Century, despite the existence of Arab traders prior to that date. "Some have suggested that the Sufi tradition–a mystical branch of Islam that emphasizes the ultimate reality of God and the illusoriness of the perceived world–may have been brought in at this time" (Frederick and Worden 1993:15). The mystic nature of the Sufi brand of Islam was more in touch with the indigenous faith that already existed, as well as more appealing to Indonesians than the brand of Islam that was introduced during the time of initial Arab merchant trade.

Islam was drawn to Southeast Asia through the trade. Because commerce was prevalent along the coasts of Sumatra, Java, and the eastern archipelago, it is not surprising that Islamization primarily gravitated to these areas. Islam existed long before the advent of European mercantilism. "An inscription from a tombstone dated 1297 reveals that the first ruler of Samudra, another Sumatran state, was Muslim; the Arab traveler Muhammad ibn-'Abdullah ibn-Battutu visited the same town in 1345 and wrote that its monarch was a Sunni rather than a Shia Muslim" (Frederick and Worden 1993:12). Europe was well aware of the Muslim dominance in trade routes in Indonesia. Southeast Asia was not only a threat to Europe economically, but religiously as well. Islam had a long established presence in this region, and it became evident that the Europeans were to face their resistance in any attempt to take over the Southeast Asian trade region. In eastern Indonesia, Islamization proceeded through the 16th and 17th Centuries, often in competition with the aggressive evangelism of Portuguese and other Christian missionaries (Frederick and Worden 1993:13).

In the late 1500s, the Portuguese were the first Europeans to come in significant numbers to the archipelago. Faith and profit, conveniently harmonized, motivated these early European explorers. "The papacy charged Portugal with converting Asia to Christianity. Equipped with superior navigational aids and sturdy ships, the Portuguese attempted to seize rich trade routes in the Indian Ocean from Muslim merchants" (Frederick and Worden 1993:15). The Portuguese came into Indonesia to monopolize the spice trade of the eastern archipelago. "Nutmeg, mace, and cloves were easily worth their weight in gold in European markets, but the trade had hitherto been dominated by Muslims" (Frederick and Worden 1993:16). The Portuguese were unsuccessful at gaining control, as Indonesian Muslim states did not hesitate to get rid of the Portuguese intruders. The predominantly Muslim region of Southeast Asia did little to ingratiate the Portuguese. "Their cruel practices of conversion by torture, their pitiless extortion, and their slaughter of the 'heathen' Hindus and Buddhists as well as their ancient Muslim foes earned them hatred" (Greaves 1990:411). It is possible that the negative response from the region was due to the religious tone Portugal set upon its arrival. Nonetheless, the goal of Christianizing Asia and Muslims continued to keep intruders on the defensive.

During the 17th Century, Amsterdam emerged as Europe's primary center for commerce and banking. Unlike the Portuguese, the Dutch concentrated their effort on trade and strayed from religious entanglements in the region. This was very effective in removing Portuguese existence in Indonesia and possibly attaining some cooperation with Muslim rulers. The Dutch came to control the largest amount of territory and population in Southeast Asia, incorporating the whole of what is now Indonesia in their colonial empire. "Dutch companies amalgamated to the Dutch East India Company in 1602 which in the following decades built a highly profitable commercial empire centered on Java, controlling the trade of Southeast Asia far more effectively than the Portuguese had done" (Greaves 1990:453).

The Dutch East India Company was strategically placed at Batavia (Jakarta), with other bases that would further oust the Portuguese disdained existence in Indonesia. "The key to Dutch commercial success in Indonesia was the security of its base of operations in Batavia. The earliest governor generals had not intended to become involved in Java's politics. They envisioned the company as a primary maritime power, consisting of a network of forts and heavily defended trading routes. But during the 17th Century and especially the 18th Century the Dutch found themselves caught up in Java's perennial political instability" (Frederick and Worden 1993:17).

While nations throughout the Islamic world are currently in greatly varying states of economic well-being at the start of the 21st Century, the vast majority are in a state of underdevelopment. While there are a number of causes for this, one of the most critical is the difficulty that Muslims faced in obeying their religious principles and still actively competing with their European counterparts due to the fact that no institutions were in place to cope with such a radically different and adversarial trade philosophy. Timur Kuran refers to this as the "Islamic commercial crisis." He explains that "the institutional evolution of the West had turned Islam's traditional commercial institutions into sources of competitive disadvantage" (Kuran 2003:415). Despite the fact that there was no way for political entities and merchants throughout the *Umma* to prepare for the onslaught of aggressive competition and predatory trade practice, the importance of finding ways to more effectively relate Islam to contemporary international economic and cultural conflicts such as this one cannot be understated. The institutional failures of the mercantilist era hold clues to how this can better be accomplished in the future, especially in the context of remarkably similar modern-day resource accumulation by the West in a predominantly Islamic region (oil in the Persian Gulf).

CONCLUSION

Mercantilist society was introduced by European countries and later imposed on Islamic communities throughout the East. However, it is very important to understand that although it is a European based socio-economic system, many of its central tenets were being practiced by Muslims long before the Europeans figured their benefits. The main difference lies in the intentions of both parties. While the Europeans sought to enrich their Crowns, Muslims tended to seek benefits for their populations, stability for their regimes, and to spread the word of Islam through trade and transport.

One of the main factors that spurred the need for a mercantilist society was the development of the nation-state. This conception is very undesirable to Muslims. It imposes on the very foundation of the concept of *Umma*, or global Islamic community. The seemingly trivial imposition of divisive lines was a concept that Muslims could not understand. During the time of the Peace of Westphalia, Muslims struggled to maintain their connections across territorial borders. Despite the restrictions that were set up as a result of mercantilism, pious Muslims continued to trade and, thus, spread the Islamic voice. It also introduced the concept of nationalism, creating a new community aside from the *Umma*. Although God was primordial, the man-made nation was now the basis for all governance and administration. This created a problem for the average Muslim living in a given state. This new form of territorial claim was threatening the connections of the entire Islamic community.

Muslims at the time were facing a struggle of identity. Although the interests of the *Umma* still existed, the new community created by the nation-state was somewhat of a distraction for the average Muslim. The struggle to maintain Islam and adapt to new ties of identity were very difficult, and resolving these issues was further complicated by the other developments made by mercantilism, as well as the effects it had on the community.

In Islam, dividing people into tribes and nations is merely adding variation to creation in order for different people to come and meet one another in a tone of mutual respect and co-operation, albeit never for the endorsement of hostility and disparity. It also calls for sharing, honorable deeds, holy virtue, the benefit of the masses, and the pleasure of Allah who protects all who honor him. The Holy *Qur'an* declares all these meanings very clearly when Allah says: 'O mankind! Be dutiful to your Lord, Who created you from a single person, and from Him He created His wife, and from them both He created many men and women and fear Allah through whom you demand mutual, and the wombs. Surely, Allah is watching over you" (*Qur'an*: Surat-an-Nisaa'). The existence of different people is something that God created; however, it was not in order to create conflict. The conception of the European nation-state was seen by Muslims as a human act of creating further division and competition, not only for social reasons, but more specifically for political and economic reasons as well.

Countries with large Islamic communities tended not to have tremendous quantities of gold, which was the motivating force of the mercantile era. However, they had other resources that were desirable to Europeans, who primarily collected them through colonization. Thus, through the seizure of Islamic goods and lands, Westerners could accrue the gold through the sale of such goods for the bullion being collected by their mother countries. European colonization imposed a new style of government, not taking into account the system of self-governance practiced by Muslims and the already existing Islamic law presented by *Shari'a*, the *Qur'an* and the *Hadith*. Along with this redefinition of community, there was also a degree of exploitation of indigenous populations present in European domains.

The concept of centralized government was also another contradiction that created much confusion for the Islamic community, which had no previous idea of government intervention. There were centers for regulation from Spain to Southeast Asia; however, there was no specific government apparatus that controlled trade on all levels. This changed the fundamental nature of trade.

Before mercantilism, trade was used by Muslims to attain necessary resources as well as expand the community of believers in Islam, through teachings, communication, and conversion. Trade was related to bartering and based around exchanging the surplus of goods or resources in return for those that were unattainable. Until the rise of Western mercantilist policy, it was never seen as a zero-sum situation where the gain of one party was to the detriment of another. Prior to mercantilism, the Muslim traders shared a very symbiotic relationship. Although it cannot be said that there were no corrupt and selfish Muslim traders, this went against every tenet of Islamic trade.

Very few religious laws or social systems have encouraged the institution of peace in the same way that Islam has. Islam orders the practice of this great virtue through respect and self-restraint even at the most trying of times. Islam provided one of the earliest comprehensive frameworks for establishing and maintaining peace and the welfare of all Abrahamic peoples. Many believe that "Islam drew for stability the most genuine guarantees; if adopted by the countries of the world, and followed by the rulers, leaders and politicians, the world would then rest and save the agonies of war" (Greaves 1990:544). It is believed that a society that embraces Islam allows the sanctity of the meanings of brotherhood and sisterhood to overcome the spirit of racism and inflexibility.

Another foundation of Islam that would promote peace and understanding is the training of the souls on the spirit of forgiveness. Islam prides itself on virtues like the absolute necessity for trustworthiness, the prohibition of subversion and the dishonor of violating treaties and agreements. Therefore, in international affairs, an Islamic country would seem to be the ideal potential ally. However, the problem in today's world is that there has not been any serious resolve by the nations of the world to balance all the needs of international actors, notably in the case of Islamic countries.

Islam sets forth a complex and rational just war principle, built around the concept of self-defense. It also stresses justice, compassion, and a respect for law and order, even at a time of war. In this value, Islam maintains the highest possible standard for itself and its followers. Allah says in the Holy *Qur'an*: "O you who believe! Stand out firmly for Allah and be just witnesses and let not the enmity and hatred of others make you avoid justice. Be just: that is nearer to piety, and fear Allah. Verily, Allah is Well-acquainted with what you do" (*Qur'an*: Al-Maa'idah).

The Prophet Muhammad emphasized simplicity, humility, and modesty with respect to one's standard of living. The *Qur'an* commands all Muslims to follow this example. This shows Islam to be inherently opposed to the European values of bullionism and extravagance. Despite this, the prayer, "Our Lord, grant us blessings in the life of this world and blessings in the life to come, and save us from the torment of the Fire" seems to avoid precluding the pursuit of affluence in life. As opposed to irrationally forbidding economic well being, it instead condemns hoarding. Islamic teachings explain that "the storing up of food stuffs with the object of selling them at higher prices in times of need and scarcity–a practice, which is considered a sin" (Ibn Hanbal 351). While one may be wealthy, if he or she has wealth in abundance, he or she must disperse it to those who are in need.

Islamic attitudes toward trade and economic development has likewise been very favorable since the religion's earliest days. The *Qur'anic* teachings are also welcoming of trade which is free from fraud. The *Qur'an* teaches that "the day is appointed for a profit-making occupation (*Qur'an* 78:11); shipping is a bounty of God to mankind (*Qur'an* 17:70) winter and summer caravans (the two most important business transactions of the Meccans) were set up for "civilizing" the Quraysh. Several passages regard frauds in trade, like short measures, to be among the despicable acts. Believers are enjoined to "spread over the land and seek the abundance of God" (*Qur'an* 62:10).

The political setup prearranged by Islam is one based on consultation among Muslims. No one person has the right to overrule the opinions of the majority of those living in the land. This refutes the notion that any form of absolute rule is acceptable to Islam, especially in the form of colonization or economic exploitation. Muslim nations can only benefit from free trade by ridding themselves of regimes that impose constraints on their internal economies, directing any benefits into their own pockets and those of their friends. Instead, it should be used as an impetus for development and prosperity that benefits the entrepreneurs, workers, and consumers in all nations. The mercantile system exploited the economic system used successfully for hundreds of years by Muslims. By imposing a centrally regulated and exploitative system, Europeans introduced an economic system that could not be reconciled with Islamic beliefs, placing Muslims at a fundamental disadvantage. It was impossible for them to successfully compete against Europeans in a system that stood in defiance of so many of Islam's central principals. The tenets of mercantilism were similar to the merchant system of the Arab world; however, while similar in aspects of theory, they were very different in practice.

CHAPTER 3

Islam and Capitalism

Lisa Livingood

INTRODUCTION

> *The great struggles of the twentieth century between liberty and totalitarianism ended with a decisive victory for the forces of freedom–and a single sustainable model for national success: freedom, democracy, and free enterprise. In the twenty-first century, only nations that share a commitment to protecting basic human rights and guaranteeing political and economic freedom will be able to unleash the potential of their people and assure their future prosperity.*
>
> –National Security Strategy 2002: President George W. Bush

The preceding quote vibrated across the globe with the George W. Bush Administration's announcement of its National Security Strategy, now also known as "The Bush Doctrine." The reality that the most powerful country in the world seeks to promote its form of Capitalism worldwide stands strong. Currently, discussions of whether Islam and Capitalism are compatible take place in boardrooms of large corporations, state departments, among military specialists and academic institutions worldwide. The topics vary but the key points revolve around the following ideas:

(1) The goal of Capitalism versus the goal of Islam;

(2) How Capitalism distributes wealth versus how an Islamic economic system should distribute wealth according to the *Qur'an*; and

(3) How Capitalism affects societies and what the *Qur'an* says regarding the goals of society.

For the purposes of this chapter, I must make clarifications distinguishing the theoretical paradigms based on Adam Smith's Capitalism and the reality of today's Free Market and mixed economies. In Smith's view, the production and exchange of goods can be stimulated, and a consequent rise in the general standard of living attained, only through the efficient operations of private industrial and commercial entrepreneurs acting without regulation. Every individual in pursuing his or her own good is led, as if by an invisible hand, to achieve the best good for all (Adam Smith Institute 2004, Encarta 2004). Adam Smith believed that a government must have a monopoly on violence to protect the state (army) and the individual's body and goods (police). A government must also have a court system to settle disputes, enforce contracts, and punish criminals. In this system, a state's concept of peace is through absence of war (Smith 1776, Capitalism.org 20 October, 2004), also known as negative peace or *sulah* (Bangura 2004).

Some academics argue that no truly ideologically capitalist state exists. In response to the bloody riots of the Industrial Revolution, caused by the extreme, obvious evils of a completely unregulated industrial complex (child labor, unregulated industrial waste and pollution), governments began to place some limits on business practices. This led to regulated Free Market economies.

The benefit of regulated Free Market economies seems obvious. Quantitatively, more wealth is produced. However, the long-term qualitative negative effects of the Western version of free-market economies are still being discovered (divorce, drop in birth-rate, suicide, non-political violent crime, isolation of the individual from the community, increased economic stratification). Many have proposed that the negative, qualitative effects may be potentially mitigated by careful thought, psychological research, and controls restricting the length a laborer's workday, minimum leave time, and overtime pay requirements.

Often, politicians throw around words like "Capitalism," "free-market economy," and "mixed economy" interchangeably. For the purposes of this chapter, the term "capitalist economy" describes the Free Market economies of today based on laissez-faire principles. The resultant culture, economic system and societal goals remain the same. Capitalism deals with the individual's needs and the means of satisfying those needs. It addresses the materialistic side of a person's life. The ideology focuses on the right of the individual to pursue wealth (Smith 1776, Malkawi 2002, Norberg 2004). Proponents of Capitalism claim that a Free Market is the most efficient system for the allocation of resources. Additionally, they claim an inevitable increase in industrial growth, production of wealth, and resultant economic freedom (Norberg 2004, Brittan 2002, Jay 2000). Using the principles of "Comparative Advantage" and "Economies of Scale," the capitalist believes that wealth increases when a producer generates product in accordance with consumers' demand and competitively with others in its industry. This result can only be achieved by Free Market production instead of government controlled production and allocation of resources. The result is the increase of produced wealth (Samuelson 1980). This is true for both domestic Capitalism, such as found in the industrialized West, and for global Capitalism.

Ironically, while the underlying purpose of government in the Capitalist model focuses on the protection of the individual, his property and pursuit of wealth, Capitalism treats the worker as a commodity that can exist in excess supply while making no provision for ensuring the individual attains wealth or even meets base needs. Consequently, Capitalism accepts poverty as an inevitable by-product. Islamic Economic Doctrine does not.

Inherently, Capitalism grants the freedom to pursue wealth but no provision to attain it. An individual's basic needs of food, shelter, education, and health will remain unmet if the person, too young, old, sick, undereducated, or unneeded, is unable to obtain a job or the required materials in order to offer a service (Malkawi 2002). In response, many moral Free Market economies have instituted within their own states social provisions to address some aspects of poverty. Contrary to popular expectations, increased production of wealth has not necessarily meant increased material well being for the poor. In the United States, for example, the poverty rate has remained on average constant through the last 35 years, if not gotten worse. Additionally, while the production of wealth has increased and the poverty rate stayed relatively constant within large industrial countries, global poverty and global stratification between rich and poor countries continues (Weisbrot, Baker, Kraev and Chen 2001). Despite economists' attempts at refutation, "The rich get richer, and the poor get poorer" still seems to hold true.

This leads to the debate surrounding Capitalism and Islam. It seems that Capitalism in its pure form with absolutely no controls cannot be compatible with Islam due to the following reason: There is an immediate clash not in the production of goods, but in the distribution of wealth (Malkawi 2002). If a view is expanded to include the regulation of corporations in order to protect society, while still allowing private ownership of corporations and private control over most aspects of production, then it appears in concept that both the economic sciences and systems of Capitalism and Islam may be compatible. At a minimum, Islamic free-market economies must have the freedom to put in place restrictions on business practices that protect their culture (such as the Christian practice of closing on Sundays), coincide with the *Qur'an's* guidance regarding usury (*Riba*), taxation (the *Zakat*), and support Islamic requirements of wealth distribution. A final evaluation of the compatibility of Capitalism and Islam may rest on questions regarding each economic system's social morality. A modern debate on this subject must examine recent research studying the effects of both domestic and global Capitalism.

In this chapter, I review relevant works from both Western and Islamic writers in an attempt to deconstruct doctrine and examine common questions surrounding the ideological goals, cultures, and effects of Islam and Capitalism. I then examine these ideas through the lens of three states pursuing a policy of free trade with majority Muslim populations. Finally, I conclude with a quick look at some questions and ways of thinking that the world community must address if it chooses to pursue peaceful co-existence in a world of global Capitalism and Islam.

REVIEW OF RELEVANT LITERATURE

In an attempt to create a well researched, scholarly work examining what these two concepts mean and how they relate, I read books, articles, scholarly journal entries, Internet sites, encyclopedias, attended lectures, visited world recognized financial institutions (such as the International Monetary Fund) and even corresponded with a scholar of Islamic Economic Doctrine. I read current articles on Globalism, Islam, Islamic Economic Doctrine, Muslim-Secular states, Islamic States, and I looked for multiple points of view in all of these arenas. To be sure, there is more information and many more points of view than can be integrated into this chapter. However, three major questions with several sub-points rose that require attention:

(1) Does the *Qur'an* support the idea of Free Trade? This subject includes discussions of economic science and economic system, the role of government, worker incentive, and concepts of wealth–distribution, ownership, and social classes. It also includes discussions of whether the cultural, economic, moral and social doctrines of Islam are compatible with the same of Capitalism. This includes the concepts of justice and rule of law, the handling of poverty, community, law, and prohibition of exploitation.

(2) Is the *Qur'an*'s requirement of Muslims to pay *Zakat* compatible with, first, Capitalism and, second, a Free Market mixed economy?

(3) Does the *Qur'anic* prohibition of *Riba* translate into incompatibility with a Free Market Mixed economy?

In exploring these questions, I hope to present, integrate and bring attention to prevalent scholarly perspectives.

Support or Denial of Free Trade in Islam

In examining whether a Free Market Economy is compatible with Islamic Economic Doctrine, scholars discuss the role of trade within a state (Abdul-Rauf 1984, Malkawi 2002, Affandi 2002, Mannan 1987, Al-Fanjari 2004). They also discuss private ownership of land, private ownership of property, wealth, means of production, and profit. As the role of government is outlined in Capitalism, it is also outlined in Islam.

Economic Science: Production of Goods

A discussion of the compatibility of Islam and Capitalism can be approached from many directions. Many scholars, Western (the industrialized West), non-Western, economists and theologians start with the discussion of economic system versus economic science. The questions asked include the following:

(1) What means of production are being used (economic science)?

(2) Who owns the means of production (economic system)?

(3) Does the worker keep her or his profit?

(4) Does the state own all companies, raw goods, and final products?

When discussing an "economic system," scholars look at the production systems. Specifically, they are looking at things like worker incentive, the rule of law, the role of government, taxation and possession of property (Abdul-Rauf 1984, Malkawi 2002, Affandi 2002). Islamic theologians and economic scholars also examine the integration of God's word and the morality of a given system.

Scholars specifically exploring the economic systems of Capitalism and Islamic Economic Doctrine diverge semantically on these two economic systems' degree of compatibility. Part of the distinction seems based in whether one looks at pure Capitalism, a mixed economy, or what Abdul-Rauf refers to as "democratic Capitalism." He writes: "Capitalism, too, has modified itself and has welcomed some socialistic reforms within its system. It is no longer simple Capitalism but *democratic* Capitalism" (Abdul-Rauf 1984). Once a scholar accepts modified Capitalism, whether defined as a mixed economy or democratic Capitalism, the idea becomes that of a Free Market Economy modified by morality as defined by the authoritative body legislating regulation on trade practices.

One scholar, Malkawi, looks at the ideology and cultures of both domestic and global Capitalism and their impact on the world today. He then describes the difference between economic science and economic system. Malkawi defines an economic system as "a set of rules and regulations, which define how to distribute the wealth, how to possess it, and how to spend or dispose of it" (2002). He concludes that as this system is based in ideology, "the economic system of Islam is different from that of socialism/communism and that of Capitalism" (Malkawi 2002). Even so, he writes: "*Shari'a* has left the matter of production of wealth to the people, to be produced according to their experience and knowledge. Islam focuses on the Economic *system* and not the economic science" (Malkawi 2002). Malkawi focuses later on the ethical failures of Capitalism and the structure for Islamic Economic Doctrine to address those failures.

Islamic theologian Abdul-Rauf credits Dr. Novak's *The Spirit of Democratic Capitalism* with thoroughly outlining the concept of democratic Capitalism. Abdul-Rauf contrasts this form of "moral" Capitalism with an Islamic concept of economics. He describes the spirit of democratic Capitalism by delineating three components of the concept: a democratic polity, a Free Market and incentive economy, and a moral-cultural system that is pluralistic and liberal. Later, he points out that the components are mutually autonomous, but interdependent systems (Abdul-Rauf 1984:27–33, 57–68). Where democratic Capitalism does not doctrinally requires one religious standard for a central worldview (each component is autonomous), Islam explicitly require the world be viewed from an Islamic perspective. The components are unambiguously interdependent. They are all centered on Islam.

For a Western thinker, this precept might appear to eliminate the possibility of reconciling the doctrine of Islam and that of a pluralistic interpretation of Democratic Capitalism. However, the unifying system of Islam preaches a positive peace where everyone has the means to successfully control his or her own social, economic and political life. This catch leads directly back to the fundamentals of "legitimacy of private ownership, the freedom of private enterprise, a Free Market Economy with effective incentives" (Abdul-Rauf 1984:37), as well as rule of law, a government of minimal control, and an economy of free trade.

While impossible to argue that Capitalism and Islamic Economic Doctrine work identically, if one dissects the components of a Free Market Economy and Islam's promotion of business, the two can overlap if not merge. In support of this idea, Affandi writes:

> Islam not only recognizes the need for business but encourages it as means of making social and economic life function smoothly in order to bring prosperity to mankind. Islam also fully realizes that in order for business to fulfill that noble objective, a market economy is absolutely essential (2002:35).

Affandi continues, arguing that the following conditions need to exist for a market economy to thrive: "1. an open market;" (freedom of individuals to produce, own, and exchange goods), "2. free competition; 3. dynamic private enterprise; 4. full operation of the forces of supply and demand; 5. honest businessmen" (not truly a requirement in the reality of today's Capitalism); and "6. minimum government intervention to be undertaken only when necessary to safeguard the broader and common interests of the community" (Affandi 2002:35). Affandi spends an entire chapter dedicated to proving "the rationale for Islam's strong support, Islamic provisions to protect it (a market economy), and the reasons why minimal government intervention is allowed" (Affandi 2002:36–44).

When discussing the role of government in both Capitalism and Islam, the idea of Rule of Law takes center stage. Nearly every scholar cited discusses its importance. Imad-ad-Dean writes: "In a law-based economy, a single set of laws or rules govern the decision making and people operate not on the basis of commands tailored to specific transactions, but on their free choice within the scope afforded by universally applied laws. This is precisely the Islamic system" (Imad-ad-Dean 1996). Imad-ad-Dean continues, reminding the reader that it was during the 7th Century "in classical Islamic civilization that the modern concept of the rule of law developed" (Imad-ad-Dean 1996).

Malkawi concurs that both the *Qur'an* and *Shari'a* support ideas of private ownership, the earning of property, free competition, the pursuit of wealth, self-reliance and worker incentive. He, too, clarifies for the reader the ways in which these basic principles of a Free Market Economy were outlined nearly 1,100 years earlier in the *Qur'an.* Malkawi writes:

> These verses, and the like, denote clearly that the divine rules (*Ahkam Shari'a)* related to the economy, aim at acquiring property and enjoying good things. So Islam obliged individuals to earn, and ordered them to enjoy wealth that they earned, so as to achieve economic growth in the country, to satisfy the basic needs of every person, and to enable to the satisfaction of his luxuries (Malkawi 2002).

A careful examination of this quote, while pointing to similarities of a capitalistic Free Market Economy, also points to the schism in ideologies. It is hinted at with the phrase "to satisfy the basic needs of every person." All modern scholars of Islamic Economic Doctrine and Free Market economies seem to agree: The general principles upon which Capitalism is based, the principles outlined by Affandi as being critical for a Free Market Economy to thrive, are approved, promoted and supported by the *Qur'an* and *Sunnah.* What Islamic scholars seem to take issue with is their perception of immorality of the culture of Capitalism. Specifically, they point to Capitalism's lack of provision for the poor, the hoarding of wealth (implied in *Riba* and *Zakat*), the isolation of the individual, the breakdown of community, and the lack of a prohibition of exploitation (Malkawi 2002, Abdul-Rauf 1984, Mannan 1987, Affandi 2002, Al-Fanjari 2004). Incidentally, while not directly pertinent to the discussion of Islam and Capitalism, one should note that throughout the history of Capitalism, Christian scholars, including several popes, have also condemned Capitalism. The issues these theologians and Christian economists raise are nearly identical to those of Islamic scholars. For example, Pope Leo XIII castigates the unequal distribution of goods. He speaks about "immense wealth for a small number and deepest poverty of the multitude." In *Global Capitalism, Liberation Theology and the Social Sciences*, Muller, Tausch and Zulehner carefully examine many of the prominent criticisms of Capitalism. Among the disparagements are lack of justice, extreme economic stratification, treatment of the poor and weak, idolatry, culture of performance, survival of the fittest and consumption (2000:4–44).

Capitalism, Islam and questions of Wealth and Poverty

Not surprisingly, Islamic scholars delineate several key ideas regarding wealth. The key production motivation for individuals in a Free Market society is the securing of property and pursuit of wealth. This pursuit, in fact, underscores the origins of incentive for the Capitalistic Economic system (Harder 2000, Norberg 2004, Adam Smith Institute 2004, Capitalism.org 2004). This form of motivation leads to the components of a healthy Free Market Economy as previously referenced by Affandi. The pursuit of wealth, therefore, is seen as moral and good in the culture of Capitalism. This concept is true in Islam as well.

The pursuit of wealth is also seen as moral and as a means of being Godly. It allows the individual to contribute to charity, to support the *Umma*, and enjoy the world God provided on earth. Islam is neither a religion of abstinence nor consumption, but of moderation. The individual should create and enjoy wealth, but not hoard it. Therefore, although the ideologies concur on the moral value of the pursuit of profit, Islam splits with Capitalism regarding the final purpose of wealth. In Capitalism, wealth is an end in itself. In Islam, wealth is created to support God's wishes that the individual enjoy God's creation and support the world community (Affandi 2002, Malkawi 2002, Mannan 1987, Abdul-Rauf 1984, Al-Fanjari 2004, Imad-ad-Dean 1993 and 1996).

How do Capitalism and Islam differ in regards to poverty? Proponents of both argue that their favored system of economics attacks poverty. Norberg, an economist and prominent proponent of Globalism, defines Capitalism as "a system where the individual is his own master and the master of his property, with the power of making contracts and starting up in business, and the ability to move about, travel and trade regardless of national boundaries" (2004:25). Norberg believes that Capitalism reduces poverty through increased production of wealth. He argues that statistics prove a global increase in production of food per capita, an increase in caloric intake per capita, a decrease in infant mortality, a decrease in illiteracy and an increase in political rights (Norberg 2004:25–37). Proponents of Capitalism would argue that as for poverty, under Capitalism, no poor man is prohibited from creating a fortune. Referencing Ayn Rand, *The Capitalism Site* argues that taking money from the rich to give to the poor is a form of robbery and immoral (Capitalism.org 2004).

Malkawi agrees that the culture of Capitalism promotes freedom to pursue wealth. However, he does not equate some redistribution of wealth as evil, but instead as Godly and moral. As Malkawi discusses, Islamic Economic Doctrine "aims at eliminating poverty from the society, rather than managing the poor" (2002). He is not alone in this line of thought. Many scholars come to similar conclusions when examining the role of the *Zakat's* provision for the poor, and some as well when considering *Riba* and its redistribution of wealth (Abdul-Rauf 1984:1–24, Mannan 1987:329–361).

Additionally, Malkawi comes to different conclusions than Norberg regarding statistics, Capitalism and poverty. While examining Census Bureau statistical trends within the United States, Malkawi finds:

> The average number of poor people averaged more than 30 million people with an average of 15% of the population being poor. In the meantime, the GNP grew from $400 billions to $10 trillions from 1959 to 2000. This very large increase in the national product did not contribute to the resolution of poverty. More than 30 million continue to be poor (Malkawi 2002).

According to the United States Census Bureau, the poverty rate has consistently fluctuated between 11.3 percent and 15 percent from 1966 and 2000 (United States Census Bureau, March 1960–2001). Malkawi points out a major fallacy of Capitalism from a Muslim perspective: "Whether the individual is or is not able to satisfy his/her needs is not of concern to the economy, as long as the production of goods continues to grow, and the wealth continues to grow" (Malkawi 2002). To be sure, this quote represents a common view accepted or promoted by most authors cited, regardless of the economic system an author supports.

To sum up the preceding thoughts, both Islam and Capitalism seem to hold the components of a Free Market Economy in high regard. Both doctrines promote ideals of individual freedom, the right to earn and own property, to produce goods, to pursue wealth (but in Islam not to hoard wealth), to trade freely with minimal government intervention, and equal protection for all individuals under a codified rule of law. However, Capitalism and Islam seem to split paths on the role and treatment of the poor, the definitions of equitable distribution of wealth, and the role of God within a state's economic and political institution. Still left for discussion are the themes and scholarly discussions of the *Zakat* and Capitalism, and *Riba* and Capitalism.

The Zakat and Capitalism: Compatible or Not?

What is the *Zakat*? Why is or isn't it compatible with Capitalism? All scholars addressing the concepts of Islam and Capitalism write about the *Zakat*, its role in Islamic Economic Doctrine, and its relationship to Capitalism. Abdul-Rauf elucidates: "The *Zakat* is an annual obligatory payment of 2 1/2 of accumulated savings remaining in one's possession for a year. The same applies to commercial goods" (1984:11). He clarifies all of the types of income to which the *Zakat* applies such as treasure, extracted minerals, and agricultural produce. He then considers the importance of the *Zakat* payment to the state (or directly to the poor) and its role in wealth redistribution, charity, community, and ensuring the basic needs of the poor are met. Abdul-Rauf also examines a side economic benefit of the *Zakat*: because it applies to surplus savings at the end of the year and not investments, investing money is encouraged and thereby helps the local entrepreneur (Abdul-Rauf 1984:11).

Mannan also discusses the previous ideas, but adds that it is the spirit of the *Zakat* to which one must adhere. He writes that the 2.5% outlined in the *Qur'an* is not adequate to ensure the assistance to all poor and that a larger percent should be taken from rich people to meet the needs of the *Umma* (Mannan 1986:68). While to some this idea may sound like Socialism, the means of production, private ownership of property and other qualities of a Free Market Economy remain.

Imad-ad-Dean refutes the idea of *Zakat* as a form of Socialism. He points out that "there is nothing in the *Shari'a* to justify state ownership of the means of production" (Imad-ad-Dean 1996). He continues, explaining that the *Zakat* "is small enough to leave most of the wealth in the hands of the most productive while offering the poorest the means to become productive themselves" (Imad-ad-Dean 1996). To a liberated mind, there seems little difference between the *Zakat* and *a* Free Market/Mixed Economy welfare tax. Both "taxes" attempt to balance the motivating forces of free trade and provide for the basic needs of all members of society.

Riba and Capitalism

Like the *Zakat,* the Islamic concept of *Riba* remains prominent in the ongoing discussions of Capitalism and Islam. However, unlike the *Zakat*, the concept of *Riba* and its translation draws heated debate among Islamic Economic Doctrine scholars. The *Qur'an* clearly prohibits *Riba* (all cited scholars). The debate often stems from the specific translation of the word "*Riba*" into English. Some translate it to mean "usury" (Imad-al-Dean 1993), others to mean "interest" (Kahf 2001), and yet others "exploitation" (Imad-ad-Dean 1996), "excess or addition," "overcharging on interest" (Imad-al-Dean 1993). Those economic scholars who distinguish between usury and interest use Islamic jurisprudence to show that interest is not prohibited (Imad-ad-Dean 1996).

In contrast, A. Ahmad and Mannan disagree with the previous authors, expressing their belief that interest and usury are differences in scale, not in kind. They propose that nit picking over a specific definition misses the entire point. Mannan and Ahmad show that scale is based in perception. What one person considers a low interest rate another considers usury (Ahmad 2004, Mannan 1987:118). The debates regarding *Riba* remain heated within the scholarly world of Islam.

While the dispute rages on as to whether the *Qur'an* allows the Western concept of interest, another debate ensues: Does a Free Market Economy require Western style banking? In other words, does the style of banking determine the type of economy (Mixed, Socialist, and Communist)? Imad-ad-Dean explains that it does not: "The essence of the market is entrepreneurship. Trade, not banking is the primary function of markets" (Imad-ad-Dean 1996). One needs only to look back to Affandi's six components of a healthy Free Market Economy to see that the style of banking is not a determinant.

For those who hold fast to the idea that it is interest that the *Qur'an* prohibits, the challenge of creating successful interest-free banking becomes a moral and economic necessity. Nearly 20 years ago, Mannan asked: "Is it possible to have an interest free society?"

(Mannan 1987:118). Perhaps unknown to him, others were already attempting to make Islamic Banking a reality. The Islamic Development Bank opened in October of 1975, but it did not appear to gain significant momentum until the mid-1990's (Isdb.org 2004). While Islamic interest-free banking remains a goal of many Muslims, the world continues to wait for the emergence of a successful Islamic state functioning solely on Islamic Economic Doctrine (Kahf 2001).

Critics of the compatibility of Islam and Capitalism often begin with pointing out that the concept of *Zakat* and prohibition of *Riba* do not exist in the ideology of Capitalism. While that may be true in the non-existent, theoretical, Adam Smith form of Capitalism where there is no taxation or government regulation, in a more modern view of a Free Market Mixed Economy, the ideologies appear able to work well within each other.

This chapter adds to the body of peace studies by illuminating some of the critical issues facing the world today. Since the year 2000, the way the world considers issues of peace, politics and religion changed drastically. Prior to September 11, 2001, many would have nonchalantly brushed aside any thought that the process of integrating Muslim societies into the Global market demands critical attention. Even now, many in the mainstream do not see the importance of understanding the similarities and differences of these ideologies. It seems enough to condemn the "Other," with no need to comprehend the humanity, the benefits or reasons for why the "Other" does things the way it does. However, if the world holds global security and the elimination of poverty as viable goals, then businesspersons, religious leaders and the masses whose opinions influence policy makers must come to understand and respect the world views of people not of their faith or culture. Additionally, if we all can agree that Free Trade increases production, that people need to have ownership of their social, political and economic lives, and that a society should have the ability to legislate taxes to assist in common goals, then how we achieve these ends becomes negotiable.

ANALYSIS OF FINDINGS

In the previous section of this chapter, relevant doctrinal issues of Islam and Capitalism were explored. This section examines the reality of how these two ideologies integrate or impact in three countries where most citizens are Muslim. In approaching this portion of my research, the questions of which states to select and why, became complex. In the end, I have chosen to examine Kyrgyzstan, Saudi Arabia, and Turkey. Factors of consideration included

(1) Percentage of population Muslim (75% or greater to be considered);

(2) Size of a state's population (Note: India maintains the third largest Muslim population. However, Indian Muslims remain politically and socially insignificant,

as they hold only 12% of the total state population. Nigeria and Ethiopia also have significant numerically large Muslim populations who remain near minorities. At 50% of the total state, these Muslims, too, cannot create a state based on faith. Even in states with majority Muslim populations, the political factions following different interpretations of the *Qur'an* often have similar divisive effects [Dougan 2004, i-20, 37, 55]);

(3) Secular or Islamic State;

(4) Length of time of current governmental institution;

(5) Colonized or conquered? By whom? With what impact?;

(6) Oil/no oil? Is the economy resource based?;

(7) Does the economy participate in international trade? To what extent?

During the course of examining these and other factors, several things became abundantly apparent. First, most predominately Muslim countries have only recently become sovereign states free of colonial, conquering, or occupying forces. The only notable exceptions are Saudi Arabia and Turkey, and even these states have been heavily influenced by the politics of the 20th century. In fact, the land disputes of Britain, Russia and the regions previously included in the Ottoman Empire continued arguably through the Soviet territorial imperialism after World War II (WWII).

One must not simply glance over the occupations as a simple fact. Many countries within the Islamic world have been fighting for sovereignty for nearly 1,000 years (since Pope Urban II endorsed "retaking" Jerusalem from the Turks in 1095). The fall of the Berlin wall and subsequent fall of the Soviet Union marked more than the beginning of the United States hegemony. It marked the beginning of an incredibly turbulent time of hope, of new secular Muslim states (Uzbekistan, Kazakhstan, Kyrgyzstan, Tajikistan, Georgia, and Azerbaijan) and the spread of American ideals promoting social, economic and political freedom. Russia had lost, and Washington won. With new independence and American support, governments began to actively reform internal education standards, trade, growth, and industry.

The last 15 years have also seen a worldwide increase in stratification of the world-class structure. The Middle East North African (MENA) countries and many central and sub-Sahara African countries have been experiencing a decrease in growth and subsequent increase in per-capita poverty rates. Additionally, because of borders drawn arbitrarily by colonial powers, which do not accommodate cultural, tribal or religious demographics and/or previously imposed colonial governments, nearly every state on the continent of Africa struggles with questions of national identity. After years of domination, many countries are still assessing who they are now and what the best form of government is for their culture. While mainstream media, students and policy makers of the West seem to throw these facts aside, they provide context critical to understanding why the states of predominantly Muslim populations are "behind" those of the industrialized West.

Finally, I selected Saudi Arabia, Turkey and Kyrgyzstan for now seemingly obvious reasons. Each is a great country in its own right. Each is a member of the Islamic Development Bank. Each has an overwhelmingly Islamic population. Moreover, each struggles in very different ways to balance the secular and non-secular Muslim political forces within. For example, Saudi Arabia fought the onslaught of British Colonialism and has remained an independent state for over 60 years, Turkey maintained its sovereignty as Europe and Russia looked hungrily to its land, and Kyrgyzstan emerged recently from communist Soviet rule to become an independent state working for democracy and transitioning to a Free Market Economy. The last 15 years have been historically significant for all three countries, and each represents vastly different cultures, current realities, and possible futures.

Saudi Arabia

> ...a preeminent economic power in the region, with an economy that ranks among the top 25 largest economies in the world, Saudi Arabia accounts for fully one fifth of the GDP of the entire Middle East, including Turkey. Whatever takes place in Saudi Arabia has an enormous effect of the region and, to some extent, the global economy as well (Naimi 2004).

Saudi Arabi plays a strong role in global trade, despite its lack of membership in the World Trade Organization. Strategically located in the center of the Arab world, not to mention its central location between the West and the East, Saudi Arabi remains a pivotal point in critical resources as well as the Islamic holy land. In exploring modern issues of peace, Islam and Capitalism, to ignore Saudi Arabia would be to ignore a keystone of struggle in the 21st Century.

For simplicity's sake, this chapter attempts to focus on Saudi Arabia using the lenses of Islam and Capitalism. First then, what type of economic system does Saudi Arabia employ? Is the private ownership product production allowed? What about private property? Does the "Rule of Law" apply? How is poverty handled?

Saudi Arabia, like any country, presents a complex reality. While the state religion is Islam, and the majority of the population Muslim, many would still argue that the country is not "an Islamic State." With that said, no sovereign state exists where most citizens practice daily the true faith of a peaceful religion. This is not to say that true spirituality, true pluralism, and *salaam* should not be pursued. It is instead to say that while many individuals say they pursue peace, their actions often breed injustice. In fact, poor legal decisions, human rights violations, extreme social stratification, and gender bias exist everywhere. Saudi Arabia is no exception and its people struggle on many levels.

The Royal family itself is split between Crown Prince Abdullah who "leads a camp of liberal reformers seeking rapprochement with the West, while Prince Nayef, the interior minister, sides with an anti-American Wahhabi religious establishment" (Doran 2004:35–51). It would be simple to assume that Wahhabism, since it is more restricting, is a better representation of Islam. However, in regarding Islamic Economic Doctrine and the four primary schools of Islamic thought, most Muslims worldwide would probably agree that "In a world of positive peace, the basis of stability is not fear; societies are at positive peace when people have the means to successfully control their own social, economic, and political lives" (Bangura 2004:3). Therefore, if the Saudi Arabian "religious police," directed by Prince Nayef, control, subjugate and abuse citizens, they fail to follow the guidelines of Islam. If institutional structures of the state do not support the spiritual intent of Islam, then the state cannot be called an "Islamic State." In addition, because a state constantly changes, one must examine it as it exists in a given snapshot of time.

Currently, the ruling leader of Saudi Arabia pursues a composite social, state, and economic structure compatible with both Islamic Economic Doctrine and a Free Market (mixed) economy. HRH Crown Prince Abdullah promotes the private ownership of land, wealth, income, and business enterprise. In the last five years alone, he initiated reforms resulting in the establishment of the Supreme Economic Council (1999), The Capital Market Authority (2003), the Foreign Investment Act (2000), the Telecommunications Law of May 2000, The Capital Market Law of June 2003, The Corporate Tax Law of January 2004, and the Privatizations Strategy of June 2002 (Naimi 2004).

Saudi Arabia also continues to pursue a long-term movement to an interest-free economy. As a strong member of the Islamic Development Bank, the Kingdom of Saudi Arabia works to understand and apply the "economic development and social progress of member countries and Muslim communities individually as well as jointly in accordance with the principles of *Shari'a*, i.e. Islamic Law" (The Islamic 2004).

Many Westerners complain that the speed of change is too slow. Those quick to judge should contextualize these events through examining recent regional and world history. Because of colonization, globalization, war, religious movements, changes in technology, economics and trade law, all nations struggle with issues of who they are in our consumingly integrated world. The complexity of this struggle rises with the newness of a nation state, with population movements and their sometimes unwanted impact on cultural exchange.

World leaders should commend Saudi Arabia and Crown Prince Abdullah for reforms underway in the empowerment of the population, democracy (even if only males may vote), education of all citizens, and the progress being sought towards responsible and moral economics. Change must occur at a pace that Saudi life and culture can accept and integrate. Their long and difficult road ahead will most likely impact the world, both because of Saudi Arabia's geo-political power in the Middle East, and because of its natural resources. Additionally, the schism between the Princes and their followers in the Saudi population could explode and spill across first the region and then globe.

With oil becoming an increasingly sought after resource internationally, some may wonder how oil production plays into the question of Islam and Capitalism. In Saudi Arabia, the state owns the oil reserves. While all citizens share in ownership of the resources and their subsequent sale, the means of production and investment are privately owned. In fact, the Saudi Arabian economy has recently opened up so that foreign investors and producers can now participate more easily. These factors combine to support both the *Umma* (with the exception of non-Saudi inhabitants of Saudi Arabia) and a global free market.

A failing of the Saudi Arabian state lies in the application of the Islamic concepts that underlie the *Zakat.* While the *Zakat* is collected and distributed to Saudi Arabian citizens in need, migrant workers are in no way cared for as part of the *Umma.* According to Human Rights Watch, vast abuse of workers occurs in an array of categories:

> In 1962, then-King Faisal abolished slavery in Saudi Arabia by royal decree. Over forty years later, migrant workers in the purportedly modern society that the kingdom has become continue to suffer extreme forms of labor exploitation that sometimes rise to slavery-like conditions. Their lives are further complicated by deeply rooted gender, religious and racial discrimination. This provides the foundation for prejudicial public policy and governmental regulations, shameful practices of private employers, and unfair legal proceedings that yield judicial sentences of the death penalty (Human Rights Watch 2004).

Neither this abuse of workers, nor the practice of overt discrimination against women, complies with Islamic or Free Market perspectives on the Rule of Law.

While 2005 marked the first municipal elections in 40 years, women were not allowed to vote. Still, even on this front, progress towards equality for all citizens is being made, even if at a snail's pace. Some evidence of this lies in the fact that Crown Prince Abdullah has allowed women to participate in a series of recent forum discussing the challenges facing the country. "Women have also recently been appointed to the executive committees of several government-controlled entities, including the Journalists' Syndicate and the National Human Rights Commission. In June, the Council of Ministers ...issued a plan to create jobs for women" (Ambah 2004).

To sum it up, Saudi Arabia, under Crown Prince Abdullah, seems to be moving towards a more peaceful existence, which, if successful, would uphold the values of both a Free Market Economy and Islamic Economic Doctrine. He will continue to have considerable opposition, as his brother continues to use clerics, the religious police, and other powerful people who fear loss if reforms continue against the Crown Prince. Regardless, the cultural doctrine of the West and that of Islam provide the foundations for peaceful coexistence both within Saudi Arabia and internationally.

Turkey

Turkey–a beautiful country located on the edge of the continents of Europe and Asia, former seat of the Ottoman Empire, and responsible for bridging the modern cultures of Western Asia and Europe (beginning with Mustafa Kemal Atatürk)–continues to forge new paths for Muslim countries. As a member of the Islamic Development Bank, the Organization of the Islamic Conference, the World Trade Organization and The North Atlantic Treaty Organization (NATO), Turkey seems to blend what some think should be a clash of civilizations into a working integration of Islamic, Western and global organizations.

Turkey maintains a Free Market (Mixed) economy. This includes private ownership of property, private means of production, worker incentive and the rule of law. Women have the same legal rights as men, as:

> The new Civil Code, adopted in 1926, abolished polygamy and recognized the equal rights of women in divorce, custody, and inheritance. The entire educational system from the grade school to the university became coeducational. Atatürk greatly admired the support that the national liberation struggle received from women and praised their many contributions .... He gave women the same opportunities as men, including full political rights. In the mid-1930s, 18 women, among them a villager, were elected to the national parliament. Later, Turkey had the world's first woman supreme court justice (Atatur.com 2004).

In addition to the reforms that Atatürk began in the 1920s, Turkey has undergone reforms recently in an attempt to comply with the standards set forth by the European Union for admittance. This has furthered progress in the treatment of Kurds and human rights in general:

> In an assessment of Turkey's progress in meeting human rights benchmarks, Human Rights Watch said today that press freedom, freedom of religion and respect for minorities in the country remain far from perfect, but show continued improvement. The Turkish government needs to take steps to eradicate torture in police stations and facilitate the return of hundreds of thousands of Kurds displaced in the 1990s (Human Rights Watch 2004).

In pursuing the honest application of the rule of law, peaceful treatment of citizens, and the respect and protection of property rights simultaneously, Turkey also pursues the ideologies of Islam and Free Market Mixed Economy Capitalism.

During 2004, the Turkish Minister of State for the Economy, H.E. Babacan, visited the United States. He spoke of the state of Turkey and its hopes for joining the European Union (EU). Mr. Babacan stated: "The political values of the EU are universal values." He added: "These values are not specific to any culture or any religion." He also recognized the strategic importance of Turkey, "which has a 98 percent Muslim population with a very well functioning democratic system …sharing the democratic political criteria of the Western world … (could) prove that it is possible to have different cultures co-existing and being centered on universal values" (Babacan 2004).

The reforms have not only been in areas of human rights, but also economically. Prior to the new government coming in 2002, the average inflation rate was 70 percent, the public net debt stock to GNP ration reached 91 percent, and the real domestic interest rates were 34 percent (Babacan 2004). However, these numbers have fallen drastically from 70 to 18.4 percent and from 91 to 71 percent. For such a short period, such a reduction seems incredible. Interestingly, this reduction of debt, inflation and interest rates seems functionally and ideologically compatible with both Islamic Economic Doctrine and that of a fruitful Free Market Economy.

Turkey, while it strongly practices policies of free trade, it simultaneously pursues its traditionally Islamic tenets through the *Zakat* and a *Riba*-free economy. While I have already discussed that some scholars maintain that only usury is *Riba*, and not interest, Turkey supports worldwide attempts in banking alternatives. Like Saudi Arabia and 54 other states, Turkey maintains an active membership in the Islamic Development Bank. As discussed earlier, a Free Market Economy does not require interest, despite its inclusion in all Western banking structures. Regardless, Muslims worldwide pursue the development of an economic system which applies principles that will, hopefully, result in provision for the world's poor and a more even distribution of wealth. Turkey is no exception and neither is the Kyrgyz Republic.

The Kyrgyz Republic

The Kyrgyz Republic, with a 75 percent Muslim population and a 20 percent Russian orthodox population, leads the other primarily Muslim, former-Soviet states in transitioning from Communist-authoritarian-atheist states to free democratic ones. While this country claimed statehood only 13 years ago and wrote a constitution only 11 years ago, it maintains a 96–99 percent literacy rate, a $1,632,293,504 GDP, and hosts legitimately free elections with all citizens, male and female, voting. It also has maintained "a strong growth of an average of almost six percent a year …has the most liberal foreign trade and has managed to join the WTO" (Aslund March 3, 2000). In 2004, the GDP rose nine percent while maintaining a low 3.5 percent inflation rate.

Like Turkey, Kyrgyzstan courts both internal and external investments. Also like Turkey, the Kyrgyz Republic seeks to progress multi-dimensionally and pursue policies in accordance with universal values. President Akaev writes: "We need to upgrade and expand the nation's economic infrastructure in order to accelerate the development of the whole economy. The energy sector should be developed on principles of fair competition, effective corporate management, reduction of losses and costs, and accessibility of services to people. Each residence must be warm and have light." He also writes that "Poverty manifests itself in many forms. These include violation of human rights. Poverty, coupled with inequality, increases the vulnerability of social, economic, and political freedoms, generates social tension ....We must consistently and emphatically reduce poverty in all its forms because it infringes on human dignity and creates an obstacle to its adequate development" (Akaev 2003–2005).

In President Akaev's statements, one can see the integration of Islamic, Free Market, and overlapping universal principles. The Kyrgyz Republic practices free trade and economic growth. It is a member of the World Trade Organization, the Economic Cooperation Organization (an organization that promotes economic and cultural cooperation between Islamic States), the UN, and the Islamic Development Bank. Like Turkey, the Kyrgyz Republic truly seeks viable progress on all fronts.

The transition to a Free Market Economy has not been easy. When the state owns all means of production, all farmland, and housing, it can be quite challenging trying to determine how to fairly distribute resources while teaching people how to handle business practices. Kyrgyzstan has also had to work to both create a democracy while "balancing between the general tolerance for beliefs that has characterized much of government policy, and the increasing authoritarianism and influence of security forces" (International Crisis Group 2003). While this seems to be a common problem worldwide, the Kyrgyz Republic appears to handle it progressively. "A middle-range policy seems to be emerging that is meant to keep Hizb-Ut-Tahrir in check but avoid too much repression for fear of radicalizing their ranks or stirring inter-ethnic tensions" (International Crisis Group 2003).

In summary, like the other states discussed, Kyrgyzstan is attempting to progress in multiple areas. It pursues growth simultaneously with the integration of Islamic principles and Western economic doctrine. While the Kyrgyz Republic seems to be significantly more secular than either Saudi Arabia or even Turkey, it maintains memberships in international Islamic organizations, pursues an interest free economy, and works for universal care of the poor in its country.

CONCLUSION

Capitalism and Islam are concepts that signify two ideologies, two systems of economics, two cultures, two belief systems, and some would say two religions (money-theism). In comparing these monolithic cognitive structures, one man-made and the other, Muslims believe, designed by God, modern tendency dictates a binary outlook. Citizens of the industrialized West often ask questions and expect answers that can be viewed as "true or false," "black and white," or "yes and no." This is termed "binary thinking" and refers to the style of thinking where there exist only two variables in answer to any question.

Cultural anthropologists often look at Western, low-context, linear culture as binary. Influenced by their culture, Westerners then think that questions must be phrased in ways of right/wrong, good/bad, and they search for quantitative data that gives weight to one answer or the other, thereby proving it is true. Unfortunately, quantitative analysis cannot accommodate the multitude of variables in human existence. Therefore, meaningful "yes/no" (compatible, incompatible) answers must be understood within the limited paradigm for which they were created.

In examining the complexity of the world, one must accept that binary thinking is not the best solution. If our leaders, scholars, and corporate executives continue to frame the world in a black/white simple solution manner exemplified by the resounding question, "Are Islam and Capitalism compatible?", we will never reach the solutions for which we are grasping. In asking questions that demand binary answers, we cut away levels meaning until all we have left is a naked, efficient "yes" or "no" which only bridges the surface of the problem and fails to ask questions like "For which sect? In which country? With which interpretations of the *Qur'an*?

Islam and Capitalism entail complex structures, belief systems, ideologies, values and even behavior patterns. The followers of each system interpret, delineate, and live their lives in as many ways as there are people. The Muslim people of the Kyrgyz Republic have a vastly different history and culture than the people of Saudi Arabia or Turkey or Nigeria or Indonesia. While people continue to have the same basic needs worldwide, the lenses of history and culture lead to vastly divergent lenses through which to view the world and their religion.

In this chapter, I have explored the paradigms of each doctrine. I have shown that if one does not refer to pre-Industrial Revolution Adam Smith Capitalism, but instead to a kinder, more responsible Free Market–Mixed Economy form of Capitalism, the underlying structures of Islam and Capitalism are compatible. A person could both follow Islam faithfully and participate in a Free Market Economy. In fact, every day, the majority of Muslim people both follow their faith to the best of their human ability and participate in some aspect of the global economy. So where is the confusion? Why is the question being asked?

Oftentimes within a culture, people believe that the ideology they profess defines them. In the United States words like Capitalism, Christianity, and Democracy are thrown about as if "we" all understand what these terms are. Yet television, radio and newspapers rarely if ever discuss the nuances and cultural implications of what it means to be a Catholic versus a Southern Baptist, an Evangelical, a Protestant or any of the other one-hundred-plus "types" of Christians. Many people believe that since they all "believe in Jesus," they are all Christian and so are "basically the same." Such people forget the hundreds of years of bloody fighting in Europe during which hundreds of thousands of people were killed or even burned at the stake because they were the wrong types of Christians.

Many Christians like to point out that the massacres of the Crusades did not truly represent the teachings as professed by Jesus: i.e. "love thy brother" and "turn the other cheek." The same can be said for the modern predatory business practices of global corporations owned by "Christian" nations. Humans have a habit of consciously believing in a given ideology or religion, while simultaneously acting on equally integrated but opposing unconscious belief systems (Weaver 2000, 72–77).

What does this mean for Islam and Capitalism? We know that the principles underlying a Free Market Economy to include Rule of Law, and the ownership of private property, means of production, and wealth are all compatible with Islamic Economic Doctrine. In reverse, the requirement of *Zakat,* the prohibition of *Riba,* and the spiritual guidance regarding the treatment of the poor can all coexist on top of and within a Free Market Economy. However, with that being said, there are still no easy answers on which boardrooms can act. The people who follow Islam live their lives struggling, as does every other human, with the influences of history, culture, politics and economics. Even so, like theoretical Capitalism, Islam clearly supports the underlying ideologies of positive peace, personal empowerment, and economic, political and religious freedoms.

CHAPTER 4

Islam and Socialism

Arshi Saleem Hashmi

Jacques Goudeau

INTRODUCTION

This chapter is about the compatibility of Islam and Socialism as a socio-economic system. An attempt has been made to discuss the important ideas in socialism and how they can be incorporated in a Muslim society. Moreover, what is relevant in the analysis is not the concept of socialism but the relevance of a socialist system to a Muslim society. Thus, it is important to discover the compatibilities of Islam and socialism, as well as reconcile the inherent dichotomy between the anti-religious Marxist foundation of socialism and the entrenchment of religion throughout the Muslim world.

Some states successfully adopted socialism, at least in part, and formulated their economies to blend both capitalist and socialist systems. These few states emerged from the Cold War with developed, state-run economies. The majority of Muslim States tried similar paths but failed to enjoy the fruits of such amalgamation. To account for this discrepancy, we must define the concept of socialism and how it differs from communism. It is also worth investigating the relatively higher Muslim societal attraction to socialism as compared to its Western counterparts. As the appeal of socialism to Muslims does not appear to be waning, it is important to extract the many compatible ideas in socialism and Islam and apply them to society in a positive manner.

While there are many definitions of socialism, one generic definition may succinctly get the point across. It is a system of social organization in which property and the distribution of income are subject to social control rather than individual determination or market forces. Socialism refers to both a set of doctrines and the political movements that aspire to put these doctrines into practice (Encyclopedia Britannica).

The term socialism, in its modern sense, made its first appearance around 1830. In France, it was applied to the writings of Fourier and Saint-Simon, and in Britain to those of Robert Owen (www.marxists.org/reference/subject/economics/owen/). However, in the Muslim world, a particular dimension of this all-encompassing definition took root. This is the concept of Market Socialism, also called liberal socialism. In liberal socialism, the particular (sometimes national) economic system represented a compromise between socialist planning and free enterprise. Specifically, the enterprises are publicly owned, but production and consumption are guided by market forces as opposed to government planning. A form of market socialism was adopted in Yugoslavia in the 1960s in distinction to the centrally planned socialism of the Soviet Union. A similar concept was applied in Pakistan in the 1970s under Bhutto whose party manifesto was "food, clothes and housing for everybody." Because the Soviet dimension explicitly rejected religion, an analysis of this type of socialism and Islam is moot. Thus, our definition of socialism will be that of liberal socialism.

Robert Owen provided the essence of socialism in the following words (although the nomenclature was assigned later): "What ideas individuals may attach to the term 'Millennium' I know not; but I know that society may be formed so as to exist with out crime, without poverty, with health greatly improved, with little, if any misery, and with intelligence and happiness increased a hundredfold; and no obstacle whatsoever intervenes at this moment except ignorance to prevent such a state of society from becoming universal" (Robert Owen: http://www.robert-wen.com/).

Through the course of modern development, socialists have made numerous critiques of capitalism, namely: (a) pre-Marxian analyses of the way capitalist development generates extreme poverty and suffering and simultaneously extreme concentrations of wealth; (b) Marx's dissection of capitalist exploitation and class antagonism; (c) Lenin's work on imperialism as the highest stage of capitalism; and (d) contemporary critiques of dependency. Socialists have also lambasted the international expansion of capitalist social relations as a process which has brought misery rather than improvements in living conditions for the vast majority of the world's people. In addition, socialists suggest that rather than "developing" the Third World, capitalism has "underdeveloped" it, that it has made conditions worse than they were when it was still "undeveloped," meaning free of the imposition of capitalist class relations.

Yet, at the same time, rather than abandoning the capitalist development project, socialists have consistently proposed the adoption of an alternative "socialist development." This has been the case primarily since the construction of socialism in the USSR provided a real life alternative to capitalism, and not just a theory. The extremely rapid (by historical standards) industrialization of the USSR, which at the time of the Revolution of 1917 was still an overwhelmingly agrarian society, convinced many of the superiority of socialist over capitalist development. This was particularly true in the Third World where anti-colonial sentiment often included an anti-capitalist backlash.

In the Arab world, the concept of Arab socialism as a political ideology was defined by Michel Aflaq, one of the founders of the Ba'ath party, in order to distinguish socialist ideology from Soviet socialism. On the one hand, Arab socialism endorsed much of the economic and social programs of Marxist-style socialism. However, the divergent intellectual and spiritual doctrines imposed limits on its revolutionary potential. For example, the ownership of the means of production was to be nationalized but only within the constraints of traditional values such as private property and inheritance. Additionally, primitive social structures such as feudalism, nomadic tribalism, and religious factionalism were to be overcome, but not at the cost of severing the social ties that constituted the Arab identity. Thus, while there were certainly Marxist ideas in the socialism of the Muslim world, there was a sincere effort to establish a distinct Islamic imprint.

Many intellectuals in the independence movements were impressed with Soviet efforts to foster socialist development and began to consider ways socialism might be adapted to their own circumstances. Such intellectuals included both revolutionaries as well as those who sought more peaceful change. Already, by 1920, Mao ZeDong had been drawn into Marxism and the struggle for socialism, in part by the Soviet example. By 1927, Jawaharlal Nehru, returning from the Brussels' Congress of Oppressed Nationalities and a visit to Moscow, was ready to proclaim that his goal was socialism as well as the independence he had hitherto pursued as a disciple of Mahatma Gandhi. In 1936, he enunciated a view of the relationship between socialism and development which would be shared by a generation of leaders throughout the Third World. In the 1950s, Gamal Abdul Nasser of Egypt and later in the 1970s Zulfikar Ali Bhutto of Pakistan coined the term Islamic Socialism to accommodate the demand at home for a more spiritual form of socialism. The problem was initiated by Islamic clergy and scholars declaring the leaders atheists. Thus, largely due to defensive political reasons, Nasser and Bhutto endorsed their allegiance to the religion in a socialist economy. The essence of Islamic Socialism was summed up by the party ideology of the Pakistan Peoples Party, which stated the following: "Islam is our Faith, Democracy is our Politics, and Socialism is our Economy, All Power to the People."

In sum, the concept of socialism has certainly mutated repeatedly over time, meant different things to different people at different times. And there have indeed been within all of its history two contradictory meanings in struggle with each other. The first is that emphasized by its capitalist critics: a tradition that honors intentional social and economic planning over the automatic adjustments of capitalist markets. The second is that emphasized by the proponents of socialism: a tradition of believing that human beings can indeed cooperate to jointly determine their collective future in ways far superior to that possible under the regime of capitalist exploitation and the markets that have always been associated with it.

REVIEW OF RELEVANT LITERATURE

The scholars and their works discussed in this part have different backgrounds. Two of them have a Middle Eastern perspective; two having a Western background have jointly worked on an analytical work on the possibility of Islamic economic system as a third way, while the last one has a practical communist perspective on the relationship between Islam and socialism. These authors in their own capacity have tried to inform and convince the Muslim world about the fundamental principles of socialism that are completely compatible with the Islamic economic system. These authors have made an effort to explain the fundamental fault in understanding socialism as a strictly Marxist political system rather than an economic system which can be applied in a Democratic structure like the Scandinavian countries and to a lesser degree Western Europe and America.

Some scholars and writers in the Muslim world are against the concept of Islamic socialist economy. They see this concept not in isolation but being part of the grand communist manifesto. On the other hand, Adel Hussein of Egypt, Ali Shariati of Iran, Mir Said Mirza Sultan Galiev of Russia are very comfortable with the notion that Islamic socialist economic system can be adapted and applied in any Muslim society. The basic difference here is between the school of thought which believes in complete separation of communist ideology and Islam, with emphasis on categorizing socialism as an economic expression of communism, and those who call themselves socialist but not Marxist. So we can have a socialist Muslim, a socialist Christian, or a socialist Jew, for instance, but it is not possible to be a communist and at the same time maintain a religious identity.

First and foremost, Rodinson was a Marxist. In addition, early in his career, he was a member of the French Communist Party. Yet, when Soviet atrocities were exposed during the Kruschev era, Rodinson began a lengthy process of reevaluating his Communist dogma, reverting back to a "purer" form of Marxism, based more in economics than politics and more tolerant of religions. Nonetheless, the revolutionary tendencies of the proletariat to bring about social collectivism remained prominent in Rodinson's beliefs. The essays in *Marxism and the Muslim World* (1981) are based on lectures he delivered to Muslims at various locations in the Arab world. The reactions he received were largely negative, but understandable in the context of the geopolitical atmosphere of the time; communists condemned him for abandoning the party, and Muslims attacked his views because he was irreligious. At the time, however, the pervasive tension of the Cold War perpetuated ideological dogma. Either one was a communist or s/he was not; either one was a nationalist or s/he was not. Thus, because of the historical circumstances from which Rodinson's ideas emanated, he evaluated the compatibility of Islam with fundamental Marxism and the incompatibility of Islam with communism. Some of his ideas can be useful, but he analyzed Islam and communism not Islam and socialism.

Therefore, Rodinson's theme can be described contemporarily as one relating Islam to a now defunct interpretation of Socialism (fundamentalist Marxism). Rodinson worked, lived, and studied in the Arab and Muslim world for much of his life. As noted earlier, his book, *Marxism and the Muslim World*, is a collection of essays taken from various lectures delivered throughout the Muslim world in the late 1950s and early 1960s. Although he was a self-described atheist, his respect for the potential influence of religion, and in particular Islam, can be understood in terms of its ability to unite the oppressed masses in the revolutionary cause. He describes Islam's religious community as "A society that resembles a nation in many respects. It forms itself, takes decisions collectively under the guidance of its leaders, defines and adapts its internal structures, attacks and defends itself, has a strategy and tactics. It gives a feeling of belonging, patriotism of the community that makes people take sides on global options with vigor, devotion, and self-sacrifice if necessary" (Rodinson 1981:139).

Rodinson's interpretation of the importance of Islam bringing about a Marxist revolution in the Arab world is difficult to understate. The revolution of the proletariat is, in Marxist theory, an essential prerequisite to establishing a truly egalitarian society. Rodinson believed that the coalescence of the Arab world which Islam brought to the region in the 8th Century instilled Muslims to unite against outside aggression. In addition, centuries of defense and struggle against the Europeans, Ottomans, and more recently the Soviets enabled Islam to be a perfect rallying point for rebellion against foreign domination, even (as in the Soviet case) when an appealing economic system was intertwined with such ideas of foreign grandeur. In short, Rodinson believed that the unification of Arabs through Islam enhanced the region's prospects of fending off the capitalist imperialism of the Europeans in the first half of the 20th Century. The resulting unity against outside influence then drove Arab nationalism, a concept not necessarily opposed to Marxist economic transformation. However, nationalist Islamic socialism, while fending off capitalist imperialism and struggling to create its own identity, was able to successfully oppose communist incursion into Islamic lands.

While Rodinson pointed out some advantages Islam brought to the spread of Marxist ideology in the Muslim world, he also examined numerous conflicts between Islam and the particular Marxist doctrine of communism. He described the notorious incompatibility of ideologies as being two-sided. First, there is communism's struggle against Islam. This is a by-product of communism's generally anti-religious attitude. Communist organizations feel themselves bound by doctrine to struggle constantly against all religions. Religion as a false ideology used by the ruling classes dulls or mystifies the potential revolutionary awareness of the oppressed classes (Rodinson 1981:97). There is no doubt that Soviet communists sought to gain influence in the Islamic world, but the religion of Islam was considered an obstacle to communism not only in the foreign Arab lands but also in the Soviet homeland.

The second incompatibility is Islam's struggle against Communism. Rodinson interpreted Islam to be aligned with certain economic and social fundamentals of communism. These include strong egalitarian attitudes and vehement anti-colonialist or imperialist designs. He wrote about Muslim religious elements that have formulated Islamo-communist "concordism." These elements attempted to bridge Islam and Communism by laying a foundation of principles on which both ideologies could agree. "Islam is desirous of the well-being of the people, does not tolerate monopolies, and condemns loans with interest and therefore capitalism as well" (Rodinson 1981:101). But the discrepancy between Islamic nationalism and communist expansionism is irreconcilable. Rodinson described Islam's initial struggle against communism as a "reaction that represented a continuation of the age-old struggle of Muslim religious cadres against medieval heresies, irreligion, free-thinking, and then against religious indifferences and laicism disseminated by Europe" (Rodinson 1981:51). Thus, Marxist appeal and strong anti-imperialist tendencies in the Arab world during the 20th Century led directly to an Islamic adaptation to communism.

Two important Muslim thinkers who were influenced by Marxism and yet maintained their identity as Islamic thinkers are important in this review of the existing works on Islam and socialism. One finds both criticism on the relationship and approval for compatibility between the two ideologies. Interestingly, scholars who have talked about Islamic socialist democracy and socialist economy never accepted the fact that they were socialist or Marxist. Adel Hussein of Egypt, a former Marxist and now a moderate Muslim thinker, is one of them. Today, scholars like Adel Hussein are often the public face of Islam–writing in leading Arabic newspapers, speaking at conferences and on television talk shows, enjoying the support of many younger, more political Muslims interested in their attempts to rethink Islam's relationship to democracy, minorities and the West.

They bring an overtly activist stance to Islam, unlike traditional scholars who tend to be more concerned with questions of religious law, for example, or what is permissible under Islam. Hussein, for instance, believes that his goals have not changed. He still believes in social justice and Third World development. But he now sees Islam, through its ability to persuade and to mobilize, as the best tool. He respects what the West has created, but He also resents its dominance over the economy, culture and politics. Hussein, for years one of Egypt's most respected leftist economists, now leads the Islamic Labor Party, which publishes *The People* Egypt's best-known Islamic newspaper. He and his former Marxist colleagues speak of Islam as the only ideology still viable for disenchanted Muslims. Some of Hussein's other contemporaries like Abdel-Wahab Elmessiri, a former leftist with a doctorate in poetry from Rutgers University in New Jersey, considers everything from pornography to pollution as Western ills for which Islam must find a solution. Sudan's Hassan Turabi, who has tried to fashion an Islamic state in his country, recalls that in the early 1960s, all his schoolmates were Marxists. Now, he says, they speak the language of Islam (Anthony Shadid 1997:www.ol.ie/afifi/BICNews/Islam).

Another Important Islamic-Marxist name in the Muslim world is Ali Shariati. He is, for many, the ideological father of the Iranian revolution. For Iranians, the genuine need for modernity and the struggle to protect Islam became a contradictory dilemma. Modernity was Westward-looking, change-oriented and anti-tradition, while Islam is the formal cornerstone of society's established traditional values, a deeply-value reliable cultural heritage. Also, Islam and modernity present a trade-off. The choice of a path to modernity–economic, political, and ideological–posed itself only after modernity is pursued at the cost of religion. This clash of powerful contradictory ideas leaves a few intellectuals–a third group that seeks a union of opposites–in a limbo of uncertainty. Ali Shariati is of this group. He is part Muslim, part Christian, part Jew, part Buddhist, part Mazdaki, part Sufi, part heretic, part Marxist, part existentialist, part humanist and part skeptic. Shariati is perfectly at ease being a nationalist and internationalist at the same time, a materialist as well as an idealist and a practicing spiritualist. Shariati is an individualist at war with individualism and a militant of social causes, ever evading the masses. A firm believer in the inevitability of change and the necessity of adaptation, he was a modernist who usually detested the persistence of outmoded traditions, customs and institutions.

Shariati is probably the only contemporary Iranian intellectual who created a socio-political momentum that gave birth to a social movement, culminating in a revolution. In the ultimate social revolution, he sees the end of all injustice, oppression and inequality: the birth of the "perfect" New Man. The revolution, he believes, would end the dualities and the binary system. It would usher in a personal, social, political, economic and religious monotheism, imposing the will of the good and divine over the evil and satanic. Shariati is a romantic and not a practitioner of revolutions (Ali Rahnema 2000). Mir-Said (Mirza) Sultan-Galiev, Stalin's protégé at the Commissariat of Nationalities (Narkomnats), writing in *The Life of Nationalities,* the Narkomnats' journal, states that Sultan-Galiev became 'the first victim of a Stalinist purge' in 1923, when he was arrested for forming an illegal nationalist organization. At the time, he was head of the Muslim Military College. Sultan-Galiev believed in the tradition of Muslim socialism. From the early years of the 20th Century, there had arisen a secularizing reform movement within Islam, known as Jadid. Within the Muslim intelligentsia was a smaller group of Muslim socialists who saw, as articulated by Hanafi Muzzafar, a Volga Tatar: "Muslim people will unite themselves to communism; like communism, Islam rejects narrow nationalism." "Islam is international and recognizes only brotherhood and unity of all nations under the banner of Islam." Now the criticism on this is while Muslim communism might make sense as shorthand for a tactical alliance or as an ethnic-religious description, but as an ideology, a worldview, a systematic understanding of the world, it is self-contradictory (as contradictory as 'socialist Zionism'–which is not to say such people can't exist, only that they are confused as to the meaning of one or the other terms (Gerry Byrne 2004: www.workersliberty.org)). "There has been criticism on the compatibility of the two socio-economic systems, as Hanafi Muzzafar spelled out: Islamic internationalism is based on the *Umma,* the brotherhood of all Muslims. It is not the same as proletarian internationalism. Communism, proletarian internationalism, links the common situation of the oppressed masses with a common aim: socialism, the abolition of classes" (Gerry Byrne 2004: www.workerliberty.org).

J. Barkley Rosser and Marina V. Rosser talk about a "third way" of economic system in which economic decision making is once again embedded to some extent within a broader socio-cultural framework, but which uses, or seeks to use, modern technology to be an advanced modern economy. According to Barkley and Marina, within the context of the old comparison between market capitalism and command socialism, the new tradition economy offers itself as a potential "Third Way." It claims to represent the best of both worlds and to be superior to either. It claims to combine the old with the new, the individual with the collective, and the ethical with the practical. There is a harking back to a mythic past of the old traditional economy and the early period of the religion when all were supposedly righteous (Rosser 1999:763). While comparing other religious traditions like Judaism, Christianity, Hinduism Buddhism, and Confucianism, both the writers argue that none of the traditions really qualify as truly new traditional movements in that they do not present fully developed systems of economic thought and practices, but merely advocate scattered injunctions to mildly modify capitalist economies. But at least, ideologically, Islamic economics puts itself forward as a complete system embedded within a fully developed religious framework. The greater comprehensiveness of the Islamic economic system initially arose from the prophet Muhammad's (PBUH) having himself been a practicing merchant, in contrast to the founders of other great world religions. But it also reflects the view of modern Islamic economists who argue that it is a potential Third Way between capitalism and socialism for developing economies emerging from colonial rule (Rosser 1999:778).

The authors we have examined all contribute to the debate on the relationship between Islam and socialism. However, there are fundamental problems in the pre-analytical assumptions made of socialism and Islam. Many scholars have blurred the distinction between political, economic, and religious structures. For example, communism and socialism are sometimes equated. This is an unfortunate consequence of the inertia of the Cold War; socialism was synonymous with communism during the decades of paranoia and suspicion of the Soviet system. We wish to make the clarification that communism is a combination of political and economic ideologies. It is rooted in political authoritarianism and collectivist economics. Thus, as the socialist democracies of the Scandinavian countries demonstrate, one can have socialism without authoritarianism. Another assumption some scholars have made is that the economic systems of socialism and capitalism are mutually exclusive to their compatibility with Islam. But why must one choose either pure collectivism or pure individualism? In fact, there is no nation on earth that fully conforms to either economic system. Why, then, are theorists constrained to analyze Islam as either socialist or capitalist? Surely, there is common ground that is not purely of one extreme or the other. Our analysis, thus, distinguishes between societal structures on three levels: political, economic, and religious. In doing so, we relegate others to compare Islam and communism because we consider it a political-economic institution and that is not our purpose. Our concern is the link between socialism (a collective economic system) and Islam (a structured yet peaceful religion).

ANALYSIS OF FINDINGS

In continuing this chapter's analysis on the compatibility of Islam and Socialism, three case studies are examined. The societies of Pakistan, Egypt, and Syria were chosen because of their Islamic identities. In addition, studying the Pakistani case allows for a non-Arab society to be investigated, thereby contributing a broader scope to this chapter. The Syrian and Pakistani cases involve socialist development throughout most of the post-war period. Economics, religion, ideology, and international influences are part of the analysis for these two societies. In contrast, Egypt is studied in a far more specific context. The era examined for this case is the 18-year rule of Gamal Abdel Nasser. In particular, the issue of land redistribution is studied in depth. Land reform, a socialist idea, was to some extent implemented in some form or another in all three societies. Therefore, it was chosen as a significant topic of interest to the compatibility of Islam and socialism.

Pakistan and Bhutto's Islamic Socialism

Pakistan has been struggling to develop an all-encompassing identity since its founding as an independent state in 1947. The nation was created by Western-oriented professionals and bureaucrats as a homeland for Muslims, a place where they would no longer be a minority community in the Hindu-majority state of India. Enthusiasm and a sense of profound moral renaissance for Muslims in south Asia accompanied independence.

The vision of promise and unity soon encountered the realities of state building. Islamists and secularists disputed the centrality of Islam in the government. In the 1950s and the 1960s, Pakistan emphasized building its industrial base to ensure both economic and political survival. Western-educated professionals and industrialists, as well as forward-looking feudal landlords who valued education became increasingly influential. A fairly liberal interpretation of Islam was supported by the state, resulting in the passage of the Muslim Family Laws Ordinance in 1961. The period of charismatic leader Zulfikar Ai Bhutto and his "Islamic Socialism" unfolded in the 1970s. The public mindset changed from being emotionally and politically tied to the concept of a two-nation theory (one Hindu and one Muslim) that provided the basis for the creation of Pakistan to a high level of material expectation. Many people believed that life would improve significantly under Bhutto and his political party, Pakistan People's Party (PPP), but from 1971 to 1972, there was little change in the standard of living.

Inter-group tensions grew, as members of the lower and middle classes became disillusioned; upper class industrialists were alienated by the government's nationalization policies; and wealthy landlords were threatened by Bhutto's land reform program which, as criticized by some, weakened only his adversaries. In order to find an answer to the question why Bhutto used the term "Islamic Socialism" instead of "Socialism," Chengappa says that it was because of the Pakistani public's level of political consciousness that the prefix Islam proved appropriate (www.ciaonet.org). Bhutto's brand of Islamic socialism was an amalgam of anti-Indianism, socialism and nationalism (Bahadur 1977:121).

The reason why it is often said that Islam and communism have a lot in common is that both ideologies believe in a classless society and an equitable distribution of wealth. Arif Hussein quotes a Muslim League leader, Mian Abdul Bari, in the book, *Pakistan, its ideology and Foreign Policy,* stating in the parliament the following: "Islamic socialism is as much above Communism and if Communism comes into contact with Islamic socialism, I am sure we may be able to convert it into the Islamic cult" (Hassan 1966:90–91). It was actually Bhutto's strategy to guarantee a popular support base by providing an ideological base with the help of Islam. The PPP was the first party to acknowledge the claims of distributive justice. The famous slogan of *Bread, Clothes and House Roti, Kapra aur Makan in Urdu* was accepted by people not as a socialist idea but something directly derived from Islamic teachings about equal distribution of resources and idea of "*Adl and Insaaf.*" It was this realization that people voted for Bhutto because in him they saw a leader pledging to deliver what has only been a long desire. The Prefix Islamic was also to pre-empt any criticism from the rightist parties, mainly the Muslim league. Bhutto's ideology in no way was an interpretation of Marxism. The idea of Islamic socialism was presented to people in a four-fold motto: (1) islam is our faith, (2) democracy is our polity, (3) socialism is our economy, and (4) all power to the people (Raza 1997:-6).

The People's Party manifesto was couched in socialist terms. When Bhutto issued the Economic Reform Order on January 3, 1972, banking and insurance institutions were nationalized, and 70 other industrial enterprises were taken over by the government. The Ministry of Production, which incorporated the Board of Industrial Management, was established to oversee industry. Investment in the public sector increased substantially, and Bhutto maneuvered to break the power of the approximately 22 elite families that had dominated the nation's economy during the Ayub Khan period. Trade Unions were strengthened, and welfare measures for labor were announced. Although Bhutto's initial zeal diminished as he came face-to-face with economic realities and the shortage of capital, he tried to refurbish his populist image with another spate of nationalization in 1976 (Chenngapha 2002).

Bhutto proceeded cautiously in the field of land reform and did not fulfill earlier promises of distributing land to the landless on the scales he had promised, as he was forced to recognize and cultivate the sociopolitical influence of landowners. However, he did not impede the process of consolidation of tenancy rights and acquisition of mid-sized holdings by servicemen. Punjab was the vital agricultural region of Pakistan; it remained a bastion of support for the government. Success of Bhutto's Islamic Socialism can be evaluated in terms of the political mobilization of the people. Bhutto was able to communicate with the masses and used the medium of Islamic socialism. Until Bhutto arrived on the political scene, the landed aristocracy had monopolized the business of politics, but none of them were able to develop the kind of equation with the common man that he had been able to achieve. This is because these elitist leaders spoke a language that did not touch a chord in the hearts of the peasants, landless laborers, urban poor, small farmers, and salaried classes. The fact that the PPP candidate, Khursheed Hassan Meer, a former Pakistan Air Force non-commissioned officer won against the high profile Asghar Khan, a former Chief of Pakistan Air Force, from Rawalpindi, a cantonment city with a large retired military population, illustrates the point clearly (Mazari 1999:171).

Another important factor to evaluate Bhutto's era of Islamic socialism in Pakistan is his government's economic performance. It is very important that his performance should be examined in the context of the Pakistan which had lost its east wing and was undergoing political, economic and social transformation after the era of General Ayub and General Yahya Khan. Bhutto's attempt to nationalize the business and financial sector did not bring fruit during his time. However, his successor, General Zia, benefited from those policies, and extensive public sector investment in industry enabled excellent economic growth in the Zia period (no doubt there were other factors involved like the enormous amount of aid due to Pakistan's pro-United States policy in the Afghan war). Some people like Bindanda Chengappa are of the view that the Bhutto regime's efforts in economic development helped Zia to continue in power (Chengappa 2002).

Chengappa (2002) further says that the Bhutto period witnessed widespread improvement of agriculture, the most vital sector of the economy. The credit, subsidy and price policies all aided the growth of agriculture, particularly the small and the medium-sized farmers. The 'tractorization' also contributed to the development of the sector. Similarly, the banking sector, which was earlier confined to the urban areas, underwent a revolution and shifted from class banking to mass banking, with an extended reach into rural areas. On the negative side, the nationalization of the agro-industrial unit proved to be a disaster both on the economic and political fronts. It was a shortsighted move and eroded the credibility of the PPP regime in addition to antagonizing its own constituencies.

It could be argued that Bhutto used Islamic socialism to change the terms of political discourse for the first time in the country. Economics took precedent over politics. Bhutto and Islamic socialism are identified with each other in Pakistan. Another important factor of Bhutto's Islamic socialism was that it involved the masses to a greater degree than the previous regimes in Pakistan. Also, since nationalization was not approved by the United States during Bhutto's first term, its influence in Pakistan was largely reduced.

Egypt and the Nasser Revolution

Gamal Abdel Nasser assumed control of Egypt in a coup d'etat in July of 1952. The preceding monarchial regime had left the economy in shambles. Wealth and property were owned by a tiny fraction of the population. There was little industry of note, and the agrarian sector was underdeveloped and inefficient. The transition from a government passively involved in economic development to Nasser's "centralized market economy" (O'Brien 1966:316) began with mixed economic tendencies and ended with broad economic state control. Early in the new regime, land redistribution efforts solidified Nasser's support amongst the population. After the Suez war in 1957, the regime began consolidating control over private enterprises. Production targets and price controls were implemented to regulate most sectors of the economy. "In every case which entailed an incompatibility between ends and means the government almost invariably reacted by increasing power of the state rather than adopting the alternative path of negotiation and compromise" (O'Brien 1966:240). The resulting economic system was termed Arab Socialism. The issue of land reform was the foundation of the socialist reforms that took place during Nasser's 18-year reign. In contributing to the prospects of compatibility between Islam and socialism, a case study of the land redistribution efforts in Nasser's Egypt is appropriate.

Land reform was one of Nasser's foremost priorities in restructuring the Egyptian economy from private to public ownership. Throughout previous decades, Egypt's society became stratified between a disproportionately small land-owning class and a vast amalgam of sharecroppers, farm workers, and tenants. Rural peasant unrest coupled with political instability in Cairo provided a fertile climate for Nasser's government to implement broad land reforms or, more specifically, land redistribution. "In 1952 (the government) initiated a phased land reform program that targeted the property of the upper class of landowners, dubbed 'feudalists' by the government, for distribution…The beneficiaries were to be tenants, estate workers, and the poorest villagers. The law also fixed rents, set tenancy duration at a minimum of three years, and established a minimum wage" (Library of Congress, http://lcweb2.loc.gov/frd/cs).

Expanded reforms in 1961 and 1969 further reduced the size of legal landownership, but this approach was one-sided. There was no effort to consolidate small parcels of land deemed insufficient to support the tenants/owners. Towards the end of the Nasser era, the beneficiaries of previous land redistribution efforts emerged with smaller parcels due to population increases and Islamic inheritance laws. In addition, the population increases resulted in an aggregate decrease in land ownership by the peasants. The temporary nature of the success of land reforms instituted by the socialist Nasser regime is not an inevitable consequence. "Land reform laws in Egypt never had a land consolidation component as they did, for example, in Jordan" (Library of Congress, http://lcweb2.loc.gov/frd/cs). Indeed, "Land tenure, however, rather than landownership reflected how land was actually operated in Egypt…The rapid changes that occurred after 1975 and the increasing mechanization and intensification of agriculture led some scholars to conclude that landownership might no longer be the sole instrument of land control or wealth" (Library of Congress, http://lcweb2.loc.gov/frd/cs). Thus, land reform in the long-term is an imperfect solution to agrarian insufficiencies in Islamic countries. It is more likely that modernization of farm capital and farm inputs would improve sector growth. However, the land reforms assisted Nasser in gaining political capital by quelling some of the rural unrest. Hosseinzadeh explains that "(Nasser) carried out a land reform that, while terminating the power of the landed aristocracy, was orderly and with generous compensation" (Hosseinzadeh 1989:108).

Short-term improvements in the agricultural industry were soon offset by a failure to invest capital for greater efficiency. There were several reasons for this. First, the land reform laws were passed without guaranteeing the finality of the measures. "Landowners never received an explicit guarantee from the government against further redistribution of land and rent control, while amendments to the original Agrarian Reform Law almost certainly engendered uncertainty and inhibited investment in the improvement of farms or the private reclamation of land. For example, the original law permitted companies engaged in reclamation to retain land above the maximum 200 *feddans* for a period of 25 years, but an amendment of 1957 compelled them to sell 25 percent of their holdings to the Ministry of Agrarian Reform" (O'Brien 1966:233). Second, broad controls implemented by the Nasser government in 1956 exacerbated inefficiencies in the industrial sector at a time when capitalists were still expected to invest in such businesses. "Industrial investment had to fall within the pattern prescribed by the Industrial Plan; a plan private business had played no part in formulating. Law 21 of 1958 prevented mangers of large industrial firms from expanding, limiting capacity, or changing the location of plant (sic) without reference to the Ministry of Industry. The minister was also empowered to define specifications and fix prices for manufactured commodities" (O'Brien 1966:233). Lastly, the business class in Egypt was never comfortable in the climate of socialism. Investors lacked confidence in doing business with enterprises that, later, may have been acquired by the government. "Egypt's leaders and press seemed unable to decide whether capitalists were villains or heroes of their new society. On the one side the government lauded their past achievements, emphasized their continuing importance, and assiduously sought their collaboration. On the other they were warned against opportunistic individualism, exploitation and monopoly" (O'Brien 1966:233).

It should be understood that throughout each stage of land reforms, Nasser kept an ideology of socialism rather than strict Marxism. The goal of land reforms was to "destroy the political power of the feudal nobility and, on the other hand, facilitate the shift of capital from agriculture to industry by transforming the wealth fixed in land into more liquid and flexible forms of capital" (Hosseinzadeh 1989:107). Yet, rather than confiscating property for redistribution as Marxist theory suggests, the Nasser government persuaded and induced wealthy landowners with generous compensation packages. "The price of land was fixed at ten times its rental value, which was inflated to extremely high levels in the years immediately preceding the reform program. Thus, ex-owners amortized the price of their land in fourteen years instead of the legally stipulated 30 years" (Hosseinzadeh 1989:107). Nasser's socialist land reforms were moderately successful in transferring property to the lower classes. However, the attempt to jump-start the industrial sector of the economy via the agrarian sector failed. The wealthy ex-landowners invested in proven profit-making ventures such as real estate, rather than risky entrepreneurial endeavors in the nascent industrial sector (Hosseinzadeh 1989:107).

Ba'athist Socialism in Syria

Syria experienced many of the same socialist tendencies and transformations of Nasser's Egypt. This is not too surprising in that both nations were swept up in the nationalization fever of the post-war period. The parallel progression of Syrian and Egyptian ideology was demonstrated when the two nations consolidated in 1958 to form the United Arab Republic. The reasons behind this union were mostly economic and militaristic. However, sentiments of pan-Arabism were strong in both countries at the time. Uncertainty in each region's political climate soon overwhelmed the nascent republic; three years after it was formed, the United Arab Republic was dissolved. Soon after, the Ba'ath party in Syria enjoyed broad support and began to implement the transformation to socialism. Land reform, as in Egypt, played a critical role in the beginning stages of the transformation. However, its impact as a socialist accomplishment has already been investigated in Egypt's case. Thus, it would be redundant for the purposes of this chapter to study the intricacies of Syrian land redistribution efforts. Instead, the examples of socialism and how they relate to Islam in Ba'athist Syria are examined from a broader, more comprehensive perspective.

It is difficult to definitively state when the socialist economy in Syria began to develop. However, it can be postulated that by 1955, Ba'athists in Syria were influential in laying the groundwork for the transition. "In August 1955, the Syrian government took its first tentative steps toward central planning when parliament approved a seven-year development budget. Although such plans were commonplace among developing states in this era and varied widely in the extent to which they corresponded with economic reality, the process of central planning elevated the position of the bureaucracy in establishing national economic priorities, broadening the authority of the state elites to define the boundaries of private sector activities" (Heydemann 1999:71).

Gradually, the industrial and service sectors of the economy grew faster than the dominant, yet somewhat stagnant, agricultural sector. The increasing importance of large industry did not go unnoticed by the Ba'athist government. After a 'spring uprising' by the remaining capitalists in Syria in 1963, the Ba'athists announced a series of extensive 'socialist decrees' that brought the bulk of large and midsized industry in Syria under government control. During the course of the month, some 22 firms were fully nationalized, including a number of those in which the government already held a minority share; an additional 24 firms were nationalized 90 percent; and 61 firms were nationalized 75 percent. The boards of these firms were dissolved and replaced with directors selected by the government" (Heydemann 1999:189).

The Ba'athist regime after 1963 continued to experience numerous coups and social unrest. This political uncertainty undermined efforts to garner international investment in the domestic economy. Consequently, "the state successfully implemented large-scale development projects to expand industry, agriculture, and infrastructure" (Library of Congress 1987). These enormous projects were partly financed by the oil boom in the early 1970s. Simultaneously, Syria was also mounting large defense expenditures dependent on Soviet and Arab foreign aid grants. The collapse of oil prices a few years later sent the economy into a tailspin. "In response, the government initiated a selective process of economic reform... (That) expanded the role of the private sector and eased some constraints on private and foreign investment" (Heydemann 1999:209). The present-day economy is still dominated by the public sector:

> Efforts by the regime to religitimate the private sector have not, however, dislodged the public sector from its privileged position as the cornerstone of what is now officially defined as a 'mixed economy.' There has been no privatization of state-owned enterprises in Syria, and leading Syrian politicians have dismissed the prospect of such moves in the future as unwarranted. The private sector has been further, though not fully, incorporated into the system of rule, but it remains a policy taker, a subordinate participant in the process of economic policymaking. It is the state, not capital, that defines the private sector's terms of engagement and the boundaries of its participation (Heydemann 1999:209).

It will serve a useful purpose to refer to the distinctions made in previous sections of this chapter between Marxism, communism, and socialism. The Ba'athists did not hesitate to reject communism, yet they borrowed ideas from Marxism. The foundation of Ba'athist ideology is a document titled *Muntalaqat.* Written in 1963, it expresses the primary slogan of the party as "Unity, Freedom and Socialism." Unity refers to the commonality of the Arab people, a harkening back to post-war anti-colonialist sentiments. "Freedom must mean primarily liberation from colonialism in all aspects and a vigorous policy of anti-colonialism abroad, including in its forefront the liberation of Palestine" (Roberts 1987:69). In sum, socialism is the Arab world's only hope to free itself from the chains of capitalism and adapt to a modern world. These ideas both employ Marxism and reject communism concomitantly. Indeed, "the *Muntalaqat* condemns 'the Stalinist application of socialism'" (Roberts 1987:73).

The failures of the Ba'athist regime in Syria are numerous. Brutal repression in the early years of the regime failed to secure power and provide a stable government. Instead, there were 13 coups over a 17-year period. High economic growth in some sectors led to devastating effects in other sectors. However, Gross Domestic Product (GDP) from 1953 to 1976 grew at a real annual rate of 6.3 percent. The ambitious authoritarianism soon led to deficits that could not be sustained in the long-term, and the collapse of the oil boom led to the collapse of the Syrian economy. Yet, throughout this uncertainty, the Syrians still have positive feelings toward the idea of socialism. Perhaps it is the ideas of collectivism, nationalism, and pan-Arabism that are at the root of their beliefs, rather than the Ba'athist tangent of socialism. In any event, the fundamentals of socialist ideology appeal to Arabs in similar ways the tenets of Islam.

Summary of Findings

In the final analysis, we can say that the case studies of Muslim-socialist societies reveal successes and failures. The repressive Syrian regime was socialist but not communist. The anti-Soviet Ba'athists in Syria resented the imperialism of communism and capitalism. However, this did not translate into widespread support within the Ba'ath party for religious expression. In fact, there were numerous protests by the religious Muslims against the authoritarian nature of the regime. In Pakistan as well as in Syria, there were commonalities in the anti-capitalist ideologies. Both societies vehemently opposed capitalist imperialism, just as Islam rejects oppression by any means. While all three societies implemented economic reforms during the transition to socialism, Nasser's land reform measures respected the rights of the original landowners by providing generous compensation for lost property.

It is doubtful if a Soviet-styled communist ideology would have approved of such conciliatory measures for the landed aristocracy. Bhutto presented the idea of a class-less society based on equal distribution of resources which, unfortunately, never materialized. Both Nasser and Bhutto embraced the ideas of Pan-Islamism and Pan-Arabism. The second Islamic summit was held in Pakistan in 1974, where Bhutto expressed his solidarity with leaders like Yasser Arafat, Muammar Qaddafi and others against the imperialistic designs of the Western regimes. It is interesting to note that Islam rejects communism, yet it has deep roots in collectivist thought, and this was the core idea of a socialist Islamic republic based on the collective approach of the socialist system applied in the societies discussed here.

CONCLUSION

Islam and Socialism are different in several ways, and yet similar in other ways: similar, for example, in the matter of honour, of loyalty, of duty, in the use of will to change oneself for the better, in the belief that there is an order to the cosmos, and a purpose to our individual lives. Both Islam and Socialism are opposed to usury and the capitalist-consumer system based upon it. Islam, being a practical religion, has evolved a complete code of life which has successfully fulfilled the requirements of the changing times. Not only in the social but also in the economic field, it has given an ideal lead to the people.

Islamic teachings are applied to the collective aspects of human life. Hence, the Islamic concepts and systems, whether they relate to political, economic, legal or social aspects, pre-date the development of modern systems in any part of the world by several hundred years. Any apparent similarities between Islam and other systems cannot, therefore, possibly be due to Islam's "borrowing" from them but rather to the "borrowing" of other systems from Islam or, more logically, to the fact that Islam's principles and laws are so obviously correct and workable that they would ultimately have been discovered by thinkers in other systems with or without any borrowing having taken place.

The Islamic economy has to a great extent similar principles as in socialism which aims at maintaining the equality of man and eliminating too much disparity between the rich and the poor. Its ideal economic principles have raised the general standard of living and have prevented the exploitation of the poor at the hands of the rich. Islam has struck at the root of the principle of making the rich richer and the poor poorer, which has been followed in the capitalist and imperialist states of the world since time immemorial. The early Caliphate proved the words of the Holy Prophet of Islam that if Muslims faithfully pay their *Zakat*, a time would come when there would be no needy person to receive the same. The unequal distribution of wealth is the basis of all human conflicts, both individual and social. Islam has evolved its economic principles on such lines to minimize these disparities and eliminate distinctions in the distribution of human fortunes. The wealthy people are heavily taxed in order to help the poor, and this taxation forms one of the cardinal principles of Islam which no true Muslim can violate.

Islam has steered midway between Capitalism and Communism–a mean between two extremes. Capitalism thrives at the cost of society and aims at building up private property. Communism has no place for private enterprise and economy. Islam, while recognizing one's right to build up private fortunes, enjoins upon its followers to voluntarily part with 2½ percent of their wealth every year for the benefit of the poor. This has greatly contributed to the removal of social inequality among Muslims in the past. It has, thus, eliminated the defects of both Capitalism and Communism while retaining most of their virtues. Ensuring equitable and fair distribution of wealth, the Islamic economic system discourages the hoarding of wealth, as idle wealth is also taxed 2½ percent a year. It, thus, provides an incentive to the investment of capital in commerce and industry, which means wider circulation of money, more employment, and greater prosperity. Islam, thus, lays certain obligations (both moral and legal) upon its rich members which reduce the possibility of accumulation of wealth.

An individual and the community are dependent upon each other. The prosperity of one means the prosperity of the other. Instead of ranging the interests of the individual and community against one another, as is found in the economic systems of Communist and Capitalist states, Islam has recognized the interests of both. It has evolved such a healthy economic system that it has to a great extent minimized the conflict between the interests of the individual and that of the community. The Islamic economic principles, if strictly followed, would eliminate the possibility of accumulation of wealth in the hands of a few and would ensure the greater circulation of money as well as a wider distribution of wealth. Broadly speaking these principles are (1) *Zakat* or compulsory alms giving, (2) the Islamic law of inheritance which splits the property of an individual into a number of shares given to his relatives, (3) the forbiddance of interest which checks accumulation of wealth that strikes at the root of capitalism. Similar to the socialist ideals, in an Islamic society, justice before the law is strictly impartial without regard to religion, race, position, wealth, or any other criteria; the head of state, officials and members of the most influential families are just as subject to its provisions as the most humble members of society. In this context, it may be remarked that every individual in a society has a certain basic responsibility to that society not to transgress against its established limits, which relate to the sanctity of life, personhood, property and sexual inviolability. In turn, each society has its own system of penalties for violating such limits which stem from its basic understanding of human responsibility and interaction.

For a Muslim, religion cannot be limited strictly to the realm of personal faith and private life. Islam has things to say about society and what it sees as the just political order that has strong implications for contemporary politics. Unlike Christianity, Islam was concerned with politics and governance from the start. The Muslim rule that developed in the lifetime of Prophet Muhammad (PBUH) required attention to principles of community life, justice, and administration, relations with non-Muslims, defense and foreign policy. A vision of what constitutes good governance, law, and a just society was among the principal new ideas. The Prophet came not to protect the status quo, but to reform it. Women, for instance, were given legal status (where they had none before) and concrete legal protection within society.

Islamists are also modern in their heavy emphasis on grassroots organization, an important aspect of socialist philosophy. Their parties are in close touch with the neighborhoods and are closely attuned to local interests. Many Islamist parties run local social welfare programs independently of governments and provide social services such as clinics, especially for women, housing for students who have come from the village to the big city, recreational facilities for youth, legal advice, educational help, and other forms of social assistance. These activities, often far more responsive than the state to social needs in the neighborhood, are generally funded from religious donations or from large Islamist-run banks and businesses. Socialism talks about common ownership, which in practice means that everybody having the right to participate in decisions on how global resources will be used. It also means that nobody is able to take personal control of resources beyond his/her own personal possessions. Current economic, technological, political and social changes reflect a profound transformation of our world. The fundamental issue we face is not whether there will be change in future years but, rather, who is going to control it and how. The socialist answer is unequivocal. It is the people of the world who should exercise control by means of a more advanced democracy in all aspects of life: political, social, and economic. Political democracy, for socialists, is the necessary framework and precondition for other rights and liberties.

The internationalization of the economy and widespread access to information and new technologies can, if brought under democratic control, provide a basis for a world society better suited to cooperation. It is obvious that a world family is no longer a utopian dream but, increasingly, a practical necessity. Peace and freedom are the products of both individual and cooperative efforts–the two aspects are parts of a single process. Each person has the right to be free of political coercion and also to the greatest chance to act in pursuit of individual goals and to fulfill personal potential. But that is only possible if humanity as a whole succeeds in its long-standing struggle to master its history and to ensure that no person, class, sex, religion, or race becomes the servant of another. We find no contradiction in Islam and Socialism as far as these ideals are concerned. Islam emphasizes justice and equality; Socialism talks about the end of all discrimination against individuals and the equality of rights and opportunities. It demands compensation for physical, mental and social inequalities, and freedom from dependence on either the owners of the means of production or the holders of political power. Equality is the expression of the equal value of all human beings and the precondition for the free development of the human personality. Basic economic, social and cultural equality is essential for individual diversity and social progress. At a collective level, Islam talks about the Muslim *Ummah*, or a global Muslim society. Socialist embraces solidarity, which is all-encompassing and global. It is the practical expression of common humanity and of the sense of compassion with the victims of injustice. Solidarity is rightly stressed and celebrated by all major humanist traditions. In the present era of unprecedented interdependence between individuals and nations, solidarity gains an enhanced significance because it is imperative for human survival.

Islam and socialism attach equal importance to these fundamental principles. They are interdependent. Each is a prerequisite of the other. As opposed to this position, liberals and conservatives have placed the main emphasis on individual liberty at the expense of justice and solidarity, while strictly communist states have claimed to achieve equality and solidarity but at the expense of freedom. Peace is the precondition of all our hopes. It is a basic value of common interest to all political systems, and it is necessary for human society.

A lasting peace cannot be guaranteed through nuclear deterrence or through an arms race with conventional forces. Therefore, disarmament and new models of common security are imperative. What is now essential is the achievement of a climate of mutual political confidence. This can be developed through cooperation on projects for our common future and a new emphasis on peaceful competition between societies with different political, economic, social and religious structures. The fundamental economic and social causes of international conflict must be abolished by the achievement of global justice and by the creation of new institutions for the peaceful resolution of conflicts around the world. Islam and Socialism can both work for global peace and prosperity. At the same time, they should engage in peaceful competition in the fields of wealth creation, welfare, and solidarity. Societies should be prepared to learn from one another. It must become the norm for the different systems to trade, negotiate, and work together.

CHAPTER 5

Islam and Social Democracy

Ava Aprin

Meaghjan Ehni

INTRODUCTION

This chapter is about how social democracy functions in Islamic societies. In order to comprehend this chapter, it is necessary to have a lucid understanding of social democracy. It is also important to understand the inherent difference between social democracy and socialism. The central difference between these two socio-economic systems is that social democracy focuses on how to create a partially socialist society out of a purely capitalistic-democratic one. Basically, it strives to attain a synthesis between socialism and democracy. It by no means attempts to produce a pure state of democracy or a pure state of socialism. Social democracy attempts to maintain an efficient balance of both systems. Socialism would encourage communism, whereas a state of democracy would promote capitalism. However, social democracy is interested in remaining capitalistic for efficiency purposes but also strives to redistribute resources more than a typical capitalistic-democracy would.

Pierson offers a more succinct definition of social democracy: "Social democracy is constructed around three key principles: redistribution, democratic economic governance and social protection" (2001:19). The emphasis on redistribution pulls more from the socialist framework, and the democratic economic governance visibly stems more from the democratic framework.

In addition, Kesselman defines social democracy in a more in depth manner: "First, an acceptance of a capitalistic economy is coupled with extensive state intervention to counteract uneven development. Second, Keynesian steering mechanisms are used to achieve economic growth, high wages, price stability, and full employment. Third, state policies redistribute the economic surplus in progressive ways" (1982:402). This explanation will clarify what social democracy is before we delve into possible arguments that arise from the advocates of pure democracy and pure socialism.

Those advocating democracy will argue that socialism is inefficient due to the fact that the citizens will not work to their utmost potential, if they do not feel righteously compensated. However, those advocating socialism will contend that their societies will be fairer due to the fact that everyone will have an equal share. The advocates of democracy would rebut that this way of life will create mediocre production, which will inevitably be detrimental to everyone.

Social democracy attempts to reach a happy-medium between these antithetical viewpoints. In reality, neither side is going to be content with social democracy. Advocates of democracy are going to argue that the amount of governmental intervention is too much and is going to decrease production nonetheless. Socialists will dispute that this way of life is not egalitarian and, therefore, it is not fair.

To explore more deeply what this chapter is actually about, it is necessary to have and an extensive comparison and analysis of how Islam and social democracy interact. In Jawed's book, *Islam's Political Culture*, he states that those who state that democracy represents Islam will also say that Islam "was close to both democracy and socialism" (1999:69). To some, it might be apparent that social democracy would be the ideal socio-economic system for an Islamic society. However, there will be counter arguments to that position as well.

Glyn defines social democracy in another manner. He demonstrates a society that has "encompassed parties envisaging a long process of transformation of capitalism into a socialist system, based on common ownership of the means of production, as well as parties accepting the authority and ownership structures of capitalism but pressing for reforms to increase economic efficiency and to reduce inequality" (2001:2). Once more, the emphasis of equality is demonstrated in connection with the idea of productivity.

Furthermore, in *Social Democracy: Global and National Perspectives,* Martell states that "social democracy perceives capitalism as both inevitable and also inherently dynamic–the source of growth and wealth creation. Thus, it also necessarily accepts the logical and structural imperatives of a capitalist market economy" (2001:30). This section of Martell's book places important emphasis on the growth of productivity and the economy.

Many scholars have given similar, yet distinct, definitions regarding social democracy as a socio-economic system. In order to take a clearer approach to this chapter, it is important to provide a synthesized definition of social democracy. The following definition is this chapter's guide for the definition of this socio-economic system. Social democracy is a socio-economic system that is based on democracy and a capitalistic economy, with an emphasis on enough governmental intervention in order to protect the community, but not so much as to suppress the productivity of the economy.

This chapter also analyzes verses in the *Qur'an* and *Hadith* that point to a specific socio-economic system. Some Muslims argue that the *Qur'an* directs them more toward socialism, and some argue that it directs them more toward democracy. There are also some Muslims who feel that their religion fits more comfortably in a social democratic society. We will expand on these viewpoints later on in the chapter.

The central aspect of this chapter is that it investigates existing works that focus only on social democracy in order to understand its foundations. A solid base is important to any work. Thus, the chapter examines works done solely on Islam and Islamic societies in order to come to unbiased conclusions with regard to the nexus between the religion and social democracy. Finally, the chapter also reviews works done on Islam in combination with social democracy. The analysis of these works begins only after a thorough perusal of an ample amount of work done in these specific, yet related, fields.

The analysis of these materials serves as a foundation for the chapter. The use of social democracy in an Islamic society is fully assessed after determining the strengths and weaknesses of these texts, examining different Islamic countries where social democracy was or is in effect, and building on this knowledge in order to add to the existing information. Although the analysis of the Muslim societies in different countries is probably the most helpful to producing new information, all three aspects of this research are of paramount importance.

This type of study is important in today's world for a number of reasons. Primarily, the more literature and knowledge that is dispersed in today's world could increase chances for more peace and less ignorance in the future among all societies. In addition, this study is important because it gives yet another perspective regarding an important issue.

REVIEW OF RELEVANT LITERATURE

The birth of social democracy would put the most important time periods into perspective. Karl Marx appears to be one of the founders of the concept of social democracy around 1864. However, Martell states that social democracy "can trace its lineage to early nineteenth, eighteenth, and even seventeenth-century democratic movements; there is no doubt that modern socialist parties emerged and became important political actors in the late nineteenth and early twentieth centuries" (2001:10). Many hypotheses exist to explain when social democracy came about. For practical purposes, this chapter is in accordance with Marx's hypothesis because it seems to be the most prevalent among the hypotheses.

Martell's book is exceedingly important to this review because it breaks down many aspects of social democracy. The other sources utilized in this section also help to explain similar aspects from different perspectives or time periods. However, all of the sources come together to create a lucid picture of what factors are important to social democracy.

This section of the chapter delves into the specific factors that arise when dealing with a social democracy. It is important to understand when and how the idea of a social democracy came about. This will help to explain this specific socio-economic system. Governmental regulation obviously plays a large part in this system, as demonstrated by community being on the forefront of this system. Some of the main aspects that are highly regulated are social security, education, the poor, and the nationalization of industries, labor, taxes, and the environment. It appears that the government regulates all aspects of the society; however, it is not important to know in how many different aspects the government intervenes. It is also important to understand the level of governmental intervention in each of these sectors. If the government were to have complete control of all of these sectors, it would be more of a socialistic society.

"Europe was becoming an industrialized, increasingly urban society characterized by mass production, factory work, and separation of work and home. At the same time economic and social inequalities generated union and organization, the growth of mass political parties, including a variety of social movements and waves of social protest. Thus demands for economic, social and political change characterized the last three decades of the 19th Century and the beginning of the 20th Century" (Merriman 1996:901). This industrialization, with its negative effects on society, was the impetus for this socio-economic system.

"Germany was the first state to adopt the key elements of modern social welfare. Otto Von Bismarck the German Chancellor viewed these measures as a way to ameliorate the conditions of workers in the industrial age" (Stearns 2001:480). Social democracy grew out of a worker based movement. August Ebel and Wilhelm Liebknecht co-founded the Social Democratic Workers Party in 1869 and merged with the General German Workers Union in 1875 to form what came to be called the Social Democratic Party of Germany (Lipset 1995:1148). The party grew political strength, and its success in Germany encouraged the spread of social democracy to other countries in Europe. The foundation of the party hinged upon many similar Marxist beliefs. However, it opposed the revolutionary basis of Marxism and emphasized an evolutionary movement for equality. The inequality in the industrialized world had sparked a need for a unified voice of the worker who, in a social democratic realm, is revered. The social democrats provided that voice. The political organization of the industrial working class to achieve radical transformation of existing political and economic structures developed to eventually produce a conflict-free collectivist society"(Lipset 1995:1148).

Social democracy is said to have come about in an evolutionary manner, as opposed to a revolutionary manner. It came about in this manner because in order for social democracy to progress, it needed to take the route of reformism. If people did not accept this approach, revolutionaries would have arisen as a result of the "insecurity of factory employment, low wages, and long hours, and the intensifying factors such as exhausting speed of work, brutal foreman… wretched housing, child labor, rising prices of necessities…" (Marks 1939:335). All of these factors would have caused unrest within society leading to a violent, rather than peaceful, transition. This approach proves to be the more rational of the two, especially with respect to social democracy where the collective society is held in high regard.

Social democracy provided a platform for workers to unite and attempt to improve their economic position in a given society. Trade unions were formed.

> The trade union movement grew rapidly in Europe among skilled workers. The goals of the unions were to raise wages and improve conditions while increasing the number of unionized workers (Merriman 1996:909).

> Workers could be hired and fired at will and had to sell their labor for whatever the going rate was–and that rate was determined by their competition with each other to work cheaply enough to gain them an advantage in the job market. Traditional rules and protections went by the board in the new factories, which often ran for twenty-four hours a day (two twelve-hour shifts), seven days a week under the most inhumane conditions. Women and children were absorbed into the work force as well, often preferred because they cost much less than men. Living standards and educational levels actually declined in many areas. Many of the industries severely polluted their environments, their machinery maimed and killed many workers, and food in the new factory towns was often of poor quality and in short supply (Braverman1998:35).

Workers as well as many aristocrats became concerned over the abject conditions under which the new working class labored.

Many workers started to show their disapproval through strikes and other forms of protests. "The rise of strike form of protest is correlated with the growth of wage labor force that became the focus of labor historians. In all European countries, the collective cessation of work became the universal weapon for labor protests. Whether demanding higher wages, eight hour [work] days, sufferance or the end of colonialism, workers struck" (Stearns 2001:256). Countries like Germany, Sweden, and the Netherlands had infrequent strikes, whereas in countries like Belgium, France, Italy and the United Kingdom strikes were common. According to Stearns, "countries with large Social Democratic Parties that have close relations with trade unions and incorporate trade unions' demands into political bargaining, by exerting pressure at the national level" (Stearns 2001:258).

Factories and higher wages had drawn many farmers to an urban civilization. Due to industrialization, the influx of workers moving form agriculture to an industrial work capacity caused pressing problems on public welfare. As a result of this increase of urbanized workers and the inequity of their lives, "some social reformers, many politicians and most workers demanded for state intervention to protect workers from the uncertainties and hardships of their labor" (Merriman 1996: 911). European leaders became fearful of losing their power in their countries, forcing many to carry out domestic policies based on compromise and conciliation between the middle class, political interests, and working class demands.

It is apparent that governmental regulation and involvement are deeply engrained in this socio-economic system. It is involved in many programs to help the welfare state. Government also intervenes to nationalize industries and to help keep smaller industries alive and growing. Seeing that equity is on the forefront of this socio-economic system, redistribution plays a primary role in a social democratic society. However, the government does not want to be in complete control because, as previously mentioned, complete control would hinder the productivity of the society and lead to apathy among the citizens.

In a social democratic society, "the government ought to aim to 'preserve a decency threshold of social security so that equal opportunities are approximated with achieving outcomes that are said to matter crucially to people's well-being and agency, mainly income and access to the immaterial benefits of paid work'" (Martell 2001:140). This demonstrates the central idea of equity that is prevalent in social democratic societies. If a good social security program is in place, the elderly portion of the society will be better off. Therefore, income distribution among all age groups tends to be more equitable.

Social democracy encompasses distinct points of view regarding most aspects of a society. The central factor in social democracy is the inherent focus on the community as a whole. Furthermore, the actual equity of this community is also of utmost importance. In a social democratic society, the government is more involved in issues pertaining to the collective rather than the individual. For example, equity is an inherent aspect of social democracy. In his book, *Social Democracy: Global and National Perspectives,* Luke Martell states that if one had to decide whether the state or the market was more important, social democracy would give "greater weight to the role of the state while along the equity-growth spectrum it gave greater weight to equity" (2001:86). Although the market might be the method to ensure the highest Gross Domestic Product and economic growth, it might not be the best way to ensure the well-being of the society as a whole. This statement demonstrates that the well-being of the community is inevitably more important to social democracy than economic growth or the well being of the market.

As previously stated, social democrats place "an emphasis on the idea of community" (Pierson 2001:128). Community is an integral part of social democracy, and the government is deeply committed to ensuring the well-being of the citizens. Although the birth of social democracy was due to industrialization, social democrats in general believe in the reforms of every aspect of social life. The reformation was initiated through labor but made its way to almost every aspect of human wellness.

"Social Democrats are strongly critical of society when it is divided, artificially divided, into classes or groups based on socio-economic position, access to education, gender, etc. Society is a place where all people are equal, and any society that does not promote that is neither a good nor a just society" (Krischheimer and Neumann 1987:184) Social democrats generally view society as equal to the sum of its parts. In other words, society is what people make of it. People are social beings, and society is where people achieve their fullest potential. For social democrats, the state has a central role to play in promoting a good, just and healthy society. Because of their firm belief in democracy, social democrats see the state as representative of the will of all; and as such, it must take the lead in upholding society's values. In this way, the state is an instrument of social change.

The social democratic argument for equality represents together the desire for equality of outcome and equality of opportunity. The case for equality has generally been based in a rejection of the penalties of inequality: economic inefficiency, social disruption, poverty, and natural justice. The welfare state was often seen as a way of sinking inequality and rising toward a more equitable society. Social democrats have a conception of freedom that accepts liberal and even some conservative notions, but it also includes the notion that people are not free if they do not have the resources to do certain things. Where a conservative might see freedom as the absence of constraint, social democrats would think that this is insufficient.

"First, they would argue that freedom requires a concern for equality. The greater the inequality of economic resources, the less free some people (the less well-off) will be. Secondly, political freedom must also mean economic freedom. Fear of being without work, of having no power in one's workplace, and of having no workplace protection mean that people are not free. Lastly, they argue that freedom is the result of government action. If government is not prepared to provide some measure of support for the freedom found in law, then people really are not free" (Krischheimer and Neumann 1987:180).

To the social democrat, it is important for each individual to contribute to the entire welfare of society and for "direct state intervention to promote these moral purposes" (Lipset 1995:1139). Therefore, social security plays an immense role in this socio-economic system. Social security is a process by which those who work pay into a system that provides money for the elderly if they have previously worked and paid into the system. This process limits the number of elderly who might become impoverished if this system was not in place.

Social security also maintains productivity because it is not a redistributive policy. If a person does not pay into social security, then s/he has no right to receive the benefits of the program. In a social democratic polity, it is vital that work be available, which is why social security works well in this socio-economic system. The primary downfall to social security is when the group paying into the system is not the same size as the group that is supposed to be relying on the social security benefits.

A society having a centralized educational system is not enough in order to be successful in this system. The educational system has to be well thought out and well run. Some of the necessary specifics required in an educational system similar to this one are the "individualization of learning strategies, flexibility in choice of subjects and independent learning to prepare for life-long learning in the newly flexible labor market" (Martell 2001: 130). The educational system has to give students a voice with respect to certain subjects they are able to take. In addition, the way that these classes are taught needs to be innovative in order to keep the student in school and wanting to learn what is being taught.

Education is also innately important to the goals of social democracy. If an equal central educational program exists, then the population should all be equally qualified for jobs. Martell emphasizes that "providing citizens with the skills they need to survive and thrive in a global information order, through equal access to life-long learning and education, conveniently unites the demands of the new global economy with the social democratic values of social justice and equality" (Martell 2001:55).

Education is a good segue into the next important aspect to social democracy, which is the poor. *Social Democracy in Neoliberal Times* by Andrew Glyn discusses how "educational achievements are lowest precisely in the areas where poverty and joblessness is most prevalent" (2001:216). Students in these societies are hopeless because the majority of people surrounding them do not have jobs and are impoverished. These factors inhibit their desire to learn.

Social democracy is a system that is devoted to equality, which means abolishing poverty. This socio-economic policy centers around the fact that "the distribution of social advantage within any capitalist society at any time can never be equitable and must be addressed through a constant imperative to redistribute" (Pierson 2001:15). The redistribution is a process of the rich giving to the poor, hopefully, in an effort to assure that everyone is living comfortably.

This main objective of the social democratic movement was to remove the imbalance of wealth developed in Europe. A great division between the aristocracy and the working middle class soon became a concern of the social democrats. With the monopolization of major urban industries, a gap in the roles of the working class developed. In the advent of industrialization, the dynamics were shifting. By the end of the century, factories had drawn a large percentage of the farmers from the countryside into a predominantly urban civilization. This caused vast problems with the distribution of wealth. The social democratic movement was in favor of bridging the unfair social and economic separation between the wealthy and the working class. Social democracy favored profitable, nationalized industries that would contribute their profits to the common good instead of to private shareholders.

"Social democracy means more democracy, but it means less socialism, did not share faith, or perhaps shed their faith in the economic prescription of classic socialism, as regards for example, nationalization of industry" (Lipset 1995:1141). However, the social democrat did feel that the government should regulate major industry to create equity among the people and the few wealthy oligarchs. The belief that an elimination of a monopoly of an essential service, transportation for instance, was to be controlled by the state echoed amongst the social democrats. However, what differentiated it from the Marxist socialist belief was the evolution towards a democracy. Essential services of the country were best left in the jurisdiction of a democratically elected official who represented the interests of all the people. The nationalization of major services left more accountability to voters. That is to say, if the telephone service is nationalized, voters can bring pressure onto the government to provide better services, and parliament may have the power to properly tend to any defficiencies in the functioning of the major government services.

"Nationalization of products and services are beneficial for the elimination of wasteful competition and transaction costs" (Clough 1968:495). Instead of four companies producing the same thing resulting in duplication and inefficiency, one nationally-owned or regulated company can make the same product more efficiently. That way, there will be equality amongst all and the focus of laborers can shift from competion to channeling that energy to making services efficient for all. Nationalization also promotes "improvement in industrial relations" (Clough 1968:495). Employees will be more inclined to cooperate with a management appointed by a government that they have a say in electing, rather than with a management representing a shareholding minority" (Clough 1968:496). Social democrats believe that a country functions best when the struggles by industrial and agricultural workers, operating according to principles of solidarity and advocating an egalitarian society, are addressed in an economic system that would serve the broad populace rather than a favored few.

One of the main concerns in social democracy is income distribution. Social democrats believe it is the role of the government to adjust the results of the market when those market results are seen as socially undesirable. It is believed that the government should regulate the fair distribution of income. The progressive tax is a major theme in social democracy. A progressive tax is one whose rates increase as a person's income increases. This is done in order to redistribute money from the rich to the poor.

The argument for a progressive tax system is that people with higher incomes tend to have a higher percentage of that in disposable income and can, thus, afford a greater tax burden. A person making exactly enough money to pay for food and housing cannot afford to pay any taxes without it causing material damage, while someone making twice as much can afford to pay up to half his/her income to taxes. The converse argument is that "too progressive a tax rate acts as a disincentive to work; in the previous (extreme) example, there would be no monetary incentive at all for the first person to try to double his or her income. In practice, however, no advocates of a progressive tax go as far as that extreme example, so they often argue that the taxes they propose have very little effect (or even no effect at all) on incentives" (Colander 2001:119).

The impact of industrialization on nature is a concern for the social democrats. They believe as do the Marxists that the environment is sacred and only should be handled accordingly. The environment and the people who inhabit it have a symbiotic relationship that should be respected. It is a major belief of social democrats and Marxists that capitalism creates much of the degradation of ecology. Although Marx, Engels and earlier social democrats were not environmentalists by nature, the desire for the betterment of the people through natural means was a major concern. In the words of Frederick Engels,

> the analysis of nature into its individual parts, the grouping of the different natural processes and natural objects in definite classes, the study of the internal anatomy of organic bodies in their manifold forms–these were the fundamental conditions of the gigantic strides in our knowledge of Nature which have been made during the last four hundred years. But this method of work has also left us as a legacy the habit of observing natural objects and natural processes in their isolation, detached from the whole vast interconnection of things; and therefore not in their motion, but in their repose; not as essentially changing, but as fixed constants; not in their life, but in their death (Marx and Engels 1992:42).

Environmentalism arose from a specific point of conflict or investigation between society and the natural world and each supplying a particular element to the all-round ecological outlook. This conflict investigation was important to the social democrats with regards to the equality and betterment of humanity. For Marx and Engels, humanity is part of nature, and nature provides humanity's direct means of life and, hence, the fact that humanity's "physical and spiritual life is linked to nature means simply that nature is linked to itself, for humanity is a part of nature," (Marx and Engels 1992:44), but nature is also the "object and instrument" (Marx and Engels 1992:44) of humanity's life activity.

As social democracy took form in Europe, the line separating the aristocracy and the upper middle class began to blur. Easy social mobility encouraged the lower levels in society to strive for greater status and income. The working class earned a voice in the sphere of social democracy. The burden of labor and all who bore the burden were the focus of many social democratic movements. The importance of job safety, employment benefits, better wages and social welfare resonated throughout the workforce. The comfort of the working class was primordial to the social democrat. This trend soon spread to other areas of the world, many of which were not prepared for its arrival.

In sum, social democracy is a socio-economic system that originated in Europe. However, many of the implications and applications of the tenets of social democracy parallel many of the precepts of Islam. Social democracy is not often referenced in Islamic countries, although it has had a strong presence in many countries in the Islamic world. The social reforms advocated in a social democratic movement are similar to that which the *Qur'an* prescribes for Muslims. The rest of the chapter offers a closer view of three Islamic countries that have functioned in a social democratic setting. It is shown that the theory of social democracy is very different from that which is practiced. In an in-depth study of Egypt, Iran, and Pakistan, their successes and failures in social democratic contexts add a different dynamic to the study of the socio-economic system and also add insight to the functionality of social democracy in an Islamic society.

ANALYSIS OF FINDINGS

This section is broken up into three different segments based on three Muslim countries that have utilized social democracy. This portion of the chapter expounds upon the strengths and weaknesses that are prevalent in Iran, Egypt, and Indonesia vis-à-vis this socio-economic system. These countries are exceedingly distinct in many aspects, but this section studies them based on their fundamental similarities. Hopefully, this segment will help to explain the peaceful practices found in these Muslim countries.

Iran

At a time when the European world was moving towards a social democratic model, Iran was still in the stages of colonization by both the Soviet Union and Britain. The wars that took place with the Soviet Tsarist regimes, the defeats and subsequent treaties that occurred as a result, led to major socio-economic repercussions "such as the loss of revenues from the lost territories, destruction of the traditional economy, transformation of the Iranian agriculture and its linkage to the world market, and the ruin of peasants, artisans, part of the merchants, and their traditional institutions, all of which led to the vast emigration of Iranians mainly to the tsarist empire" (Chaqueri 2001:183).

Unlike the situation in Europe where the population moved form a rural life to urban life within the same country, the Iranians were migrating to countries outside of Iran to acquire some wealth for themselves. "The disintegration of the traditional economic system and the concomitant ruination of the peasantry and artisans led to the release and unemployment of labor, particularly from among the peasantry" (Chaqueri 2001:77). Also, "ruined peasants and artisans from Iran emigrated to Central Asia, and as far as America. The most significant part of this emigration appears, however, to have been to the southern provinces of the Russian empire where capitalism was spreading" and industrialization was taking form (Chaqueri 2001:78). Unlike Europe, "Iran's new economic system was not conducive to the creation and growth of industrial enterprise" (Chaqueri 2001:77).

During the time away from the country, Iranians were settling for worse conditions because they were trying to support their families back home. This cheap labor that they provided caused conflict between the various ethnic groups in the region. There was a widespread hostility in Asiatic Russia toward Iranian immigrants largely due to their role in keeping the wage level down. "Hostility was based on the contradictory economic interests of the two wage-earning population groups: Muslims, i.e. Iranian immigrants and native Tartars; and non-Muslims, i.e., Armenian, Georgians and Russians" (Chaqueri 2001:85). Iranian immigrants' gradual politicization made their mobilization for social democratic causes a real possibility. Their participation in industrial strikes and political events gave them the experience that they could never have acquired at home, where both the economic and political conditions for such actions were lacking. This new found knowledge made its way back to Iran in an attempt to improve the social and economic conditions of the Iranians. There were certain guidelines for labor and life to which the Iranians were not privy that made a huge impact in the beginning of the 20th Century.

"While peasants and artisans continued to emigrate, other social forces, such as clergy, disconnected merchantry, and their allies pressured the royal court and the government to administer reforms"(Caqueri 2001:98). Internal demand for reform was slowly growing. "Naser ad Din Shah's reign was characterized by growing royal and bureaucratic corruption, oppression of the rural population, and the indifference on the Shah's part" (Chapin and Metz 1989:22). There was increasing opposition among the clerical classes, merchants and the people of Iran. This widespread reform and new ideas emerged in the country in the form of social democracy. The first was in the form of a constitutional revolution. The people began to demand a tight control over royal authority by enforcing a rule of law to combat external influences as well as assist in upward mobility by the masses.

"The Shah's failure to respond to the protests by the religious establishment, the merchants, and other classes led the merchants and clerical leaders in January 1906 to protests by taking sanctuary in mosques in Tehran and outside the capital. When the Shah reneged on the promise to permit the establishment of a "house of justice," or consultative assembly, 10,000 people, led by merchants, took sanctuary in June in the compound of the British legation in Tehran" (Chapin and Metz 1989:23). In 1906, "the Shah gave in to popular demands and promised the creation of a national consultative assembly, the Majles as well as a decree promising a constitution" (Omidivar 1993, Online)

In 1904, in order to organize revolutionary social democratic activities among the people of Azarbaijan and other Iranians, a political group called Hemmat (Aspiration) was founded in Baku. The Hemmat group for the first time translated the term "Social Democracy" into Persian, in order to make it more understandable for the Iranian people who had no knowledge of European languages (Tajbakhsh 2000).

"From the ranks of clergy rose numerous revolutionaries who threw themselves, with an admirable devotion, into the fray for the renovation of their country" (Chaqueri 2001:140). To emphasize the degree of importance of the clergy in the Iranian revolution when the "Caucasian socialist movement spread to Iran and a socialist party was organized, this declared itself the defender of Allah and the great prophet" (Chaqueri 2001:140). Soon after the constitution was granted, the honeymoon between liberals and clergy was over. The Persian clergy was at the head of the constitutional revolution.

"The anjomans had become a rallying point of the popular forces and the basis of grassroots democracy, an eyesore for the shah and his reactionary camarilla" (Chaqueri 2001:100). The popular political associations (anjomans) and municipal and provincial associations played a critical role in the Constitutional Revolution. "The Constitutionalists considered representative participation in official anjomans in the form of provincial assemblies and municipal councils an essential aspect of democratic government. Popular political societies and provincial assemblies must be considered an important component of the constitutionalist movement and one of its primary goals" (Arjomand 1988:38–9).

In the aftermath of the Constitutional movement, both the anjomans and the nascent political parties declined, finally to be eclipsed by the centralized state building of the democratic Constitutionalists and then by the authoritarian centralism of Reza Khan Pahlavi (Tajbakhsh 2000).

> FEAM; lit., Social-Democratic Party, an organization was founded in 1905 by Persian emigrants in Trans-caucasia with the help of local revolutionaries. It played an important role during the Constitutional Revolution by introducing radical ideas and by taking part in the struggle for the restoration of the Constitution in 1908–09. Members of the organization maintained close links with the Hemmat party. Close ties were also maintained with the Baku and Tbilisi committees of the Russian Social-Democratic Workers party (RSDWP). Nariman Narimanov, the prominent Azeri leader of Hemmat, headed the FEAM. He apparently translated the program of the RSDWP from Russian into Azeri for the Hemmat party and then, with some modifications, adopted it as the party program for the FEAM. The FEAM created its own form of European socialism and indigenous ideas. It upheld liberalism and nationalism, was critical of the conservative *ulama*, but also maintained some religious beliefs. The first commitment of the Mojaheds was to protect the Constitution and the Majles. At the same time, they advocated changes beyond the limited reforms of the Majles and demanded the redistribution of lands to peasants, reforms in child labor, an eight-hour work day for factory employees, and other similar social democratic measures (Afary/Iranica 2000).

The Mojahed organizations between 1905 and 1907 released drafts of their demands of their program in Tbilisi and Baku. "Of these demands, the most important of which can be summarized as; limiting power of the absolute monarch; granting workers the right to vote, irrespective of their income or wealth; holding parliamentary elections based on universal suffrage; distributing the large landed estates among peasants and introducing legal protection for peasant ownership in land; and granting democratic rights to workers, such as the freedom of association, speech, and assembly and the right to strike" (Chaqueri 2001:123).

In 1908, "workers had put forth the following demands: the increase of their piece-work by one shahi, the employment and dismissal of workers only in consultation with workers, sanitary conditions for the work place, medical care to be paid by the management during worker's illness, payment of regular wages during illness, the reduction of overtime work, overtime work payment at twice the normal wage, no replacement of workers on strike with other workers, payment of wages during strikes, and no dismissal of workers for taking part in a strike" (Chaqueri 2001:92).

It is almost one hundred years since the Iranian Constitutional Revolution of 1906, the first event of its kind in the Middle East. The Revolution opened the way for a cataclysmic change in Iran, heralding the modern era. It saw a period of unprecedented debate in a burgeoning press. It created new opportunities and opened up seemingly boundless possibilities for Iran's future. Many different groups fought to shape the course of the Revolution, and all sections of society were ultimately to be in some way changed by it. "The old order, which Naser al-Din Shah Qajar had struggled for so long to sustain, finally passed away, to be replaced by new institutions, new forms of expression, and a new social and political order" (Iranian Heritage Foundation 2003).

Egypt

Egypt is a prime example of a Muslim country that uses social democracy. Although social democracy has been implemented fairly recently in this society, Egypt provides a good base for how Muslim societies can function in this socio-economic system. It has practiced social democracy since the 1950s. Muslim societies can easily adapt to social democracy for the most part. However, some setbacks do exist as it is with adjusting to any type of new system.

The majority of ideals discovered when studying social democracy greatly parallel some of the central themes of Islam. As previously stated in the chapter, socialism and democracy are the two socio-economic systems preferred by a vast number of Muslims. Social democracy works well in Islamic societies because "Muslims identify Islam and their social institutions and find it difficult to adjust themselves to pressures making for social change because they can only think within the sphere of ideas expressing the traditional ethos of Islamic culture" (Trimingham 1964:175). Seeing that social democracy is almost a synthesis of the two socio-economic systems, it is relatively easy to understand how Egypt's Muslim society fits into social democracy. This socio-economic system holds a lot of the same values that are prevalent in Islam.

Using what we already know about social democracy from the previous section, we can create a connection between Muslim societies and social democracy. More specifically, this sub-section focuses on how the different aspects of social democracy relate to Egypt. It examines the key aspects important to social democracy prevalent in Egypt, which are the community, the birth of the socio-economic system, governmental regulation, social security, education, labor, and taxes. These aspects have been explained in great detail, they will not be iterated here so that this sub-section does not bore you with those specificities. However, it does examine how these specific aspects occur and affect the Muslim society in Egypt.

The birth of social democracy in Egypt occurred in the 1950s. This movement was started by the 1952 Revolution, led by Gamal Abd al-Nasir "who took control of the Egyptian government in 1952" (Voll 1994:175). Nasir believed in most of the same ideals of social democracy. The school of thought of "Nasserism symbolizes the direction of liberation, social transformation, the people's control of their own resources, and the democracy of the people's working forces" (Voll 1994:175). Therefore, "Nasserism" is similar to social democracy with respect to the themes of freedom, social change, and citizens being in charge of their own capital.

Community is an exceedingly important facet of Islamic life. Muslims refer to the community as the *Umma,* which is "the nation of Islam and of the Muslims, incorporating all their peoples, ethnic groups and races" (Sagiv 1995:107). Social democracy does a lot to protect the Egyptian community. Egypt tries to treat everyone the same and is not biased against some based on ethnic issues. In contrast, Syria operates on a different socio-economic system and is favorably biased towards Arabs. Syria privileges "Arab over non-Arab foreigners in various respects, including the investment of capital as well as the acquisition of citizenship and political rights, while fewer, if any, advantages of this sort were granted in Egypt" (Kienle 1995:53). Muslims do not view ethnicity as a means of discrimination; they believe that all ethnicities are equal. This is only one of many examples of how Islam interacts well with social democracy in Egypt.

Egyptian society puts a strong emphasis on education. The *Qur'an* states that people should go to great lengths to be educated. David Sagiv states that "Only by deepening education and embracing science and technology, the liberal intellectuals aver, can Egypt stride toward a better future" (1995:151). Although Egypt strives to provide what is best for its community, education needs to be reformed in order for it to be a pure social democracy. Although "competent specialists had begun to appear in the natural and social sciences" in Egypt, only one fifth of thc population was literate (Issawi 1956:38). This information was obtained at the brink of social democracy in Egypt, so the society has had time to improve its statistics. This statistic demonstrates one of the many benefits of social democracy on Egypt.

The government is also an interesting aspect to look at when studying the effects of social democracy in Egypt. Egypt elects its officials, and those officials govern the citizens. The *Shari'a* states that a "civilian government rules in the name of the people, and not a religious government with the pretensions to being the rule of God; for only the Messenger or the Prophet governs according to the rule of God" (Sagiv 1995:86). Muslims should not even seek out a leader who is trying to enforce the "rule of God." They should want a leader that will look after the people and let God take care of carrying out his rule at the proper time.

As previously stated, taxation plays a large part in social democracies. These taxes are used to redistribute income or to provide benefits to the citizens of Egypt. Many Middle Eastern countries are "undertaxed while Israel and Egypt exceed or approximate taxation levels of advanced industrial nations" (Entelis 1997:152). Taxing also relates back to the idea of the *Umma* because Egypt is taxing in order to take care of its people.

As already mentioned, Egypt progressed greatly after the 1952 Revolution and its acceptance of social democracy. The community became an integral factor of the Egyptian society. The colonialist system became obsolete, and Egyptians had full freedom. The rights of the people became consequentially more important. Education also became a free entity open to all, and Egypt's infrastructure was on the rise. All of these factors came about as a result of this socio-economic system, which follows the majority of the beliefs regarding Islam.

Indonesia

Indonesia is also a relevant example of a Muslim country that lives under social democracy. "National consciousness emerged gradually in the archipelago during the first decades of the twentieth century, developed rapidly during the contentious 1930s, and flourished, both ideologically and institutionally, during the tumultuous occupation in the early 1940s, which shattered Dutch colonial authority" (Frederick and Worden 1993:31).

The 1824 Treaty of London defined a British sphere of influence on the Malay Peninsula and a Dutch sphere on Sumatra, although its provisions placed no restrictions on British trade on the island. Sumatran trade became an issue of contention, however, because the British resented what they saw as Dutch attempts to curtail their commercial activities. One provision of the Treaty of London was the independence of the north Sumatran state of Aceh. But Aceh (Muslim ruled) controlled a large portion of the pepper trade and alarmed the Dutch by actively seeking relations with other Western countries. A new Anglo-Dutch treaty, signed in 1871, gave the Dutch a free hand in Sumatra concerning Aceh. Two years later, talks between the United States consul in Singapore and Acehnese representatives gave Batavia the pretext for opening hostilities. Dutch gunboats bombarded the sultanate's capital, Banda Aceh, and troops were landed. The capital fell under Dutch occupation the following year, but Acehnese forces undertook guerrilla resistance. The Aceh War (1873–1903) was one of the longest and bloodiest in Dutch Indonesian history (Frederick and Worden 1993).

During the 19th Century, militant or reformist Islam posed a major challenge to Dutch rule, especially in Sumatra. The *padri* of Minangkabau, for example, were returned pilgrims from Mecca who were inspired by Wahhabism–a Western term given to the strict form of Islam practiced in Saudi Arabia–that stressed the unitary nature of God. The *padri* were determined to cleanse their society of non-Islamic elements, such as the traditional system of matrilineal inheritance and consumption of alcohol and opium. The Acehnese, the most rigorously fundamentalist of Indonesian Muslims, also had close contacts with Mecca. "The principal architect of colonial Islamic Policy was Christiaan Snouck Hurgronje, a scholar of Arabic who had gone to Mecca to study Indonesian pilgrims and served as an adviser to the Netherlands Indies government form 1890 to 1904" (Frederick and Worden 1993:28).

As in other parts of colonial Southeast Asia, nationalism was preceded by traditional-style rural resistance. The Java War, joining discontented elites and peasants, was a precursor. "Around 1900 the followers of Surantika Samin, a rural messiah who espoused his own religion, the Science of the Prophet Adam, organized passive resistance on Java that included refusal to pay taxes or perform labor service" (Frederick and Worden 1993 30). Militant Islam was another focus of traditional resistance, especially in Sumatra. National consciousness was not homogeneous but reflected the variety of Indonesian society. Dutch subjugation and the shock of war from 1942 to 1945, however, fused diverse groups into something similar to a unified whole.

The responses of Islamic communities to the new political environment reflected their diversity. Pressed by ethnic Chinese competition, especially in the batik trade, Muslim merchants formed the Islamic Traders' Association in 1909.

> In 1912, this group became Sarekat Islam (Islamic Union) under the leadership of a former government official, Haji Umar Said Cokroaminoto. Sarekat Islam became the first association to gain wide membership among the common people. By early 1914, its membership numbered 360,000. Committed in part to promoting Islamic teaching and community economic prosperity (anti-Chinese sentiment was a major appeal), the organization also drew on traditional Javanese beliefs about the return of the "Just King," and Cokroaminoto went so far as to cast him in the role of a charismatic, if not divine, figure. Cokroaminoto's advocacy of Indies self government caused the Dutch some anxiety. By 1916 Sarekat Islam had some eighty branches both in Java and in the Outer Islands. The modernist or reformist trend in Islam was represented by Muhammadiyah (Followers of Muhammad), a group established at Yogyakarta in 1912. It was particularly strong among the Sumatran Minangkabau, and a number of modernist schools were established there. Its importance is reflected in the fact that Minangkabau, such as Mohammad Hatta, were surpassed in numbers only by Javanese among the leadership of the Indonesian revolution. In 1926 the Nahdatul Ulama (Revival of the Religious Scholars and sometimes known as the Muslim Scholars' League) was organized as a conservative counterweight to the growing influence of Cokroaminoto's syncretism and modernist ideas among believers (Frederick and Worden 1993:35).

Islam was a unifying force not only in the social reforms of Indonesia, but also for political advancement as well to fend off potential returns of intruders after its independence. Social democracy was laying its seed way before the birth of the parliament and constitution where it was becoming realized, in lieu of very poor adjustments that were to be made with the rmoval of colonial forces. "In May 1914, Hendricus Sneevliet (alias Maring) established the Indies Social-Democratic Association (ISDV), which became the Communist Association of the Indies (Perserikatan Komunisi di Hindia) in May 1920 and the Indonesian Communist Party (PKI) in 1924. Backed by the Communist International (Cominterm) in Moscow, the PKI became active among trade unionists and rural villagers" (Frederick and Worden 1993:36). The Government worked hard to surpass any communist popularity in Indonesia. This resistance, although shedding some light to social democracy for the region, was ironically the same reason social democracy was initiated to stop it as well.

The birth of social democracy in Indonesia occurred when it gained independence and created a constitution in 1945. Indonesia set up a government that "shall protect the entire Indonesian people and the whole of the land of Indonesia, and in order to promote the general welfare, to improve the standard of living, and participate in establishing world order founded upon freedom, eternal peace and social justice" (Hooker 2003:17). The constitution emphasizes well-being and the citizens' right to a decent life. It strives to increase the standard of living for all citizens, not just the elite.

The myriad factors that have been repeated regarding social democracy also are important in Indonesia. The *maslahah*, or public benefit, is an integral part of the society that encompasses insurance and medicine. The *Zakat*, or taxes, also contribute to the overall well-being of the society, especially the poor. In addition, relief of poverty plays a significant role in Indonesia under social democracy. The aforementioned aspects parallel social democracy and Islam.

The *Zakat* plays an integral role because the money is redistributed throughout the society for the social benefit of all. More specifically, "*Zakat* is property being transferred from one person to another or to a named class recipient" (Hooker 2003:112). In Indonesia, the key source of property is land. The poor do not own any property and do not pay *Zakat*. Hooker states that "to demand that the poor pay *Zakat* is not rational, nor is it required by religion" (2003:114). In Indonesia, there is a certain percentage of each source of property that a citizen has to pay. This money goes directly to helping the less fortunate citizens of the society. The payment of the *Zakat* is a prime example of *maslaha*. "*Maslaha*–now usually translated as 'interest' or 'benefit' for the *umma*. It is not self-interest, but a *good for society*" (Hooker 2003:3).

The Islamic terminology can be difficult at times because of the different interpretations. For instance, the definition for *maslaha* in Egypt and the aforementioned definition could be completely similar or completely different. This is also something that is reflected in all aspects of cross cultural communications. Different countries tailor their vocabularies to suit the needs of their respective peoples.

Indonesia also had an interesting adaptation period while trying to adjust to correlating Islam into its new socio-economic system. Indonesia had to seek out other means of reference besides the *Qur'an* in order to answer its economic questions. Hooker states that the "answers from within Islam were not sufficient in the new conditions. The solution was to support changing the conditions–to look for an Islamic polity, to encourage or force the individual to become a good (better) Muslim" (1993:45). This demonstrates the fact that Indonesia understood that there is room for interpretation and change in order to better adapt to new surroundings.

In sum, social democracy made its way eastward rapidly. However, many Islamic countries were not prepared for industrialization and the ramifications of that rapid move toward capitalism. It is almost as though Islamic countries had no concept for the way the world was developing. Islamic countries were founded on many structures, rules, and regulations based on Islamic faith. The way the world was progressing and its impositions and contradictions with the Islamic faith caused many issues for the development of this socio-economic system in countries like Iran, Egypt and Indonesia. Although these countries were singled out as Islamic countries that developed strong social democratic environments, the conceptualization of all the causes and effects of industrialization were very foreign to the average geographically disadvantaged Islamic states.

CONCLUSION

Social democracy uses evolutionary measures to control capitalism. It was in essence a response to the direction the world was taking in light of industrialization and growing economies. Although states were driven by the quest to acquire wealth, that wealth was compromising the health and welfare of the people. The importance for the value of the human life started gaining a stronger role globally, and the social democrats were extreme advocates during late 19th and early 20th Centuries.

The individual voice gained importance in the creation of a unified community of people as a whole. The community worked together to improve the living condition, working conditions, and overall welfare of the people. In order to nurture this concept, social democrats organized the people to take an evolutionary stance for their conditions as well as the conditions of their neighbors. Reform is one of the most effective measures that the social democrats used. These reforms were done to maintain some equity among the people of a given county. This disparity of wealth was magnified through the institution of capitalism and all that it encompasses. The disconnection of the people from the few wealthy ones was evident, and measures were being taken to narrow the gap between the haves and the have-nots.

Islam is both a theoretical and a practical religion, and upon its many tenets, the foundation for its civil rights and laws have been built through which Islam managed to accomplish what it called for in terms of worldwide humanity and true brotherhood among people, despite the differences in skin color or national identity. Any Islamic society is primarily characterized by the religion itself. The egalitarian theory of Islam stresses that "there are no distinctions as to the ranks of the members of the *umma*, but only distinctions in function" (Chaqueri 2001:33). Allah says in *surat* Al-Hujurat (verse 13): "O Mankind! We have created you from a male and female, and made you into nations and tribes, that you may know one another. Verily, the most honorable of you in the sight of Allah is he who has most *taqwa* among of you. Verily, Allah is All-Knowing, All-Aware." The Qu'ran and the Hadith have very subtle as well as some blatant views about equality among wo/men. However, many are based around the oneness in community and under Allah. "The Prophet said: "O people! Verily your Lord is One and your father [Adam] is one. An Arab is no better than a non-Arab, and a non-Arab is no better than an Arab; a red man is no better than a black man and a black man is no better than a red man–except if it is in terms of *taqwa* (piety)..." (Reported by Imam Ahmad 22391 *al-Silsilat al-Saheeh* 2700).

As with social democracy, Islam is centered on the *umma*, the community. The importance of the communal standard of living is laid out in the tenets of both systems. Therefore, the social democratic model of life is one that is very conducive to the Islamic way of life.

As seen in the case of Iran, the social democratic platform was one that gave way to the change. It was on the reforms that were already carried out by the social democrats that Islamists gained ground to bring an end to the reign of the shah and impose a theocratic government instead. This theocracy is centered primarily on Allah and all that Islam encompasses in the daily lives of the citizens of Iran. It is a platform that has enabled reform and, thus, the revolution of change in Iran as well as in other Islamic areas of the world.

Similarly with Egypt and Indonesia, the social democratic system is one of the most adaptable systems for Muslims. Egypt and Indonesia are better examples of states that are incorporating Islam into the social and democratic spheres of society. Value is placed on the living standards of people. It is a priority in these Islamic countries that the people are treated well and respect the role of the individual in the community but uphold the community as a whole.

A social democratic system in an Islamic society can promote peace in today's world and the future in a variety of ways. Primarily, this socio-economic system is able to promote peace by showing that Muslim societies can live under a socially democratic system. This system allows Muslims to have a voice and the full authority to live as they please. A common myth of Muslim societies is that since the religion is demanding, the people are forced to practice every last aspect of it or they will be punished by the law of the land. However, in social democracies, that is not the case. People do have a voice and the right to choose. That point focuses more on the democratic side of the socio-economic system. However, the socialist aspect of the society helps to alleviate poverty and other societal ailments, leading toward a peaceful nation. Poverty and crime lead to a society of chaos because one leads to the other. These ailments are repaired by the redistribution of resources and a fair amount of government involvement. A nation has to be domestically at peace before it can even think about promoting peace to the world.

It has been said that democracies hardly fight one another. Countries participating in social democracy historically do not have to worry about going to war with these democratic countries. By knowing that they do not have to worry about war with a number of countries, it puts less stress on the given societies. If their worry is diminished, these socially democratic societies can channel their energies into more productive methods of keeping peace and order.

If Islamic people living under social democracy are content overall, then it will paint a better picture to the rest of the world that Islam is not to blame for the problems that we are having in today's world. Terrorist attacks are not the fault of a specific socio-economic system, but are the fault of an unwieldy group of people. A society cannot be blamed for this specific faction of individuals, if the society or country did not preach the ideals of the group. The more knowledge people have and are able to understand about a certain society can lead to a decrease in blame and animosity toward a socially persecuted people. Different parts of the world have different beliefs regarding Muslims worldwide. It is found that the erudite people of the world do not despise or blame the religion for the horrendous acts of terrorists that use the religion as a scapegoat for their cowardly deeds. However, if one is to survey a random sample of Americans, for example, many of these respondents will associate the words Muslim and Islam with hatred and war.

In this chapter, there were three country case studies that were used to examine the myths of an unmerciful, peace lacking Islam. Egypt, Indonesia, and Iran are all Muslim societies that have used or are functioning under socially democratic systems. These countries were peaceful with their approach to the socio-economic system. The wars that may have arisen with these nations were either during a different socio-economic system or not as a result of the society being predominantly Muslim. These were wars that could have been had by even the most peaceful and powerful of nations. By propelling the findings of this chapter into today's world, we can hope that the less informed people will better understand the peaceful side of Islam. Although three countries seem like a small starting point for such an immense issue, everything has to start somewhere. Hopefully, this chapter will lead to more extensive research that will further dispel the myths some people have about Islam.

CHAPTER 6

Islam and Self-Reliance

Mubarka Haq

Nicole Rowsell

INTRODUCTION

> It takes only the merest acquaintance with the facts of the modern world to note that it is now an interactive system in a sense that is strikingly new (Appadurai 1996: 27).

Encapsulated in Arjun Appadurai's quote above is a growing unease in the global system predicated on gross economic imbalances which are bleeding over into social disenfranchisement and growing unrest. A sense of urgency exists to address these imbalances, both through detailed analysis of economic and social factors–including the increasing predominance of religion to be considered as a motivator–and structured responses which go beyond the dominant paradigm of international political economy. This chapter seeks to address the key components of self-reliance as a socio-economic model which, by its very nature, opposes dominant economic structures, and assess its complementarities (or lack thereof) with the tenets prescribed in Islam–a religion which is also opposing the dominant Western paradigm at present. Self-reliance is investigated in order to determine its historical value and assessed in terms of what could possibly be considered as its reemergence today. The first step in our analysis then must be to define the socio-economic system of self-reliance.

While the literature on self-reliance as a socio-economic system is not extensive, there are several authors who have discussed self-reliance, with different levels of care and complexity, and sought to define it as they perceive it in the context of their individual scopes. This is not to equate all the texts that have been analyzed, nor is it to equalize their strengths and weaknesses. The basis of our analysis is the similarity that comes about from all of the sources to derive a consolidated definition of what we perceive to be key components of self-reliance.

In his writings countering the dependency theorists of the 1960s and 1970s, J. Friedman defines a self-reliant society as "an inclusive, non-hierarchical society that stresses cooperation over competition, harmony with nature over exploitation, and social needs over unlimited personal desire" (Friedman 1986: 205). Here, Friedman defines self-reliance as the alternative to the endogenous or self-directed development and possibly the only hope for peripheral regions that lack economic growth and bargaining power.

Similarly, Yusif Sayigh considers the socio-economic system to be a viable system and strong opposition to the centre-periphery paradigm, dominant at the time of his writing. "Self-reliance... is a strategy for development characterized by, and likewise influencing, both those economic and non-economic areas of decision and action which together express the determination of a society to seek regeneration, and for that purpose to depend on itself, to the maximum extent possible" (Sayigh 1991:94). Sayigh sets up his definition of self-reliance, which later he dissects into seven distinct aspects, and emphasizes that basic human rights, freedoms and social justice are the prerequisite for initiating self-reliance.

One of the foremost scholars on self-reliance, Johan Galtung, in his seminal work on the topic, defines this socio-economic system and identifies its antecedents as follows: "Self-reliance is not merely an abstract recipe, a way of organizing the economy with heavy emphasis on the use of local factors, but a very determined struggle against any kind of centre-periphery formation with the ultimate goal of arriving at a world in which each part is a centre" (Galtung 1980:20). Galtung's thesis lays down the foundation of his research; he later goes into an in-depth analysis of what is required to achieve self-reliance and what self-reliance transports with it.

Self-reliant development has different connotations for different people, depending on their experiences and relationships to the 'centre.' For some, it suggests the traditional meaning of economic growth; for others, it symbolizes an individual's self-worth. However, in all of these texts, self-reliance is defined as the answer to the dependency bondage in the Third World. In assessing the different viewpoints, the authors consider it inherent that self-reliance is not just a socio-economic system but also a psychological state which defines how the individual views the world and his or her role in the immediate social environment. An individual can be of no use to others if s/he does not contain the bare essentials that allow him/her to feel competent in his/her own psyche. It is at this stage in which true self-reliance is born. It is imperative to understand that this process must begin from the individual level and then evolve into the other levels, such as the local, regional, national and international levels. Perhaps Johan Galtung puts it most eloquently when states the following: "To withstand normative/ideological power emanating from some kind of centre self-confidence, self-respect is needed–a faith in one's own values and own culture and civilization: the traditional one and the ability to create a new culture" (1980:20). Thus, the scope of self-reliance goes beyond the economic structure and can be translated into a vehicle for social action.

Economic aspects of self-reliance are also encapsulated in several examples of struggles for social justice, such as Gandhi's *Satyagraha*, a philosophy based on the Hindu notions of 'truth' and 'holding firmly.' "The potential of *satyagraha* to change an opponent's position, Gandhi believed, came from the dependence of rulers on the cooperation of those who had the choice to obey or resist" (Ackerman & Duvall 2000:66). While some would consider the Gandhian struggle an internal matter, the substantive resistance to the Raj–and by extension the British colonial institution–utilizing the village as the primary locus of direct struggle, presents compelling avenues for comparison. This example is raised here in an attempt to highlight the extrapolation which can be made from the socio-economic construction of self-reliance, which is the inherent propensity for nonviolent struggle against international economic pressures. In this way, too, we see potential linkages to Islamic tenets of personal and social responsibility, which will be explored in greater depth later.

Contemporary economic flows usually include the undermining of local initiatives for subsistence, in order to meet global demand. In turn, a relationship of dependency, entrenched in the discourse of center-periphery inequalities, is repositioned today in terms of Third/developing/non-Western world opposing the 'modernized' West. To put it in other words, essentially 'the West versus the Rest.'

In his book outlining the emerging cultural flows (often referred to as globalization), Arjun Appadurai articulates *deterritorialization* as a process that "brings laboring populations into the lower-class sectors and spaces of relatively wealthy societies, while sometimes creating an exaggerated sense of criticism or attachment to politics in the home state" (Appadurai 1996: 37–38). In the context of this pressure to conform to Western-dominated models of capital flows, the anti-globalization movement is in essence a conglomeration of numerous 'self-reliant' communities and organizations that have developed a forceful counter argument. While conceptualized in the 1960s and formalized into a discourse in the 1970s, the basis for self-reliance draws parallels to contemporary dissatisfaction with the imbalance of power in economic flows and could offer insights into potential alternative methodologies.

There are those who take a morbid view of current world affairs, implying a *clash of civilizations*, which will have destructive ends (e.g., Huntington 1993). While this view may be skewed, and indeed possibly based on racist misunderstanding of cultural and religious differences, the contemporary global reality requires that questions of economic, political, social and religious motivations be addressed. In this tenuous environment, this analysis hopes to offer points which can be extrapolated to present a vision for peaceful resolution of conflicts in the current world order, particularly when the rift between the West and Islamic cultures seems to be growing.

REVIEW OF RELEVANT LITERATURE

Historically, many schools of thought have influenced the way we think about the Third World and its development such as economic principles, various incursions of thinking from particular epochs in time, and many years of historical baggage. It is through these types of lenses that different theories of development have emerged. Remnants of dependency paradigm and its framing of the center-periphery dichotomy are still quite present in contemporary development discourse. Development theories have seen their own internal revolution and evolution over the years in trying to cope with the conflicts and criticisms of their own partial and subjective views as well as the eccentric problems of their times. Still there are many valid points that have been introduced by the different theories. In our analysis, we concentrate on self-reliance as a development theory as well as a socioeconomic system and take into consideration its numerous facets and links to the multifarious complex 'Third World.'

Similarly, the movement which emerged in opposition to the realist model (self-reliance) has also adapted to present-day economic and social linkages, often encapsulated in the term 'globalization.' In order to adequately address the relevance of self-reliance and Islam's response to it, several theoretical frames need to be addressed in order to offer a solid platform for analysis. Yusif Sayigh notes the inherent complexities of this socio-economic model and highlights the three levels for consideration:

> At the nation-state or collective (that is, regional) level, self-reliance is viewed as a strategy for development. On the other hand, self-reliance at the micro-level is more of a principle of cooperation within villages and communities, first, for the purpose of self-help internally, and then for co-operation and exchange with neighborhoods. Furthermore, at the micro-level, self-reliance involves the inculcation of these principles and values, and the establishment of those structures and avenues of action, that together promote the sense of identity and authenticity (Sayigh 1991:97).

While his analysis focuses specifically on the nation-state development level, Sayigh's contributions have much broader implications. Using Sayigh's quote to frame this analysis, self-reliance is considered within three contexts: (1) a large-scale development framework, (2) socio-political considerations, and finally (3) the psycho-social implications. In their approaches to large scale implementation of self-reliant development, theorists have offered several jumping off points from which to view self-reliance. We will begin with an outline of Sayigh's model, recognizing that his analysis is multi-dimensional, and then highlight John Friedmann's alternative approach.

In his comprehensive analysis, *Elusive Development: from Dependence to Self-Reliance in the Arab Region* (1991), Yusif Sayigh outlines seven interrelated aspects through which self-reliance as a strategy for economic development in the Arab context can be viewed. The first aspect Sayigh identifies is a need for 'Third World' societies to liberate themselves from the neo-classical economic and sociological model of development, which posits the Western capitalist industrial example as the ultimate goal for any society hoping to advance.

At its core, Sayigh's first principle of self-reliance is "a return to one's own sources of strength, resources, capabilities and interest, in the hope of achieving an inner-directed development, through the pursuit of the independence of decision-making in a national economy which subordinates external relations to the needs of internal accumulation, production and interests" (Sayigh 1991:102). The second aspect of self-reliance to consider is specific to the Arab region and, therefore, particularly relevant in this analysis as it refers to Muslim countries: there is a deep need to find a harmonious balance between the values of 'modernity' and those of religious fundamentalism. Sayigh suggests that Muslims who take an orthodox view towards Islam are often members of the same group that vehemently opposes dominant models of development. The third aspect of self-reliance lies in a deep awareness of dependency, understanding of its meaning, its nature and origins, and its implications on social structures. Awareness of the nature and role of dependency is a necessary condition for the assessment of the feasibility of a movement to stop its spread and then to force it to retreat on the various fronts where it is entrenched. The fourth aspect of self-reliance is the need to develop concepts, positions and courses of action appropriate to the conditions of the Arab region and the correction of its economic, social and political structures. The fifth aspect of self-reliance reaches beyond the imperative of elaborating a self-generated view of development and the ensuring that this development is inner-directed and will cater to external markets only in so far as internal needs and interests have been catered to. The sixth aspect of self-reliance is the need for the adoption of an Arab regional prospective in the conceptualization, design and pursuit of development. Essentially, a method for acculturation must be implemented in order for self-reliance to be effective; this is really the cornerstone of the theory. The seventh and final aspect is the determination of a society to seek self-reliant development with resolve and intelligence. The intelligent and well calculated and graduated pursuit of self-reliance requires a well calibrated mix of idealism with realism, of ambition with practicality (Sayigh 1991). Sayigh emphasizes that none of the first six aspects, and not all of them together, can alone make the pursuit of self-reliance serious and promising. Only when the seventh aspect is added to the other six will the pursuit become meaningful and promise to help society pull gradually out of dependency.

Friedman addresses how originally it was thought that economic development would lead to a 'good life,' but this was equated to material consumption which "...uprooted people from their communities, alienated them from their cultural traditions, poisoned their environment, destroyed their natural resources, and concentrated power in the hands of multibillion-dollar corporations that were increasingly accountable to no one but themselves" (Friedmann 1986: 206). He dissects Third World development into two parts: those who have and those who do not. He asserts that those who have bargaining power and 'function as centres of control' undergo an endogenous or self-directed development, and those who do not have the means to hold their ground are weak and must resort to self-reliance: "the only viable option peripheralised populations have for their survival and well being"(Friedmann 1986: 212). He agrees that it must start from the bottom, but he also illustrates this as a part of society that is invisible and refers to it as the 'informal markets.'

He emphasizes that this is where most of the internal uprisings can take place to help overcome inherent weaknesses. Friedman sees women as being the main 'actors' or driving force of self-reliance in this huge unaccounted 'civil society' and will help "…change reality, not administer it" (Friedmann 1986: 212). He views that women, through active participation in these invisible economies of households and communities, can create a large dent into the existing system of dependence. He acknowledges that each peripheral region may view self-reliance in different ways, but he also sees some common viable outcomes such as "an orientation that assigns priority to the basic material and psychological needs of people…, social recognition of the value of voluntary work in households and community…organizations such as the instruments of production and good health, adequate space for life, work and political assembly, strategic information, social networks, and financial resources" (Friedmann 1986: 212). Transitioning away from the dominant definition of self-reliance as an alternative vehicle for development, we will now address the concepts within the framework for socio-political responsibility within a society.

In general, theories of self-reliance have often been scrutinized for focusing on the individual as opposed to the group, encouraging total independence, and imparting the breaking of all ties. The notion is that self-reliance brews anti-capitalistic behavior, brings anarchy, and hinders innovative progress. But in actuality, self-reliance has been an accepted social behavior of existence for humankind across the world, throughout history. Then it was not a development theory or a socioeconomic system, it was a way of living–a way of surviving. Survival is based on the fulfillment of basic human needs–the most well known are food, health, education and shelter. And the lesser acknowledged, yet crucial, needs are safety, freedom, development, and acceptance. But it is no secret that more than half of the world's population is impoverished and unable at attain these very same basic human needs, and that there is a "…growing gap between survival needs and their fulfillment, and the failure of growth to trickle down to the poor…" (Sen & Grown 1987:38). There are more than several hypotheses for why this persists even with all of the technology, wealth and growth the world has seen, but Gita Sen and Caren Grown suggest that "the interests of powerful nations and classes, both internationally and nationally, are enmeshed in these structures, and therefore often have a vested interest in their persistence. As a result, the survival of large sections of the population in the Third World has become increasingly uncertain and vulnerable" (Sen & Grown 1987:26).

Johan Galtung speaks about these vulnerabilities and how self-reliance is the solution to extricate the 'Third World' from this epidemic of dependency. The first assertion he makes is that there are three essential things that are needed to become self-reliant: "... self-respect, ability to be self-sufficient and fearlessness/invulnerability..." (Galtung 1980: 21). He emphasizes that self-reliance is more entrenched in "...psycho-politics than in that of economics" (Galtung 1980:21). One should not envy the Western mores and castigate or marginalize his/her own traditions, values, culture and civilization. This exacerbates the West considering itself the 'center' or pinnacle of the world, which feeds right into the dependency theory by creating desires for the center's products, and introduces vulnerabilities. One must attempt to deflect these vulnerabilities by creating "...independent taste-formation, being less susceptible to 'tastes' generated from the centre and satisfiable with the centre goods only" (Galtung 1980:21).

And, if each person were to create what s/he needed, local factors would be more efficiently utilized, creativity would be stimulated, there would be more diversity in development, less ecological misuse and exploitation of natural resources, and decreased inequalities. But self-reliance must begin at the individual level, and it "...cannot be at the expense of the self-reliance of others; it only implies the autonomy to set one's own goals and realize them as far as possible through one's own efforts, using one's own forces, including economic factors"(Galtung 1980:22). In essence, self-reliance is a system that makes each person actively participate in becoming self-sufficient and fearless, encourages an attitude and a structure of defense, and in turn creates mass participation that pours over into self-reliant communities, regions, and nations.

But becoming self-reliant does not in any way imply total independence or seclusion from all. Except in the case of basic human needs, where it is imperative to be self-reliant so that it is not wielded as an instrument of coercion over one at a time of crisis, self-reliance signifies restructuring the thought and process of participation and solidarity. "The point is not to cut out trade but to redirect it and recompose it by giving preferences to cooperation with those in the same position, preferring the neighbor to the more distant possibility, cooperation to exchange, and intra-sector to inter-sector trade" (Galtung 1980: 26). The idea is to try to have collaboration and deal with your equals, to have camaraderie with others at the same level, whether it is a neighbor or a nation. Moving horizontally as opposed to vertically will allow more compatibility with local conditions, have positive externalities internalized or given to neighbors at the same level, and help withstand trade dependency manipulation. This will allow the center and periphery ground to be leveled and deter future centers from being created or eventually having every part become a center. And hence, a way of becoming autonomous by "...resisting centre-periphery formations, including the penetration, fragmentation, marginalization and segmentation supporting mechanisms" (Galtung 1980:21).

In contrast to Galtung's detailed analysis, Stokes offers a concise text on self-reliance, outlining a practical reference guide for small communities to empower themselves through subsistence level development and harnessing of natural resources. This text supports the claims of other theorists cited earlier. "The building of a more equitable global society is proceeding in localities where people participate in, rather than just observe, the solving of their problems" (Stokes 1978:7).

Building on this level of analysis, Sayigh applies the discourse of self-reliance to a particular region. Linking self-reliance to the largely Muslim Arab world, Sayigh offers summative remarks about prerequisites for Arab states to successfully pursue self-reliant development:

> ...the orientation of nationalism should be progressive, in the sense that nationalism should be supportive of the struggle for liberation and for social justice; it should respect human freedoms and rights and allow meaningful political participation for the broad masses; it should motivate the people to protect Arab territory from external incursion and to liberate areas already usurped; it should be a force in the struggle to free the economy where ownership of the means of production is broad-based, with a strong public sector, alongside a sizeable and active private sector and a wide-reaching co-operative sector, within a pattern of division of labor which is not tampered with arbitrarily and irresponsibly (Sayigh 1991:209).

Sayigh's words offer a potential view of how Arab (and by extension Muslim) society may best manage a program of deliberate self-reliance. This analysis will act as a starting point later in this chapter to frame case studies of Islamic countries which have engaged in self-reliance.

As one of America's greatest literary figures, Ralph Waldo Emerson, constructed a psycho-social and political philosophy which has deeply influenced the United States' view of democracy. It is interesting to note that while Emerson certainly outlines a self-centered view of self-reliance, his perspective is decidedly Western and steeped in the notion of the individual as the center. While this does not create an inherent contradiction with other self-reliance authors who are clearly aligned against the dominant dependency paradigm emulating from the West, it is critical to recognize the origins and, therefore, the potential intentionality informing Emerson's work:

> He who knows that power is in the soul, that he is weak only because he has looked for good out of him and elsewhere, and, so perceiving, throws himself unhesitatingly on his thought, instantly rights himself, stands in the erect position, commands his limbs, works miracles; just as a man who stands on his feet is stronger than a man who stands on his head (Emerson 1841:23).

For Emerson, while there is certain emphasis on the community, which will be addressed shortly, the ultimate actualization of self-reliance is the lack of substantial connections to others, even in one's immediate community. In this way, Emerson is espousing the sort of political structure which other transcendental writers such as de Tocqueville revere in American political society. Kateb views Emerson's philosophy towards self-reliance as one with intrinsic links to a political doctrine, "...urging the elevation of democracy to its full height, free of the aristocratic, but also free of the demonic" (Kateb 1995:18).

While our hypothesis is that the role of the individual and self-reliance as a philosophy of being needs to be emphasized more, Emerson's work leaves something to be desired. As Kateb notes, "He [Emerson] does not ask what happens to active self-reliance when the moral motive overrides all else and when therefore persons are supposed to devote themselves to the direct achievement of moral good, even to the point of self-sacrifice" (Kateb 1995:200). While Emerson's vision of self-reliance and its relationship to democratic principles is somewhat naïve by today's standards, he offers an ideal state of being. However, as Kateb notes, Emerson's interpretation does not effectively address the question of ethics in the didactic relationship of an individual and a larger community or society (Kateb 1995).

On the other hand, Galtung digs deep into the various faces of self-reliance and acknowledges that it must be a bottom-up process, but his analysis fails to address how this insurrection of genesis will take place. How does one create compassion and respect in another, motivate a person, build self-confidence, erect courage, and make people care?

His theory also implies that resources are available to each person and that the individual chooses not to realize them. To some extent, this may be true, but one cannot overlook the fact that land, wealth and resources are not equally distributed. "Existing economic and political structures tend to be highly inequitable between nations, classes, genders and ethnic groups" (Sen & Grown 1987:25). And all other things held constant, how does one acquire these useful assets to become self-reliant? If each person takes care of his/her own interests, then who takes care of the indigent masses that are unable to become self-reliant?

And although Friedman agrees with Galtung's bottom-up philosophy, he also falls short in explaining how to instigate this ideology of self-reliance in the invisible economy with women, who "...constitute the majority of the poor, the underemployed, and the economically and socially disadvantaged in most societies" (Sen & Grown 1987:23). Women are not only subjected to the oppressions of the centre-peripheral problems as men, but they are also trying to cope with the internal anguish of gender-based inequalities and subordination. As Gerda Lerner stresses, "As long as both men and women regard the subordination of half the human race to the other as 'natural,' it is impossible to envision a society in which differences do not connote either dominance or subordination" (Lerner 1986: 229). Friedman portrays women as an untapped resource, but he fails to acknowledge their own struggles of internalization that have allowed them to be defined and confined in the very same surroundings in which they subsist. So, then, in this bottom-up system, how do we change the way people think?

While addressed by self-reliance theorists, the issue of basic human needs (a foundation of conflict resolution theory) has yet to be fully explored, and it is an area which we feel could offer new and innovative insights into the application of this development model. Bruce Stokes' reference to meeting basic human needs certainly peaks the interest of those in the conflict resolution field due to the likely orientation towards John Burton's cannon of literature on the topic. Whether Stokes was specifically referring to Burton, or simply referencing the same terminology, is of little consequence, as the underlining need for psycho-social frame for analysis is inherent here (Stokes 1978).

Building on the work of earlier theorists, Burton highlights basic human needs as a means by which to view all conflicts. Ranging from the interpersonal to the international, he offered a truly universal approach to human nature and framework for conflict resolution (Burton 1993). He proposes that humans need a sense of security and identity in order to maintain positive self-esteem and abide by norms within their immediate environment–these are non-negotiable and fixed for the most part. These needs–or values–are at the core of an individual's identity and, therefore, go beyond positional interests. The theory is based on the following prerequisites: (1) need for response, (2) stimulation, (3) security, (4) distributive justice, (5) consistent behavior in others, (6) meaning deduced from consistent responses, and (7) role defense (Burton 1979). Therefore, our contribution to the discourse on self-reliance is based on the field of conflict resolution, by outlining the imperative of the role of the individual vis-à-vis the community. Indeed, this is actually the fundamental core of the paradigm.

ANALYSIS OF FINDINGS

In order to uncover the implications of self-reliance methodologies being implemented in a Muslim society, we will now consider three case studies, analyze the findings for each, and provide some final thoughts which highlight crosscutting themes. In the scheme of Islamic ethics, a free person establishes three simultaneous relationships: with God, with their own self, and with the society. Providing direct connections to the precepts of self-reliance outlined earlier in this chapter, we will attempt to draw out these three levels of analysis in each case study. The cases deliberately represent a broad range of political, religious and regional factors. For example, Libya and Iran offer two vastly different interpretations of Islamic law in society, which is used to mobilize both communities. Alternatively, the Nyerere era of Tanzanian history is a critical period, both for the development of that post-colonial state and also for the self-reliance school of thought which emerged in direct opposition to colonial repression. The Tanzanian example also looks at a society in which the Muslim population is a sizable minority and, therefore, faces additional dynamics in implementation of this socio-economic system. The similarities and differences of these case studies will now be addressed in greater detail, beginning with Tanzania.

Tanzania

Often considered to be one of the fathers of self-reliance, Julius Nyerere occupies a critical place in Tanzanian history and in development discourse. As the nation's first president after independence from colonial rule, Nyerere had the unique challenge of developing a governing structure which would provide adequate support to its citizenry, while also creating a framework for unity within the fledgling state. Emerging from a long and painful history of colonial rule, Nyerere emphasized a return to the base and reclamation (both literally and figuratively) of the land. By actively developing this connection, Nyerere underscored the foundations of self-reliance and enacted social and political reforms to engage Tanzanians in empowering their communities (McDonald & Sahle 2002).

While Tanzanian society has the potential to be highly factionalized along tribal lines, cohesiveness has been steadfastly maintained throughout the country's post-colonial history, including the Muslim inhabitants predominantly located along the coastal region of Mombasa. This is in part likely due to the loose ethnic affiliations which have not engendered deep solidarity along those lines. Similarly, the large number of ethnic groups has created a sociological state of affairs in which no one group has a large power potential, thereby encouraging unity through diversity. In actuality, the development of the overarching Swahili culture which transcended ethnic divisions has fostered a larger solidarity and commitment to the nationalist project. In order to foster this environment, Nyerere implemented his theory of inclusion, defined in the following manner: "This theoretical framework can be described as the philosophy and practical management of different parts of society by making them part of the decision-making process of one and the same group" (Omari 1995:29). Therefore, this analysis, by focusing specifically on the coastal Muslim communities, has a high level of transferability to the larger national experiment with self-reliance.

Islam came to what is present day Tanzania as it did too much of the African continent, through conquest; however, conversion was not simply based on the desire to conform to the new paradigm. "Most Muslims in East Africa converted to Islam through the attraction of brotherhoods and became either formal or informal adherents of the *tariqas* [Sufi Muslim communities]" (Nimtz 1980:172). With respect to Tanzania, and in many respects other areas of Muslim Africa, Islam was a vehicle for self-reliance to take root, as a matter of solidarity and survival. Religion acted as a coagulant within communities and protected against cleavages which could have potentially proven divisive.

In one of his central writings, the *Arusha Declaration,* Nyerere articulated his vision of the linkage between socialism and self-reliance. These nuances are highlighted here in order to address the components of his vision and to provide a platform from which to provide an analysis from the Islamic perspective: (1) The need to build a society where no person exploits another, everybody works and reaps a fair return for his labor, all major means of production and exchange in the nation are controlled and owned wholly or in part by the peasants through their democratically elected government and co-operatives;

(2) the need to de-emphasize the importance of money and industries by the establishment of co-operatives; (3) the need to de-emphasize urban development and focus on rural development (Komba 1995:37). The first point articulated in the *Arusha Declaration* is directly compatible with Islam and can be seen in the *Five Pillars* (*Iman*–faith, *Salah*–prayer, *Sawm*–fasting, *Zakat*–charity, and *Haj*–pilgrimage).

"After the *Arusha Declaration* the Government hoped to adapt the technological advances of the non-African world to the traditional system and to transform the traditional system to make *ujamaa* the communal basis for the development of the village life, replacing the scattered homesteads of traditional Tanzania with their extended families and mutual-aid work units" (Brown 1995:17). Despite the unifying nature of Islam, this somewhat utopian perspective has been clouded in the case of Tanzania. The colonial legacy of 'divide and conquer' has created an historical inequity within Tanzanian society, which has favored Christian populations. Therefore, it is unclear if Muslim communities within Tanzania were successful due to religious commitment or principled engagement with self-reliance based on socialist ideology.

Tanzania's socialist underpinnings obviously fly in the face of an Islamic ethos of ethics and economics, by delegitimatizing the role of religion in political discourse. Nonetheless, communities implementing the *ujamaa* philosophy of strength through small group cohesiveness were certainly in line with Islamic teachings. And while Nyerere's philosophy of self-reliance was certainly not based in whole on Islamic tradition, there is no denying the tremendous legacy the religion left on Eastern Africa. In many ways, the *ujamaa* closely emulates the conception of *umma* in Islam, both in scope and purpose. According to Khadduri, "The conception of the *umma* or brotherhood constituted the basis of the Islamic community in whose membership alone the believer obtains prosperity in this world and salvation in the next" (Khadduri 2001:30).

Libya

In Libya, from the time Muammar Qaddafi came to power in 1969, through a bloodless coup which overthrew King Idris Al-Sanusi, he was interested in implementing what could be termed self-reliance with significant Islamic moorings, inspired by the Nasserite movement of the time. His tour de force leadership style, coupled with an overtly hostile stance towards former colonial powers propagated an international community with little esteem for the forceful leader. Additionally, abhorrence for the Lockerbie bombing in 1988 effectively isolated Libya from many countries, and United Nations sanctions cemented a need to enact policies of self-reliance in order to survive, as it was clear Qaddafi was not interested in softening his posture.

However, before delving too deeply into the ramifications of this charismatic leader's dictatorial grip on the Libyan nation, an outline of his musings on a socio-economic system, much of which has been captured in his various writings, is presented. *The Green*

Book is a manifesto of political, economic, and social concepts formatted by Qaddafi into a socialistic system of direct participatory democracy which he defines as "The Third Universal Theory." Although nowhere credited in his book, Qaddafi has officially verbalized his theory's Islamic connections, notably in response to his religious critics, who openly declared the book to be incompatible with Islam, partly, they charged, because its stipulations on private property flouted Prophet Muhammad's (Peace be Upon Him; henceforth, PBUH) words and practices encapsulated in the *Hadith*. In order to address his many critics, a brief presentation of Qaddafi's framework for self-reliance is needed. As he puts it,

> Man's freedom is lacking if somebody else controls what he needs, for need may result in man's enslavement of man. Need causes exploitation. Need is an intrinsic problem, and conflict grows out of the domination of man's needs (Christman 1988:72).

In Part II of *The Green Book, The Solution of the Economic Problem*, Qaddafi rejects capitalism and communism for being fundamentally corrupt and, in their place, proposes a socialism of sorts. Qaddafi's system guarantees a home, a basic income, and a vehicle for everyone. His goal is an egalitarian, non-collectivist society in which man either works for himself to supply his needs, is a partner in a socialist corporation and shares in its production, or performs a public service for society which, in turn, provides his needs. Embedded in his analysis is a stringent distaste for any foreign intervention, to the extent that the removal of all traces of imported ideologies was a conscious project of the nation.

The *Jamahiriya Society*, loosely translated as 'state of the masses,' addresses development on the economic level as fulfilling and liberating man's needs. It views man's freedom as incomplete if it is dominated by someone else. Therefore, Libyan plans for development are squarely based on self-sufficiency: "There is no freedom for a people fed from overseas" (Christman 1988:29). In order to operationalize this perspective, the monarchy and any remnants of Italian colonialism were dismantled and devalued, which often involved reclamation of private property. By 1979, the ownership and control of the industrial base had been transformed; and in the early 1980s, domestic private trade was phased out, to be replaced by people's distributive committees supplied by the state's General Marketing Company. Similarly, local community-level institutions called Revolutionary Committees were formed to invigorate the populace and design a process of reiteration of core Libyan revolutionary values throughout the country.

While Islamic precepts such as the primacy of the *umma* can be seen in Qaddafi's writings, many religious figures have strongly questioned his theories and consider them gross misrepresentations of *Qur'anic* teachings. In 1978, Qaddafi debated Islamic doctrine with a group of Muslim religious scholars (*ulama*) in Tripoli. Much of the talk focused on the extent to which the *Hadith* should complement the *Qur'an* as a source of spiritual guidance, a central problem being how to know which of the various *Hadith* traditions associated with Prophet Muhammad (PBUH) to accept. "This is the familiar problem of theological exegesis: human beings must stand above the texts if they wish to evaluate them; in which case there is a paradox that the text, once evaluated, cannot serve as a *primary* ground for truth" (Simons 1993:231).

Libya under Colonel Qaddafi's reign certainly does present a convincing case of self-reliant communities developing an intricate network of support and mutual benefit. However, Libya remains dependent on foreign companies and labor and there is no sign that it will achieve the desired levels of self-sufficiency in the short or medium term. There can be little doubt that the Libyan position has changed in many areas, although debate is still possible about the extent of the transformation. "Economic policy has discernibly shifted in the direction of liberalization, there is an evident move away from moral and practical help for dissident groups throughout the world, and constructive steps have been through discussion and real initiatives to improve relations with other countries" (Simons 1993:290).

Seemingly going against his own philosophy, Qaddafi has consolidated much power at the level of elites within Libyan society, thereby encouraging a ring of supporters vigilantly willing to curtail any opposition to the leader before it gains momentum. While this abuse of power is clearly un-Islamic, Qaddafi has always maintained a strong linkage to religious underpinnings and insisted on a devout allegiance to faith on the part of the Libyan nation.

As a closing caveat, statements coming from Qaddafi and the Libyan government demonstrate essentially an about-face with respect to much of the state's foreign policy under his tutelage. Reparations to the families of the Lockerbie bombings after more than two decades and a denouncement of weapons of mass destruction have so jolted the international community that United Nations' sanctions were lifted in the fall of 2003 and relations among staunch enemies of the state are beginning to normalize, albeit slowly. While it is too soon to be able to adequately reflect on the nature of Qaddafi's shift, the question of his motivations–be they religious or purely strategic–will likely prove fruitful in an analysis of potential methodologies which contribute to de-escalation processes (an area which requires much attention from conflict resolutionists).

Iran

In Iran, the Islamic Revolution of 1979 was a pivotal period in its history and illustrated a country's journey from a monarchy to a self-reliant Islamic Republic. For some, under Pahlavi's regime, "Iran had just completed nearly two decades of rapid economic growth and impressive social development" (Amuzegar 1993:3); for others, "the Islamic Republic inherited 'a semi-peripheral country following almost three decades of dependent capitalist growth…'"(Amuzegar 1993:16). We neither attempt to concur or oppose either position, nor do we intend to revisit the manner in which the regime change occurred. For the purposes of this analysis, we concentrate on whether post–1979 Iran was able to attain an Islamic self-reliant state.

"There were two goals of this 'Islamic Revolution': first, to remove the Shah and his administration from power and second, to bring Iran into an Islamic state" (Hussain 1983:97). After Ayatollah Sayyid Ruhollah Musavi Khomeini came into power in 1979, he sought to recreate a truly Islamic society and economy: "a complete code of life and thus directly, and strongly, affects all aspects of life" (Saeed 1994:46). Khomeini steered away from the Western and concentrated on the Islamic economic model. He perceived that the Western economic model correlated development to modernization and modernization to secularization, associating a monetary value to development and/or the 'good life'; whereas, in the Islamic economic model, development was achieved through self-reliance as prescribed by the *Qur'an* and the *Shari'a*. So then Khomeini set "all civil, penal, financial, economic, administrative, cultural, military, political, and other laws and regulations in the country to be based on 'Islamic criteria'" (Amuzegar 1993:26).

Khomeini began the Islamization of Iran by restructuring the framework through the Constitution. The preamble of the Constitution clearly stated that an overall 'human development' is to be attained, where not just secular but also spiritual development will be essential to bring people closer to God. It sought to establish a 'just society' through independence from 'foreign domination' and the elimination of 'poverty and deprivation.' The Constitution speaks of three distinct levels of reform: (1) the individual, (2) the domestic, and (3) the international, in the scope of 'public, cooperative, and private.' Chapter One defines the government's role in ensuring that everyone obtains basic human needs such as food, housing, jobs, and health care. It also emphasizes how various sectors, such as the industrial, agricultural, military, and technology, need to become self-sufficient. There are several Articles contained in the Constitution that discuss the ownership of private property and its uses, and business practices, profits and prohibitions under the Islamic law. Chapter Three discusses the 'Right of the People' and economic rights. It addresses how the government needs to take an active part in making the people of the country self-sufficient, such as providing schooling up to high school, and providing every citizen with land on which to reside. Chapter Four of the Constitution goes into foreign economic relations. The Articles detail the endorsement of the Majlis (the Iranian parliament, which consisted mostly of *mullahs*) to all 'international treaties, conventions, contracts, and agreements,' and parliamentary approval on any governmental foreign borrowing.

And although Khomeini vowed on several occasions to return his appreciation to women for their support during the revolution and "in various places, the constitution makes reassuring statements about the future of women in Iran's post-revolutionary society"(Meyer 1995:109), "the Assembly of Experts devised a framework in which the Islamic rules were vague and not in favor of women.…the 'Islamic system' had suppressed the democratic rights of women for compulsory veiling, preventing women from holding judicial posts, sexual segregation, ...execution and the flogging of women on charges of prostitution and adultery, re-establishing polygamy and temporary marriage, and practically annulling the Family Protection Law..."(Hussain 1984:53). And "in the first three years of the Revolution, twenty thousand girls and women were executed" (Goodwin1994:115).

The objectives and policies of an Islamic society and its economics were communicated to the people through the Friday sermons at mosques across the country. And although the Constitution *seemed* to reflect all of the precepts and principles of Islam, there were several problems which made it difficult to implement. The steps taken towards self-reliance made the administration more dependent on external powers in the years directly following the Revolution than before. As if the drastic 180 degree change in the structure of Iran all at once was not severe enough, many internal and external problems unforeseen by the new administration caused an additional push of the economy into a downward spiral and made Khomeini's vision difficult to materialize. The many factions–religious and secular–like the center-right groups of liberal-democratic secularists, the industrial and agricultural bourgeoisie, the conservative clergy, and the orthodox Shi'ite communities who aligned with Khomeini because they did not have the connection with the masses or the ability to overthrow 'The Shah,' later became a source of tension for the new government. Most of the disputes between these factions were said to be based on the interpretation of the *Qur'an*: "for every verse in the scripture calling for redistribution and sanctioning a command economy, there is another, sanctioning the right of property, decreeing inequality to the natural order of things" (Ajami 1993:30), signifying a lack of clear enough method of interpretation (Saeed 1994:61); a subjective divergence in interpretation "often arriving at meanings that violate the spirit of the *Qur'an* when seen in its totality" (Saeed 1994:59).

Instead of making the social and economic environment of Iran better, Iran immediately started feeling the negative repercussions of the new Islamic Republic. United States led foreign sanctions and embargos, set by President Jimmy Carter, caused wild fluctuations in the price of crude oil in foreign markets. The war with Iraq quickly diminished any chance of the economy recovering any time soon. The Gross Domestic Product was rapidly falling, inflation was on the rise, unemployment increased, and the dependence on external markets to provide basic human needs grew, primarily in the realm of basic food items. "A country that was once sufficient in food products now had major shortages....the regime's own statistics showed heavy industry functioning at 25% of its pre-Revolutionary capacity"(Goodwin 1994:121). And because the Ayatollah had denounced professional expertise as being without value, there were dramatic shortages of doctors, dentists and other professionals (Goodwin 1994:105).

All these developments not only caused the economy to dive into recession, but they also brought "human suffering, personal hardship, and individual sacrifice..." (Amuzegar 1993:59). As frustration grew, so did protests and riots against the Khomeini government.

To some, Khomeini was a religious leader; to others, he was another dictator who existed within an administration instead of an individual monarchy. Whatever the 'Claim of Truth' may be in this case, one thing is clear: "the Revolution of 1979 held forth to the Iranian populace the promise of 'national integrity' through 'self reliance.' Although intended to change Iran's economic and political course, the Revolution had produced no structural changes in the economy by late 1987" (www.parstimes.com).

Table 1: Cross Country Analysis of Exports (US$ millions)

Country	**Major Exports** **Total exports (fob)**	**2002**	**2003**
Tanzania	Coffee	35	40
	Total exports(fob)	903	999
Libya	Petroleum and petroleum products	10,614	13,544
	Total exports(fob)	11,604	14,527
The Islamic Republic of Iran	Fuel	22,945	24,057
	Total exports(fob)	28,324	28,283
fob=(free on board)			

Table 2: Cross Country Analysis of Foreign Trade (US$ millions)

Country	Total	2002	2003
Tanzania	Imports (cif)	1,661	2,107
	Exports (fob)	903	999
Libya	Imports (cif)	6,250	6,663
	Exports (fob)	11,604	14,527
The Islamic Republic of Iran	Imports (cif)	23,786	29,547
	Exports (fob)	28,324	28,283
cif= (costs, insurance and freight) fob= (free on board)			

Summary of Findings

Looking at Tables 1 and 2 along with our case studies, we illustrate a factor that plays a major role in a country's ability to achieve self-reliance, mainly its supply of resources. Tanzania's largest exports are coffee and then cotton, it imports approximately twice what it exports, and its imports consist of capital goods, fuel and energy, and food. Libya's largest exports include crude oil, refined petroleum products and natural gas, and it exports about twice as much as it imports; imports include manufactured goods, food and primary products. Iran as an exporter "is OPEC's second largest oil producer and holds 10% of the world's proven oil reserves. It also has the world's second largest natural gas reserves (after Russia)" (http://www.eia.doe.gov/emeu/cabs/iran.html). And in the ratio of imports to exports, Iran runs about even, with imports in industrial supplies, machinery, and consumer goods.

It is no secret that global interdependence is just as important to the survival of the developed countries now as self-reliant development is for the developing countries. The notion that self-reliance brews anti-capitalistic behavior, brings anarchy, and hinders innovative progresses is completely unfounded. It is an attempt to discourage the progress of self-reliant behavior, because self-reliance obstructs the center's dependency on the periphery and its resources. In fact, true global interdependence is an ally of self-reliance, and there is "no fundamental conflict between self-reliant development and increased international cooperation" (Parmar 1975:5). Global interdependence is supposed to be egalitarian, promoting mutual benefits and gains to all parties involved. "But in practice the history of trade has been one of domination by the strong and deprivation of the weak...an engine of growth for developed nations and an instrument of exploitation for the developing" (Parmar 1975:4). So then self-sustaining growth is perceived as the antithesis or antagonist to this suppressive state, currently the most prominent method for the center to muscle the Third World.

CONCLUSION

> It is my inmost conviction that Islam is *amal, yakeen, muhabat* [work, faith, and love] and without these the name 'Muslim' is sounding brass and tinkling cymbal. The Koran makes it absolutely clear that faith in One God, without a second, and good works are enough to secure a man his salvation (Abdul Ghaffar Khan [Easwaran 1999:63]).

Abdul Ghaffar Khan encapsulates the value of work in the quest to be a good Muslim and fulfill one's duty to the *umma.* The case studies highlighted earlier illuminate both support for and challenge each Islamic country's ability to deal with a self-reliant socio-economic system, and there are several factors that contribute to this disjuncture. First, given the countries' histories, they tend to lean towards their feudal past and have been unable to break those bonds; hence, transporting historical and cultural baggages from generation to generation makes us 'victims of evil customs'–Jinnah (Goodwin1994:55). Second, during the Prophet's time, Islam coexisted with many other religions through peace treaties; and because there was only *one* Islam, it could play a powerful social role as a unifier. But after the Prophet passed away, the divergence of thinking created many sects of Islam, and nationalizing a country under one banner became problematic and began to hinder the freedom of the other factions (Weiss 1998:141). Third, because of the bond between government and religion, extremism has played a big role in wielding people in the name of religious conviction and "...the blurring of religion and governance, the increasingly militant Islamic revivalist movement is dictating how people should think, behave, dress, and live; it is also increasingly influencing how nations are governed...as they call for a return to an earlier, more spiritual (and certainly idealized) form of Islam, their rhetoric has more to do with demagoguery than purity of religion" (Goodwin 1994:8). Fourth, the lack of knowledge about the *Qur'an* has perpetuated the misuse of the text and its message, and has created a haven for manipulation and destruction. "The biggest weakness in the application of the *Qur'anic* doctrine has been in its interpretation. As a consequence, interpretations and regulations are made arbitrarily. This is believed in, practiced, and presented as an 'Islamic way of life' and has thus devastated societies" (Saeed 1994:58). Fifth, the supply of resources a country encompasses tends to directly determine the quantity and quality of attention it receives from external sources, irrelevant of its nature. Sixth, if any government chooses not to conform to the centers' norms and "persist in orientating policy to citizen needs over those of 'the economy'...are likely to be disciplined...quickly bringing these governments to heel" (Green & Voyageur 1999:148). And seventh, because of all of these things, we cannot disregard the fact that religion has been misconstrued to be used and abused over the years to fulfill personal and political agendas–"For political ends, the Prophet's intent regarding women is both misinterpreted and misapplied, and his sympathy for women's rights is frequently no longer reflected in the law and practices of modern government" (Goodwin 1994:9).

Badawi, in *Gender Equity in Islam*, states that "women at the Prophet's (P) time and after him participated with men in acts of worship, such as prayers and pilgrimage, in learning and teaching, in the market place, in the discussion of public issues (political life), and in the battlefield when necessary" (Badawi 1995:32). He stresses that Islam teaches modesty and moderation; the liberal West and the ultra-restrictive regions of the Muslim World are extremes, and "both extremes seem to contradict the normative teachings of Islam and are not consistent with the virtuous yet participative nature of both men and women in society at the time of the Prophet Muhammad (P)" (Badawi 1995:32). He asserts that seclusion is not divinely based but rather socially imposed restrictions, and "nowhere in the *Qur'an* does it say that women have to veil so obsessively"–Nilofar Ahmed (Haeri 2002:357). Most verses emphasize the parameters defined for modesty and behavior of both men *and* women. "These are to ensure morality and modesty in social living" (Patel 1979:x). Badawi adds that "…Islam regulated and restricted polygamy, it is neither required nor encouraged…and demographic data indicate strongly that monogamy is the norm and polygamy the exception" (Badawi 1995:27). And as for temporary marriages, "it was firmly prohibited by the Prophet six times on six occasions" (Nasir 1990:16). The Prophet abolished such sex-discriminating practices as female infanticide, slavery, and introduced concepts guaranteeing women the right to inherit property, and the right to exercise full possession and control over their own wealth (Goodwin 1994:30). It is "ironic that the most outstanding contradiction regarding the inequities suffered by Muslim women is that Muhammad (PBUH), the founder of Islam, was among the world's greatest reformers on behalf of women.…Islam, in fact, may be the only religion that formally specified women's rights and sought ways to protect them" (Goodwin 1994:30).

Each country is unique in its exquisiteness and predicaments, and it is evident that there are many levels of self-reliance and each one equally important to the final outcome, from the structural changes to the economy and to the recalibration of the individual psyche. But perhaps the most essential concept at every level is that each country, like each person, must develop its own path and model to self-reliance, and that "the formulation of concepts and policies of development be based on its own socio-economic realities"(Parmar 1975:8). Enhancing one's own country by captivating certain aspects and ideals from history and other countries may be helpful in the reformation process, but emulating the progressive patterns of the 'center' in totality or seeking to only do the exact opposite of the 'West' may find itself incompatible and/or detrimental to the existing country and its civilization.

Writing on the interplay between Islam and economics in a society, Naqvi remarks that "Man is free; but he should also be committed to the betterment of the society. Thus, driven by a strong ethical impulse, he is supposed to discharge his social and economic responsibilities for his own good and that of the society" (1994:1). In this way, we can see that Islam provides a clear path to fulfillment of the individual's responsibilities to God through accountability to his or her own community and through (among other things) a commitment to economic betterment and inter-dependence.

The central idea that defines Islamic economics, and which sets it apart from positive (neoclassical) economics, is its insistence on the *explicit* inclusion of an ethics *based on religion* in a unified analytical framework. Naqvi outlines four elements of Islamic economics: unity (*tawhid*), equilibrium (*al 'adl wal ihsan*), free will (*ikhtih'ar*), and responsibility (*fardh*). Unity refers to a binding arrangement, both within the individual and as a contract between members of the Muslim community. Equilibrium encompasses both the desirable state of affairs and the process to get there. Naqvi refers to free will in the following manner: "Indeed, quantitatively and qualitatively, the Islamic (relative) freedom may even be greater than the Kantian absolute freedom; greater quantitatively because it depends in an important way on man's freedom from avarice and greed for worldly possessions and from the slavery of the self" (Naqvi 1994:31). Responsibility to one's community takes considerable effort on one's part to ascend to this lofty station–indeed, it takes doing good acts, which mostly take the form of giving to the poor and the needy. The Islamic pillar of *Zakat* is the primary vehicle for fulfilling this responsibility. Naqvi goes on to note that "while this principle implies making a sacrifice, it is *not* the kind of sacrifice that one would consider a hardship" (Naqvi 1994:32).

With a total population of 4,994,000 in Libya, and 66,250,000 in Iran, out of which, 97 percent (4,844,188) and 99 percent (65,587,500) are Muslim, respectively, it is no surprise why they are considered Muslim states, but they are "by no means Islamic states... .A real Islamic state will naturally breed Islamic consciousness" (Hussain 1984:216), which has not been the case here. In reality, most states are Muslim in name; but in practice, they are far from the true Islamic precepts. Islam is based on the *Qur'anic* teachings and is an all encompassing religion for all times. It is a part of the internal and external existence, touching not only the spiritual but also the secular life in which we live. It is believed that "...the downfall of Muslims started when Islam became a habit with them and ceased to be a socioeconomic program of life" (Saeed 1994:49). There are three major problems currently affecting Muslims across the world–the interpretation, application, and observance of the *Qur'anic* teachings.

The interpretation of the *Qur'an* has been one of debate for many centuries and is only further divided by the multifarious subjective mores throughout the world over time. The isolation of words and phrases does not allow one to appreciate the essence of the word, which can only be comprehended from reading and understanding the text in its totality, and "the literal interpretation of the *Qur'an* over the past several centuries, which continues almost unabated in the present Muslim countries, has done the greatest harm to Muslims" (Saeed 1994:57). And if the interpretation breaches the heart of the ideology, then how would the implementation be expected to have a positive effect on humanity? It is essential that the application should not only be in line with the letter of the *Qur'an* but also in its spirit.

The observance of the *Qur'anic* teachings is a crucial element and one that is often overlooked. Islam is about self-actualization; realizing the word and applying it to all parts of one's 'own' existence. The six articles of faith: (1) the Belief in one God; (2) the Belief in His Angels; (3) the Belief in His Books–the original *Zabur* (Psalms), *Torath* (Torah), *Injeel* (Bible), and *Qur'an*; (4) the Belief in His Prophets and Messengers; (5) the Belief in the Day of Judgment; and (6) the Belief in God's Divine Decree–*Taqdir*, and the five pillars of Islam discussed in Chapter 1 were sent as guidance for humankind and sought to create righteousness and a civilized society, in which both men *and* women were accountable for their actions and behaviors. But many people forgot the *Reasons* for the teachings, the *Meanings* behind the words, and the *Purpose* of the message:

> Instead, all emphasis has been placed first on 'minimal Islam'–that is, the profession of faith, prayer, fasting, *Zakat,* and pilgrimage. These various items were arbitrarily linked together and focused on in isolation. Thus, Islam was made the sum of those items. As far as the integral teaching of the *Qur'an* and the historic struggle of the Prophet were concerned, which provided the socio-moral context for these provisions and institutes and cemented them together, it had already been lost sight of (Saeed 1994:58).

So then people became more conscious of what society thought rather than what God sees, the external images were accentuated and the internal reflection forgotten; and hence, acceptance was sought from the created instead of the *Creator.*

Islam insists that its ethical philosophy dominate the economic realm. Islam further stipulates that not just ethics but an ethics based on religion must be accepted as the source of the basic postulates needed to make valid economic generalizations. The practices of Muslim societies do reflect, however imperfectly, the dominance of Islamic ethical beliefs. To be seen on the side of 'right,' Muslims must be committed to a societal framework in which human freedom is guaranteed and selfishness is not accepted as a virtue. Reminding themselves of this basic characteristic of the Islamic society, its members must expand their inner selves to reach out to higher social ideals.

CHAPTER 7

Islam and Globalization

Yoseph Nasser

INTRODUCTION

This chapter investigates the widely debated issue of Islam and globalization. It attempts to refute the widely held conviction that Islam is inherently incapable of adapting to globalization and the secular standards that are applied within it. In an attempt to contest this assertion, this chapter focuses on the Islamic sources that may embrace some of the idealism in globalization, yet reject the unfair practices it can entail. The chapter also takes a close look at thoroughly examined case studies of Islamic societies that have participated within the realms of globalization.

Within a globalized community, popular Western thought condemns Islam as anti-modern, and with it promotes only secularism as a viable tenet of modernity. However, a closer look reveals the possible positive ramifications of Islamic inclusion. According to Sean L. Yom, "Islamic revival is part of a world-wide religious resurgence that corrects the secularist bias of European modernity. Globalization is a driving force within this process" (Yum 2002). In this excerpt taken from the text, globalization will play a pivotal role in shaping a more balanced world order that includes religious doctrine in political systems. Indeed, even in Western cultures, such as America, there seems to be a revival of political Christianity working within the democratic framework. Similarly, Islamic revival is the catalyst for tipping the balance on a global scale, as it attempts to influence political policy.

Before delving into a more nuanced appraisal of the relationship between Islam and globalization, it is imperative to define globalization. A number of definitions can encompass its contemporary application:

(a) Globalization can thus be defined as the intensification of worldwide social relations which link distant localities in such a way that local happenings are shaped by events occurring many miles away and vice versa (Anthony Giddens, Director of the London School of Economics).

(b) Globalization compresses the time and space aspects of social relations (James Mittleman, Professor at the School of International Service at American University).

(c) The concept of globalization reflects the sense of an immense enlargement of world communication, as well as the horizon of a world market, both of which seem far more tangible and immediate than in earlier stages of modernity (Frederic Jameson, Professor of literature at Duke University).

(d) Globalization may be thought of as a process (or set of processes) which embodies a transformation in the spatial organization of social relations and transactions–assessed in terms of their extensity, intensity, velocity and impact–generating transcontinental or interregional flows and networks of activity, interaction and the exercise of power (David Held, Professor of Political Science at the London School of Economics).

(e) Question: What is the truest definition of Globalization? Answer: Princess Diana's death. Question: How come? Answer: An English princess with an Egyptian boyfriend crashes in a French tunnel, driving a German car with a Dutch engine, driven by a Belgian who was drunk on Scottish whiskey, followed closely by Italian Paparazzi, on Japanese motorcycles, treated by an American doctor, using Brazilian medicines! And this is sent to you by an American, using Bill Gates' technology which he enjoyed stealing from the Japanese. And you are probably reading this on one of the IBM clones that use Taiwanese-made chips, and Korean-made monitors, assembled by Bangladeshi workers in a Singapore plant, transported by trucks driven by Indians, hijacked by Indonesians, unloaded by Sicilian longshoremen, trucked by Mexican illegal aliens, and finally sold to you. That, my friend, is Globalization! Finally, an explanation in English (http://www.manbottle.com).

(f) Globalization refers to a multidimensional set of social processes that create, multiply, stretch and intensify worldwide social interdependencies and exchanges while at the same time fostering in people a growing awareness of deepening connections between the local and the distant (Manfred Stege).

What is found to be common in most of the preceding definitions is the emphasis of the compression of time and space, implying that increasingly events in one place can affect events occurring somewhere else. As seen from the satirical depiction of globalization which involves a set of events occurring from a global event (the tragedy of Princess Diana's death), globalization often occurs without many people being aware of its intensity. Another common feature that can be delineated from the preceding quotations is the focus that globalization is not a single process, but a set of processes.

Islamic faith addresses concepts of peace, equality and human rights that are imperative to consider within the processes of globalization which focuses on economic and technological factors. With the inclusion of Islamic components in the processes of globalization, worldwide communities could benefit from globalization instead of experiencing the negative or exploitive impact.

Western perception of Islam is seen as such that it counters globalization, in that globalization is essentially about the expansion of common ideals based on economic enhancement. During this process, however, it challenges and threatens many social, spiritual and cultural elements that are currently present in an "un-globalized" society. This is a strong view that is shared by many Western academics, such as the renowned columnist of the *New York Times*, Thomas Friedman, author of the controversial publication, *The Lexus and the Olive Tree.*

The ideals of contemporary globalization are also predominantly those of the West. While much of globalization is focused on the technological advances which occur, there must be other factors to consider when shaping its justification: namely, globalization of the human condition, civil society, of governance; and of expansion of time and its elimination of space; all concerns to the future of Islam (Inayatullah 2002).

Islam proposes an alternative paradigm in regards to the recent trend of globalization and includes nine major focus points: *twaheed* (unity of thought, action and value across humanity, person, nature and God), *khalifah* (God's ownership of the earth), *ibadah* (worship based on the larger needs of the people), *ilm* (knowledge of self and others), *halal* (one's actions are blameworthy), *adl* (there is social justice), and *zulm* (tyranny), *istislah* (there is public interest), and not dihya (waste) (Inayatullah, 2002). These actions can be considered as an alternative global community, but adaptive to many facets within it can promote its own paradigm for globalization–one which is more concerned with the preservation of God's world and the people in it.

The ideals of Islam are already global. They regard equality, justice, human rights and dignity which should be considered throughout globalization (Khan 2002, Cheref 2002).

REVIEW OF RELEVANT LITERATURE

The study of the association between Islam and Globalization is one that produces a dichotomy of two differing and distinguishable psychoanalyses relating to coexistence:

1. The *global disorder* theory: Scholars who argue that there is no coexistence between Islam and Globalization. Such theorists assert their argument by using theoretical and empirical observations on radical Islam's political systems and behaviors. Writers, such as: Fukuyama, Hadar, Kaplan, Lewis and Huntington conform to such a premise.

2. *Islamic revival* and its correlation with Globalization: Scholars who seek to weigh arguments about the religion's significance within the globalization process. They conclude that the capacity of Islam to adapt to exogenous influences and pressures not only can prosper with globalization but also has the capability to contribute to it.

In this section, I examine the arguments of both theories of the dichotomy through a thematic approach by focusing on the major grounds of arguments from each of the authors. I then summarize and attempt to relate each of the mentioned arguments and how it relates to the topic.

What is lucidly apparent during the course of my research is that Islam for the most part differentiates itself from the other major faiths. It is a faith that revolves around the moral principles of the *Umma* (community) to implement the organized set of legal and moral rules for the organization of collective and individual behaviors. It stresses the importance of the role of the community and clearly delineates various individual responsibilities with reference to that of the community. Islam addresses both spiritual and material issues, in the theological and political realms. It is not simply a set of functional values and beliefs, but a pervading element of reality that shapes the obligations of the Muslim in relation to God. The revival of Islamic identity and the emergence of new Muslim political movements, including the radical fundamentalist groups, make up only a minor factor of what is a broader significant trend: the resurrection of religion as a significant force that has been shaping collective behaviors and identities during the current processes of globalization.

Global Disorder

Scholars who prescribe to this school of thought generally depict Islamic civilization as one that is incapable to peacefully coexist with other "civilizations" in the age of globalization, where integration of cultures and behaviors occur. Such scholars essentially point to the increased sense of religious symbolism as a major cause for wars in the post-Cold War era. Acknowledging this, resurgences in religions such as Islam will unquestionably bring about more conflict and a significant impediment to the advent of globalization.

Francis Fukuyama's "The End of history and the Last Man" piece argues that the history of humankind has been modeled through the dialectical clash of political ideas. Because of this, the collapse of the Berlin Wall which signified the end of communism demonstrated a victory of Western ideas and the exhaustion of other ideologies (Fukuyama 1992). Idealistic challengers, such as socialism, had attempted to structure society according to a detailed outline, but they were ultimately defeated by Western liberal democracy. The argument implies that the engines of globalization (technology, communications and capital) are significantly entrenched in the West; and with no competing ideologies evident, then the path of globalization will undoubtedly occur through Western values, beliefs, and norms.

In response to this, other scholars such as Leon Hadar and Benjamin Barber claim that not only had the end of history never occurred, but new ideological forces would develop sources of violent conflict that would disrupt the stream of globalization. Hadar describes Islam as the "Green Peril." Green embeds the symbolic color of religion and illustrates the monolithic perception of Islam as "a cancer spreading around the globe, undermining the legitimacy of Western values," as represented by the "Muslim fundamentalist," a super-empowered individual armed with radical ideas and nuclear weapons, fully intent of launching a *Jihad* (Hadar 1993). Barber highlights this dissension more despairingly, in his piece on a "*Jihad* vs. McWorld" struggle, in which globalization has confronted the "retribalization of large swaths of humankind by war and bloodshed," implying that Islam functions as an obstinate force against a global identity (Schultz 1996).

Nevertheless, the most derisive diatribe to Islam's compatibility with globalization has been launched by scholars such as Bernard Lewis, Robert Kaplan, and Samuel Huntington. Bernard Lewis is a Middle Eastern historian who argues that Islam had historically experienced periods of inspired hatred and violence and that "it is our misfortune that part, though by no means all or even most, of the Muslim world is now going through such a period, and that much, though again not all, of that hatred is directed against us" (Lewis 1990:45). The modern day "political language" of Islam, from its political body to its authoritative governance over communities of faith, revolves around the great disappointment with the "Talismans" of constitutional governance and post-colonial independence (Lewis 1988). An immense wave of anger rampaged through much of the Muslim world due to its "traumatic domination by the West," and many Muslims were thus vehemently opposed to Western culture and its ideology: capitalism, democracy and even liberalism. Lewis notes that:

> It should by now be clear that we are facing a mood and a movement far transcending the level of issues and policies.... This is no less than a clash of civilizations: the perhaps irrational but surely historic reaction of an ancient rival against our Judeo-Christian heritage, our secular past, and the worldwide expansion of both (1988:67).

Throughout his work, Lewis frequently asserts that secularism and its "worldwide expansion" are flashpoints on which the Muslim world would wage a resistance. (Lewis 2001).

Huntington asserts through the "the clash of civilizations" thesis that if large parts of communities reject the "superiority" of Western ideas, it is because of deeply ingrained incompatibilities in the collective composition and value systems of their own civilizations. Some ideas have remained so incompatible that any form of rapprochement would lead to further conflict. For example, the Islamic notion of a global *Umma* that connects and bonds Muslims across borders by faith alone threatened the normative basis of the Western concept of "state sovereignty." This implies that Islamic governance and civilization will clash with the West, given the strength of current Islamic revivalism, which he defines as a "broad, intellectual, cultural, social and political movement" that aims to revive "Islamic ideas, practices and rhetoric and the recommitment to Islam by many in the Muslim world" (Huntington 1997:63). This essentially, endangers the forces of globalization, which he calls the result of "broad processes of modernization that have been going on since the eighteenth century" (Huntington 1997:63). Furthermore, Huntington asserts that the "Muslim propensity toward violent conflict," evident by various contemporary conflicts involving Muslim societies, indicates the growing violence that would portray Islam's relations with other religions and civilizations (Huntington 1997).

Kaplan, in his piece, examines the distinction of value origination that is apparent between Western culture and other cultures, such as Islam (Kaplan 1994). He contends that Western values originate from secular humanism, whilst Islamic cultures derived much of their values from religion. These differences lead to conflict, resistant to logical restraint, and exemplified in the interstate conflicts that have been waged in much of Africa, Southern Asia, and the Balkans. Moreover, Kaplan argues that historical rifts between cultures and religions influence present day events; the ancient enmity between Islam and Christianity, for example, guided the horrific ethnic pogroms in the former Yugoslavia (Kaplan 1994).

The "House of Islam" will clash with other civilizations in a series of violence that could "ripple across continents and intersect in no discernible pattern" (Kaplan 1994:31), implying that Islam operates as a destabilizing element in the globalized world because globalization exposes and unleashes tensions that were previously hidden. While Huntington and Lewis claim that the West would endure the impact of Islamic reactions, Kaplan also incorporates the entire non-Muslim world, essentially expanding the scale and scope of the conflicts that may be launched with the continued globalization processes.

Islamic Revivalism

Unfortunately, the aforementioned arguments are based on gross oversimplifications of radical Islam and the deep rooted revivalism it entails. There is an apparent unilateral attempt to depict the actions of the radicalists as a collective cultural and societal transformation based on the actions of a few. There only exist a few sources that attempt to tackle the deep rooted cause of the transformation and its religious revivalism.

Jillian Schwedler describes Radical Islam as "a political agenda where the application of *Shari'a* is central" (Schwedler 2001) and is marked as a mobilized political movement transcending borders that is willing to use violence and aggression to execute its objective. Ghadbian suggests that the various leaders that enact these objectives aspire to "shift the frame of reference in the public realm to one in which Islam, in its various interpretations, is a major shaping force" (Ghadbian 1997). This means that they wish to follow the paradigm used for the Iranian revolution and incorporate a theocratic political system based on the *Shari'a*, with political structures that would revolutionize their civilization into the idyllic versions of a Muslim polity in the route exemplified by Prophet Muhammad's (PBUH) *Umma* in the early 7th Century AD. Its vivacity and rapid growth from the "subaltern" has led scholars like Sisk to believe that the last 30 years have been the most exciting period in Islamic religious history since the 12th Century (Sisk 1996).

It is evident that the majority of Muslim governments have had the obligation of tackling the Islamist trend over the past several decades. However, despite the arguments and assertions of some scholars who believe that Islamism is unable to last as a viable ideology due to its lack of comprehensive political action beyond mere violence, the movement has not only endured but has grown and entrenched itself.

It is imperative to avoid the seductive appeal of assuming that the growth of radical Islam implies that the entire religion has somehow undergone a violent transformation, based on some hidden "truth" in the *Qur'an*, which legitimizes radical Islamic ideology. Nair asserts that "In accepting that a singular definition of Islam is impossible, its variety of thought and practice must also be accepted. . . . However, the contexts in which Muslims find themselves are as likely to influence their behavior as the sense of the universality of their faith. The senses of community which derive from faith and practice are necessarily interpreted and shaped in distinct ways in different places, times and societies" (1997:142). Acknowledging this, it is evident that Islamism is a heavily contextual phenomenon whose main objective is to articulate and address the various grievances held by various Muslim societies across the Islamic world. The underlying causes to this are incorporated within social and political contexts of different Muslim actors, not in any textual reference within Islam.

This is exemplified in the authoritarian regime of Saudi Arabia. Radical Islam's rise can be explained by the frustration of middle-class activists who constantly felt repressed by the government and, therefore, engaged in more militant actions, with the objective to topple its political system (Wright 1996). Thus, Islamism did not burgeon as a new, distinct division of Islam, but rather as a reactionary train of thought by the middle-class who sought to clarify and elucidate the injustices through powerful means of action.

Moreover, in the present day, almost every Muslim government rejects radical Islam. This validates the dissimilarity between mainstream Islam and its radical component. Most Muslim states are largely secular, as Nasr argues: "the secular state in the Muslim world, through oppression and accommodation, has by and large stayed its ground and in large measure contained Islamic revivalism" (1999:60). As demonstrated with the Iranian revolution, Nasr asserts that the capture of power by openly radical Islamic groups does not "reshape the existing state system in any significant way." Radical Islam is easily manipulated by governments in their interactions with their domestic resisters and foreign opposers.

Another utilized method of confrontation with Radical Islam by Muslim governments is to use brutal force as a course of action. As seen with the case of Algeria, efforts to execute this action lead to cases of internal terrorism and violence, but not an attempt to invoke a mass revolution (Kashan 1997). In other cases, such as Jordan, compromises are manifested between groups that instill an Islamist element and the state. These include inclusion in government and restraint. In yet other cases, demonstrated by Turkey, Islamism does not even manage to attain any credibility of governance, beyond a few civil movements.

Therefore, it is evident that Islamism and its radical components do not enjoy uniform support from Muslims in most Islamic countries. Conversely, there are extensive efforts by Muslim governments to suppress these groups. This action proves to be the main engine for radical Islam's grievance and rage, not globalization. Despite the views of Huntington and Lewis amongst other global disorder theorists, only a diminutive element contests globalization. The radical Muslims, who their governments disparage, do not share common values with the vast majority of Muslims. However, another dynamic aspect of Radical Islam's curious pre-emergence is the broader rise of religion around the globe. Islamism can be contextualized as a component of two larger phenomena–the Islamic revival which has swept the Muslim world and the global religious reawakening that counts Islam as only one interlocutor among many. The next two sections discuss these trends and their relevance to Islam's relations with globalization.

ANALYSIS OF FINDINGS

In order to construct an in-depth analysis of Islam's compatibility with globalization, the three Islamic societies I have chosen are based on the globalization index developed by A.T. Kearney of *Foreign Policy* magazine. The Globalization Index for 2004 includes rankings of 62 countries for 14 variables grouped into four categories: (1) economic integration (trade, portfolio, FDI, Investment Income), (2) personal contact (telephone, travel, remittances and personal transfers), (3) technological connectivity (internet users, internet hosts and secure internet servers), and (4) political engagement (international organizations, UN peacekeeping, treaties signed and government transfers). I will look at the ranking for each country and other macro data that can establish an empirical snapshot of the country's adaptability and inclusion into globalization.

The three Islamic countries chosen are: (1) Saudi Arabia, an overall ranking of 41 out of 62; (2) Tunisia, overall ranking of 35 of 62; and (3) Singapore, an overall ranking of 2 out of 62 (see Tables 1, 3 and 5).

Saudi Arabia

In 2002, Saudi Arabia celebrated its 70th year of existence and the 20th year anniversary of King Fahd ibn Abd al Aziz Al Saud's appointment to the throne. Rather than adopting the title of King, Fahd was titled Khadim al Haramayn, which in Arabic means "custodian of the two holy mosques" (Library of Congress). This action was done to stress the Islamic aspect of his governance. It also resembled the partnership between the religious and political elements of Saudi Arabia's society developed in 1744 by Muhammad ibn Saud, the amir Abd Diriyah near Riyadh, and Muhammad ibn Abd al Wahhab, the sheikh who promoted the doctrine of the oneness of God in true Islam. Consequent to this partnership, political rule was under the authority of the House of Saud (Al Saud), whose leader was also given the title of Imam, and religious authority was under the hands of the Al ash Sheikh (the family of the Sheikh, Muhammad ibn al Wahhab). This arrangement, however, did not give unrestricted political power to the ruler; because in accordance with the precepts of Abd al Wahhab, secular authority must conform to divine law and produce civil order in order to be legitimate (Library of Congress).

The significance of the Al Saud is reflected in the name of the country: Saudi Arabia, the only one in the world to be named for the ruling family. The present kingdom of Saudi Arabia develops its naissance from the campaigns of its founder, Abd Al Aziz ibn Abd al Rahman Al Saud, who initially captured the capital city Riyadh with his Bedouin followers in 1902. Subsequently, with the organizational help of the Ikhwan (brotherhood), a fervent group of Bedouin Wahabbi warriors, Abd al Aziz recaptured the rest of the central region (Najd), defeating the Al Rashid forces in 1921, and in 1924 he conquered the Hijaz, including the holy cities of Mecca and Medina. Abd Al Aziz was later chosen king of these territories in 1927 and, with the request of Britain, was obliged to continue and defeat the Ikhwan military in 1929, because they had begun to encroach on the borders of neighboring states. In 1932, Abd Al Aziz proclaimed the Kingdom of Saudi Arabia. The discovery of oil by Americans in 1938 ultimately transformed the lives of the people living in Saudi Arabia. During his sovereignty, however, Abd al Aziz sought to obtain "the iron of the West without its ideas" (Library of Congress), as the King phrased it. He sought to make use of Western technology; but at the same time, he sought to sustain the traditional ideals associated with Islamic and Arab life.

Saudi Arabia had gone through a transition of leadership leading up to the early 1980s. Subsequent to Abd al Aziz's death in 1953, his son, Saud ibn Abd al Aziz, succeeded to the throne. His rule lasted only 11 years, greatly due to his lavish lifestyle which led to the depletion of the kingdom's treasury. In 1964, the Royal family, with the support of the

Ulama, or religious community leaders, overthrew Saud and appointed Faisal as King and Khalid ibn Abd al Aziz Al Saud, another brother, as the Crown Prince.

Faisal was a devout Muslim and sought to modernize the kingdom, particularly in terms of economic development, education and defense, whilst moreover playing a significant role in foreign policy (Library of Congress). During the Yom Kippur War between Israel and the Arab states of Syria, Jordan and Egypt, Faisal assisted in initiating an oil embargo against those countries that supported Israel, which included the United States. He also supported the education of girls and the opening of the government television stations to promote education. Despite these accomplishments, Faisal was assassinated in 1975 by a deranged nephew. Subsequently, Crown Prince Khalid ibn Abd al Aziz became King and appointed his brother, Fahd, as Deputy Prime Minister. Khalid's legacy was eventful, as it involved an attempt by Islamic fundamentalists to capture the grand Mosque in Mecca in 1979, alleging that the Royal family had been corrupted by Western influence. Khalid, however, died in 1982, and Fahd assumed the throne, with Abd Allah, his brother, becoming Crown Prince.

There has been an increased role of a centralized state in Saudi Arabia, which apparently has weakened Saudi tribal allegiance and its Bedouin heritage. This is due to the growth of urbanization and the industrialization that had accompanied the finding of oil. Simultaneously, the impact of Islam on different elements of its society has varied.

Many of the educated and technology-oriented younger people feel the need to adapt Islamic principles to fit the demands of modern technology. Others, who are more conservative, as well as the elderly and those with a more traditional Bedouin lifestyle, have condemned the isolation from Islamic values and the corruption they perceive that is entrenched in Western ways and their presence. This sensation has induced Islamic revivalism by many Saudis and action by the government to implement aspects of Islamic law. These include the mandatory wearing of the *Hijab* (a long black cloak and veil) by women and the more active role of the *Mutawwiin* (Committees for the Spread of Virtue and Prevention of Vice) in enforcing standards of public morality.

The Saudi notion of legality and legitimacy is highly related to the Bedouin concept of a tribal democracy, in which the individual exchanges views and seeks advice from the tribal Sheikh (Library of Congress). Saudi rulers and many of its traditionalists generally reject the Western notion of a participatory democracy, because they believe that it establishes the people as the source of judgment rather than the will of God, as found in the *Shari'a* and as interpreted by the Ulama (Library of Congress). Furthermore, they perceive Western democracy to be lacking the stability that a Muslim form of government can provide. Therefore, the government has tended to repress many students and religious figures that belong to such organizations as the Organization of Islamic Revolution who have been active in criticizing Saudi Arabia's ruling family and government.

Table 1: Segment Rankings of Saudi Arabia

Overall Ranking: 41 **Change from 2003: No Change**			
Economic Ranking 49	Personal Ranking 24	Technological Ranking 43	Political Ranking 59
Trade 34	Telephone 26	Internet Users 40	International Organizations 55
Portfolio 28	Travel 26	Internet Hosts 47	U.N. Peacekeeping 42
FDI 57	Remittances and Personal Transfers 9	Secure Internet Servers 48	Treaties 44
Investment Income 42			Government Transfers 53

Economic Overview

Saudi Arabia is an oil-based economy with strong government controls over major economic activities. It has one of the largest reserves of petroleum in the world (26 percent) and ranks as the largest exporter of petroleum. It plays a leading role in the Organization of Petroleum Exporting Countries (OPEC). The petroleum sector accounts for roughly 75 percent of its budget revenues, 45 percent of its Gross Domestic Product (GDP), and 90 percent of its export earnings (see Table 2). Foreign workers, who roughly amount to four million people, play an important role in the Saudi economy, particularly in the oil and service sectors.

The Saudi government announced plans to begin privatizing its national electricity companies in 1999, which followed the announcement to privatize its telecommunications entity. The government is promoting private sector growth in order to lessen its dependence on oil and to increase employment opportunities to the vast middle class (www.nationmaster.com). Government priorities for spending in the short-term include additional funds for the water and sewage systems and for education. Water shortages and rapid population growth have constrained the government's efforts to increase self-sufficiency in agricultural products (www.nationmaster.com).

Table 2: Saudi Arabia Macro Data ($)

Economy		**World ranking**
GDP	268.9 billion	29 of 229
per capita	11,068.64	63 of 236
Export items	*Petroleum and oil, 90%*	
Export partners	*US 18.6%, Japan 15.6%, South Korea 10.1%*	
Exports	71 billion	22 of 225
per capita	9697.93	45 of 157
Import items	*machinery and equipment, foodstuffs, chemicals, motor vehicles, textiles*	
Import partners	*US 11.2%, Japan 8.8%, Germany 7.6%*	
Imports	39.5 billion	31 of 225
per capita	1625.92	85 of 225
Personal		**World ranking**
Telephones–Main lines in use	3.9 million	37 of 231
per capita	160.53 per 1000 people	105 of 230
Telephones–mobile cellular	2.9 million	31 of 209
per capita	119.37 per 1000 people	57 of 209
Annual tourist arrivals	3.6 million	29 of 153
per capita	147.93 per 1000 people	64 of 152
Technological		**World ranking**
Internet users	1.5 million	40 of 202

per capita	59.80 per 1000 people	73 of 202
Internet hosts	0.2	89 of 122
Internet service providers	22	44 of 229
per capita	0.23 per 10000 people	73 of 202

Opportunities

The major opportunity for Saudi Arabia to further its participation in a globalized economy is the significance of its political stance and policies on major regional issues such as the Israeli-Palestinian conflict and the War on Iraq. If Saudi Arabia plays the key role of mediator between Israel and Palestine, it can definitely gain certain advantages from the international community. The credibility of the Royal family, seen by many as a repressive and irresponsible regime, would increase, and a potential peace treaty would induce a certain measure of stability into the region, in which an attractive market for foreign direct investment may be developed.

With the War on Iraq, Saudi Arabia faces a more compromising role, as Iraq's occupier (i.e. the United States) is perceived to be one of its closest allies. However, it can still play a key role with the transition of Iraq's new government. If Saudi Arabia supports such a government and does not alienate its participation from regional aspects, peaceful prospects are apparent, and Saudi Arabia can furthermore increase its regional influence as a prominent Arab beacon of leadership.

Other opportunities include the further advent of the technology sector of Saudi Arabia, and specifically the Internet and cellular phone industries, ranking on a per-capita basis in the top 50 and 60 of the world, respectively. These industries can be further developed through foreign involvement. Furthermore, it adds an additional element to Saudi Arabia's economy and may allow for the creation of more jobs within Saudi Arabia's increasingly marginalized middle class.

Threats

Threats to Saudi Arabia embracing globalization include domestic elements and the significant reliance on oil as its economic livelihood. The domestic elements include the increased frustration of its middleclass, as unemployment amongst that age group is constantly rising. Moreover, the net influx of Asian immigrants, who are generally employed for low-wage service-oriented jobs, is continually depriving regular Saudis from such jobs and further increases its unemployment rate. This deprivation encourages regular, middle-classed Saudis to adhere to alternate means of self-enrichments which include radical Islam.

This phenomenon can induce unstable forces within Saudi Arabia's business environment and act as a counter-measure for attracting global capital from foreign direct investment.

Economically, Saudi Arabia faces a significant threat due to its heavy reliance on oil for its exports. As illustrated earlier, more than 90% of Saudi Arabia's exports are oil and oil-related products. By being heavily reliant on one industry for exports, an increased level of risk perception will be generated within Saudi Arabia's business environment.

Another significant risk includes the growing instability of the region associated with the Israeli-Palestinian conflict, the War on Iraq and the growing emergence of Islamic radicalism. Market health perceptions are invariably influenced by these factors and are undoubtedly affected by them.

TUNISIA

Tunisia is situated in the Mediterranean in the centre of the North African seaboard. It incorporates the northernmost part of the African continent and is only 50 miles from Sicily.

Tunisian history is dominated by the figure of Habib Bourguiba, who headed the Neo-Destour Party, formed in 1934, and was at the forefront of opposition to the French colonial rule, taking place from 1881to 1956. After some years of repression, the French finally signed a treaty in March of 1956 recognizing Tunisia as a sovereign independent monarchy. Bourgiba became its first prime minister; and after the monarchy was overthrown in 1957 and republic declared, he then became its firs President (CIA World Fact Book).

The Bourgiba government implemented extensive policies to modernize and secularize the country. These policies succeeded in helping to raise Tunisia's living standards through social, educational, and legal reforms. Bourgiba was markedly a strong supporter of women's rights, as he sought to end the practices of polygamy and divorce by renunciation. He also restricted the wearing of the *Hijab*, a controversial action, which prompted a great deal of anger from many religious groups. Bourgiba was generally opposed to the role of religion in politics; and during the 1970s, political opposition was largely repressed, which at that time turned from being liberal to Islamist. In 1974, Bourgiba declared a one-party state and made himself president for life. This hardened political stance changed at the end of the decade as economic problems beset the country.

A multi-party political system was reintroduced in the 1980s; however, popular discontent was apparent due to the obscure electoral process, which consistently returned the governing party to power with overwhelming majorities. As the decade progressed, Bourgiba was perceived to be erratic in his decision making, as it was evident that he was suffering from senility. He was eventually deposed in 1987, after being declared unfit to govern, and spent much of his retirement years in the Monastir Palace, where he died in April of 2000 (Reuters AlterNet).

Bourgiba was succeeded by his appointed prime minister and former army general, Zine El Abidine Ben Ali, who set out to liberalize Tunisia's political structure by abolishing the life-long presidency, declaring a wide range of political pardons and allowing greater media freedom. Despite this, the main Islamic opposition group, which is now called the *Hizb al-Nahda* (Renaissance Party), has yet to be legalized. Political fault lines were exposed during the first Gulf War in 1991, when official support for the United States-led alliance was contrasted by popular opposition on the streets. The 1990s were characterized by slow political liberalization. The government was keen to allow more political diversity but was reticent of influence from nearby Tunisia.

Although many abroad have criticized the Ben Ali government, the comparative stability of political life and more recently the perception in the West of the "dangers of Islamic fundamentalism" have established some level of credibility to the government's strategy. Ben Ali won presidential elections in 1994 and in 1999, confirming his own position and that of the ruling Rassemblement Consititutionnel Democratique (RCD). In a referendum in 2002, changes were made to Tunisia's constitution, which enabled Ben Ali's right to run for the presidency and improving political transparency by reforming the electoral process.

The government has looked increasingly to the West for its economic reforms and financial support. Despite many of his repressive tactics employed against fundamentalists, Ben Ali is in general popular amongst Tunisians, a reflection both of the relatively high domestic standard of living and of social stability that has been maintained in a period of high regional volatility. Tunisia is regarded as the regional beacon of prestige within this regard and is continually working to improve relations with the other countries of the Maghreb region, with an emphasis to strengthen economic and political integration (WHO Tunisia).

Table 3: Segment Rankings of Tunisia

Overall Ranking: 35
Change from 2003: Up 4

Economic Ranking	Personal Ranking	Technological Ranking	Political Ranking
25	31	46	42
Trade 17	Telephone 32	Internet Users 42	International Organizations 37
Portfolio 57	Travel 28	Internet Hosts 60	U.N. Peacekeeping 32

FDI 24	Remittances and Personal Transfers 15	Secure Internet Servers 44	Treaties 30
Investment Income 34			Government Transfers 46

Economic Overview

Tunisia encompasses a diverse economy, with vital and vibrant agricultural, mining, energy, tourism and manufacturing sectors. Government control over the economy has gradually abridged over the past decade, with increasing privatization, simplification of the tax structure, and a prudent approach to debt. Real growth has averaged 5.4 percent through decreasing investment and a reduction in tourism. Increased rainfall in 2003 portends higher growth levels, but the continued regional tension from the war in Iraq and a terrorist attack in an ancient Synagogue have somewhat decreased tourist earnings (see Table 4).

Tunisia has gradually agreed to remove trade barriers against The European Union (EU) over the next decade. Broader privatization, further liberalization of the investment code to increase foreign investment, improvements in government spending efficiency, and the reduction of the trade deficit are among the challenges for the future (www.nationmaster.com).

Table 4: Tunisia Macro Data ($)

Economy		World ranking
GDP	67.13 billion	62 of 229
per capita	6,763.90	97 of 236
Export items	*textiles, mechanical goods, phosphates and chemicals*	
Export partners	France 31.3%, Italy 21.6%, Germany 11.5%, Spain 4.8%, Libya 4.7%, Belgium 4.3%	
Exports	6.8 billion	69 of 225
per capita	685.15	96 of 225
Import items	textiles, machinery and equipment, hydrocarbons, chemicals, food	

Import partners	France 25.6%, Italy 19.5%, Germany 8.9%, Spain 5%	
Imports	8.7 billion	64 of 225
per capita	876.59	107 of 225
Personal		**World ranking**
Telephones - Main lines in use	654,000	76 of 231
per capita	65.89 per 1000 people	149 of 230
Telephones - mobile cellular	50,000	106 of 209
per capita	5.03 per 1000 people	146 of 209
Annual tourist arrivals	4,263,000	25 of 153
per capita	429.53 per 1000 people	39 of 152
Technological		**World ranking**
Internet users	400,000	61 of 202
per capita	40.30 per 1000 people	85 of 202
Internet hosts	n/a	n/a
Internet service providers	1	191 of 229
per capita	0	205 of 226

Opportunities

The opportunity for Tunisia's economic advancement in the globalized world is undoubtedly based on the strategic alliance it has established with the EU. Five of its top six trading partners include EU members, and further pacts have been signed to allow more flows of free trade between them. This was vastly facilitated by France, as it already had preceding relations with the North African state. The manufacturing sector is set to benefit extensively and may allow a further transition from a labor-intensive to a capital-intensive economy.

Tunisia can also act as a gateway and mediator between its North African neighbors and the EU, which have long had strained relations with countries such as Libya and Algeria.

Threats

The threats that are evident to such advancement include the radical elements within Tunisian society. The government has consistently and aggressively repressed opposition Islamists, and it has yet to legitimize the opposition group. Such action may establish a level of political uncertainty.

SINGAPORE

The modern nation of the Republic of Singapore is said to be founded by Sir Thomas Stamford Raffles as a British trading post on the Strait of Malacca in 1819. Its location on the major sea route between India and China, the exceptional condition of its harbor, and its free trade status has established the port as an admirable success. By 1900, the multiethnic population attracted to the island had grown from a few thousand to 2.6 million. Singapore's first prime minister, Lee Kwan, safeguarded the founder's vision through the first quarter century as an independent nation, providing the leadership that turned it into a global city that offered trading and financial services to the region and the world (CIA World Fact Book).

Modern Singapore has established itself as a city encompassing towering skyscrapers and modern expressways which have replaced much of the tropical forests and mangrove swamps that originally existed. Many hills have been leveled and the island itself lengthened in size through extensive land reclamation projects to allow room for further development. Despite the paucity of land for development, the government has worked to maintain and expand the island's parks, gardens, and other green spaces. The government houses 88 percent of its population in mostly multistoried public housing. Raffles' town plan back in the early 1800s consisted of separate areas that were designated for the various ethnic groups that lived in Singapore during that time, which mainly consisted of Malays, Chinese, Arabs, and Europeans. Government resettlement plans began in the 1960s, essentially breaking up the former ethnic enclaves by requiring that public housing projects reflect the ethnic composition of the country as a whole. As a result, modern Singapore's three main ethnic groups (Chinese, Malays, and Indians) live next door to one another and share the same housing development facilities, shops, and transportation.

Singaporean identity, as envisaged by its leadership, calls for durable individualism with an emphasis on excellence. Thus, education, home ownership, and upward mobility are all collectively considered as suitable values and objectives. Many Singaporeans collectively see themselves as a modernized society; however, they are also encouraged to retain a foundation of traditional Asian values and culture.

The government, although secular, perceives religion as a positive element for inducing moral values in its society. Simultaneously, it is watchful of social and political activism within religious groups. Overzealous Christian proselytizers and Islamic fundamentalists are kept under cautious scrutiny, lest they disturb the religious and ethnic harmony of the country.

In terms of trade, the principles that were established by Singapore's founder, Raffles, are still recognizable in its modern economy. Only a few revenue tariffs are still imposed on such products as tobacco and liquor. Trade has sustained the island's livelihood, as in 1998 the value of Singapore's international trade was triple the total of its Gross Domestic Product (GDP). Although a few aspects of trade have changed, most have remained the same. Singapore's initial success derived from its role as a conveniently located and duty-free haven for the three-way trade of China, India, and various parts of the Indo-Malay archipelago. In early colonial times, silks from China, manufactures from Europe, incense from India, and spices from the Moluccas were all items that were significantly traded in Singapore. Consequently, deriving from its vibrant trading, a host of banking and financial service businesses emerged (Library of Congress).

Singapore officially became independent from Malaysia in 1965; and during that time, its economic prospects looked relatively unfavorable. Singapore had faced significant problems such as high unemployment, slow economic growth, a decaying infrastructure, and labor and social unrest in the era of post-World War II. Severance from Malaysia meant the loss of its economic hinterland, and Indonesia's aggressive military policy directed at Singapore and Malaysia had severed its highly reliant trade prospects from that direction. Subsequently, Britain announced the closure of its bases in 1968, which led to a loss of 20% of jobs within Singapore's workforce. These troubles led Singapore's leadership to take the difficult task of guiding the nation's economy. The government aggressively promoted export-oriented, labor-intensive industrialization through a program of incentives designed to draw foreign investment. By 1972, one quarter of Singapore's manufacturing firms were either foreign-owned or joint-venture companies, with the United States and Japan both emerging as significant actors. These developments again established Singapore as a country instilling a positive market-oriented environment and allowed the country to enjoy double-digit GDP growth during the period of 1965 through 1973. By the late 1970s, government officials strived to adopt a policy that would replace labor-intensive manufacturing with skill and technology-intensive, high value-added industries. The Information Technology (IT) sector was highly targeted for expansion; and by 1989, Singapore has emerged as the world's largest producer of disk drives and disk drive parts. In that year, earnings from manufacturing accounted for approximately 30% of the country's GDP.

Singapore's other fastest growing economic sectors are international banking and financial services, which accounted for nearly 25 percent of the country's GDP in the late 1980s. It is widely ranked as one of the top Asian financial centers, along with Hong Kong and Tokyo. The government provided incentives for the continuing diversification and automation of financial services, and Singapore's historical record of political stability and superior infrastructure were important attractions for international bankers and investors (Library of Congress)

By the last decade of the 20th Century, the former colonial port had become a global financial, trading and industrial center, much like it had been reputed and developed in the last part of the 19th Century. Singapore's leadership and people have always been capable adapting to the changing demands of the world economy, upon which an immense amount of their livelihood is dependent.

Table 5: Segment Rankings of Singapore

Overall Ranking: 2
Change from 2003: Up 2

Economic Ranking	Personal Ranking	Technological Ranking	Political Ranking
2	3	10	40
Trade 1	Telephone 1	Internet Users 3	International Organizations 59
Portfolio 6	Travel 6	Internet Hosts 10	U.N. Peacekeeping 21
FDI 7	Remittances and Personal Transfers 48	Secure Internet Servers 9	Treaties 44
Investment Income 2			Government Transfers 38

Economic Overview

Singapore is a highly developed and successful free-market economy that enjoys a remarkably open and corruption-free environment, stable prices, and one of the highest per capita GDPs in the world. The economy depends heavily on exports, particularly in electronics and manufacturing. The 2001–2002 global recession and slump in the technology sector adversely affected Singapore's economy. The government hopes to establish a new growth pathway that will be less vulnerable in its exposure to the external business cycle, rather than the current export-oriented model, but it is unlikely to abandon its efforts to establish itself as Southeast Asia's financial and high-tech center (www.nationmaster.com).

Opportunities

Singapore's opportunities include the further advancement of its high-technology industry and its financial services industries (see Table 6). Its economic model is extensively touted by many scholars as a developmental success. A significant opportunity exists with the advent of the expanding wireless sector. Furthermore, the financial industry can certainly gain from China's increasing role as a significant actor in the international trading system. Expansion of economic and political relations with the country should be highly considered. Another emerging opportunity for Singapore to further enhance its already extensive global image is to publicly demonstrate the ethnic harmony prevalent within its social structure.

Threats

It is evident that Singapore suffered a great deal from the global recession that vastly damaged the global high-technology industry. It demonstrated Singapore's significant reliance on international trade flows relating to this industry. With China emerging as the new Asian tiger, there could be foreign direct investment (FDI) diversion into China rather than into Singapore. This does not pose an immediate threat, as China's economy is still labor-intensive. However, if China successfully shifts its economy from one that is labor-intensive to one that is capital-intensive, it could threaten Singapore's economy.

Table 6 Singapore Macro Data ($)

Economy		World ranking
GDP	112.40 billion	56 of 229
per capita	24,389.21	29 of 236
Export items	*Machinery and equipment, consumer goods, chemicals, mineral fuels*	
Export partners	Malaysia 17.4%, US 15.3%, Hong Kong 9.2%, Japan 7.1%, China 5.5%	

Exports	127 billion	15 of 225
per capita	25,557.20	2 of 225
Import items	*Machinery and equipment, mineral fuels, chemicals, foodstuffs*	
Import partners	Malaysia 18.2%, US 14.3%, Japan 12.5%, China 7.6%, Thailand 4.6%, Taiwan 4.6%	
Imports	113 billion	16 of 225
per capita	24519.3	5 of 225
Personal		World ranking
Telephones–Main lines in use	1.95 million	54 of 231
per capita	423.12 per 1000 people	49 of 230
Telephones–mobile cellular	2.74 million	32 of 209
per capita	594.54 per 1000 people	8 of 209
Annual tourist arrivals	6,531,000	18 of 153
per capita	1417.13 per 1000 people	15 of 152
Technological		World ranking
Internet users	2.31 million	37 of 202
per capita	501.23 per 1000 people	16 of 202
Internet hosts	45.2	12 of 122
Internet service providers	9	93 of 229
per capita	0.00 per 1000 people	114 of 226

CONCLUSION

The functionality of Islam as a "means of disciplining ambiguity, creating boundaries and constituting, producing and maintaining political identities" (Sadowski 1998) must be acknowledged by the "global disorder" theorists, who have attempted to demonstrate that globalization excludes Islam. Their thesis is inherently inaccurate, demonstrated by their use of deficient and simplified methods of Islamic text extraction. Moreover, the failure of not recognizing the contextual element that Islam embodies within value and political systems is largely ignored and, therefore, proves to be invalidated.

The emergence of radical Islam can evidently be seen as part of a global resurgence towards religious revivalism, not as a singular force that is seen to hinder the immense effort to implement global secularism embodied significantly in contemporary globalization. The theoretical incompatibilities that may emerge between the processes of globalization and Islamic ideals may be due to the failures of globalization enforcers of the West, who vehemently contest the inclusion of any religious element, let alone Islam. It is evident that there are many facets within Islam that embrace the general ideals of globalization based on the provisions of the *Umma*. However, many in the West desire to ignore such intendancies, as they themselves even strive for religious exclusion domestically. Essentially, what needs to occur is equilibrium of ideal enforcement between secularism and religion, so that globalization can effectively be embraced by Islamic communities and its appreciation expressed. Furthermore, many in the West must understand the essential needs of Islamic communities, which extend beyond the aspiration to attain material wealth. As soon as the processes of globalization are modified to include religious sensitivity, Islam will certainly embrace it, thereby becoming a significant model for its implementation.

The argument that surfaces around Islam and its role in the globalized world is one that confronts issues of secular modernity and how it interacts with religion. It is clear that there exist facets of anti-modernity in radical Islam; however, it must be acknowledged that most Islamic revivalists disagree with them. Islam cannot merely be characterized as a "self-contained collective agent" (Sadowski 1998) and one that seems to have a "life of its own." Islam does not function as an anomaly that threatens the world and must not be treated as such. Globalization is very much part of Islam's heritage and future and, therefore, a crucial component in infinite opportunities that await the globalizing world.

BIBLIOGRAPHY

Note: some of the URL's listed below may no longer be available

Abd-El-Khader, Cheref. November 30, 2002. Globalization, Islam and Democracy. Available: http://septemberhearts.com/2002B/globalizationislam.htm.

Abdul-Rauf, Muhammad. 1979. *The Islamic Doctrine of Economics and Contemporary Economic Thought*. Washington, DC: American Enterprise Institute for Public Policy Research.

Abdul-Rauf. 1984. *A Muslim's Reflections on Democratic Capitalism*. Washington, D.C: American Enterprise Institute for Public Policy Research.

Abousenna, M. 1996. "Ibn Rushd, Founder of Hermeneutics." In M. Wahba and M. Abousenna, eds. *Averroes and the Enlightenment*. Amherst, NY: Prometheus Books.

Aburish, Said. 1998. *Arafat*. New York: Bloomsbury.

Ackerman, P. and J. Duvall. 2000. India: Movement for Self-Rule. *A Force More Powerful: A Century of Nonviolent Conflict*. New York: Palgrave.

Adam Smith Institute. 2004. *The Wisdom of Adam Smith*. Available from Adam Smith Institute: Available: http://www.adamsmith.org/smith/quotes.htm

Affandi Bin Nik Yusoff, M. 2002. *Islam and Business*. Selangor, Malaysia: Pelanduk Publications.

Ahmad, Abdel-Rahman Y. 2004. *Riba, Its Economic Rationale and Implications* [Shari'ah Rulings]. Available from Islamic Banking.com: http://www.islamic-banking.com/aom/shariah.ar_yousri.php.

Ahmad, Aziz. April 1976. "The Shrinking Frontiers of Islam." *International Journal of Middle East Studies*. 7, 2:148. Apr. 1976.

Ahmed, Akbar. 1999. *Islam's Crossroads–Islamic Leadership. Islam for Today*. Available: http://www.islamfortoday.com/akbar02.htm.

Ahmed, Akbar. 1999. *Islam Today*. New York, New York: I.B. Tauris.

Ahmed, Akbar. 2003. *Islam Under Siege*. Malden, MA: Blackwell Publishing Ltd.

Ahmed, Monzur. 18 July 1998. Abu al-Hasan al-Mawardi. *Islamic Gateway*. Available: http://www.ummah.org.uk/history/scholars/MAWARDI.html.

Ahmed, Musnad Al Imam Ahmed. Circa 1000 AD.

Al-Fanjari, M. S. 2002. *The Essence of Economic Policy in Islamic Economics* [Online Book]. Available from Witness Pioneer, http://www.witness-pioneer.org/vil/Books/MF_EEP/default.htm.

Al-Ghazali, Imam Abu. 2001. *On Faith in Divine Unity and Trust in Divine Providence: Kitab at-Tawhid Wa Tawakkul.* Louisville, KY: Fons Vitae.

Ali, A. 1993. *The Meaning of the Holy Qur'an*. Baltimore, MD: Amana Corporation.

Allama Iqbal. Available: http://www.allamaiqbal.com.

Allan, J. A. 1981. *Libya: The Experience of Oil.* London, UK: Croom Helm.

Al-Mawardi, Abu al-Hasan. 1996. *Al-Ahkam as-Sultaniyah.* Translated by Dr. Asadullah Yate. London, England: Ta-Ha Publishers Ltd.

AIqbal, Muhammad." *Britannica Student Encyclopedia* from Encyclopedia Britannica Online.

Ambah, Faiza S. 2004. *A Woman Runs for Office in Saudi Arabia* [In the first elections in 40 years, one woman jumps in. But can women even vote?]. Available from *Christian Science Monitor*. Available: http://www.csmonitor.com/2004/0916/p01s04-wome.htm

Appadurai, A. 1996. "Disjuncture and Difference in the Global Cultural Economy." In *Modernity at Large*. Minneapolis, MN: University of Minnesota Press.

Armstrong, Karen. 2000. *A History of God: the 4000 Year Quest of Judaism, Christianity, and Islam*. New York: The Ballantine Publishing Group.

Asante, Molefi Kete. 1993. *Malcolm X as a Cultural Hero and Other Afrocentric Essays.* Trenton, NJ: Africa World Press, Inc.

Aslund, A. March 3, 2000. *The Reforms in Kyrgyzstan Go Well* [Nezavismaya Gazeta]. Available from The Carnegie Endowment for International Peace. Available: http://www.ceip.org/people/Nezavisimayagazetakyrgyz.htm.

Assy, Hassan. 1993. *Divine Governance of the Human Kingdom*. Beirut, Lebanon: Cultural Bridges Press.

Atatur.com. 2004. *Women's Rights*. Available from Mustafa Kemal Atatürk: http://www.ataturk.com/women.htm.

Baali, Faud, & Ali Wardi. 1981. *Ibn Khaldun and Islamic Thought Styles: A Social Perspective*. Boston, MA: G.K Hall and Co.

Babacan, H. E. Ali. October 1, 2004. *Reengineering The Turkish Economy* (Turkish Minister of State for the Economy, Lecture). Washington, DC: Center for Strategic and International Studies.

Badawi, J. 1995. *The Social Aspect. Gender Equity in Islam*. Burr Ridge, IL: American Trust Publications.

Baffes, J. 2002. *Tanzania's Cotton Sector:* Africa Region Working Paper Series No. 42.

Baker, R. W. 1978. *Egypt's Uncertain Revolution Under Nasser and Sadat.* Cambridge, MA: Harvard University Press.

Baker, R. W. 1990. *Sadat and After: Struggles for Egypt's Political Soul.* Cambridge, MA: Harvard University Press.

Bangura, Abdul Karim, ed. 2002. *Unpeaceful Metaphors*. San Diego, CA: Authors Choice Press.

Bangura, Abdul Karim, ed. 2004. *Islamic Sources of Peace*. Boston, MA: Pearson Publishing.

Bangura, Abdul Karim. 2003. Lecture on Islamic Concepts of Peace.

Bangura, Abdul Karim. 2003. *The Holy Qur'an and Contemporary Issues*. San Jose, CA: Writers Press.

Bangura, Abdul Karim. 2004. *Surah Al-Fatihah: A Linguistic Exploration of Its Meanings*. San Jose, CA: Writers Press.

Barber, Benjamin and Andrea Shultz. 1996. *Jihad vs. McWorld: How Globalism and Tribalism are Reshaping the World.* New York: Ballantine Books.

Barbour, Violet. January 1930. "Dutch and English Merchant Shipping in the Seventeenth Century." *The Economic History Review*. 2, 2:290.

Barks, Coleman. 1997. *The Essential Rumi*. New York, New York: HarperCollins Publishers.

Basgoz, Ilhan. 1981. The Life of Yunus Emre. In *Yunus Emre and His Mystical Poetry.* Bloomington, IN: Tulip Tree Publications.

Beattie, K. J. 2000. *Egypt During the Sadat Years*. New York: Palgrave.

Bergh, S. 1954. *Averroes' Tahafut Al-tahafut.* Oxford, England: Oxford University Press.

Bickerton, Ian. 2001. *A Concise History of the Arab-Israeli Conflict*. Upper Saddle River, NJ: Prentice Hall Publications.

Binder, Leonard. 1958. "The Problems of Islamic Political Thought in the Light of Recent Developments in Pakistan." *The Journal of Politics*. Southern Political Science

Association. Available: http://www.jstor.org/gifcvtdir/di000535/00223816/di976508/97 p0403i_1.1.gif?jstor.

Biographical information on Ibn Rushd. Available: http://www.ibnrushd.org/English/ biographicalinfoibnrushd.html

Black, Antony. 2001. *The History of Islamic Political Thought. From the Prophet to the Present.* New York. Routledge.

Botman, Selma. 1988. *The Rise of Egyptian Communism 1939–1970.* Syracuse, New York: Syracuse University Press.

Braverman, Harry. 1998. *Labor and Monopoly Capital: the degradation of work in the 20th Century*, New York: Monthly Review Press.

Breitman, George. 1965. *Malcolm X Speaks.* New York: Merit Publishers.

Brown, I. and R. Brown. 1995. "Approach to Rural Mass Poverty." In C. Legum and G. Mmari, eds. *Mwalimu: The Influence of Nyerere.* London, UK: Britain-Tanzania Society.

Brzezinski, Z. 2004. *The Choice.* New York: Basic Books.

Bukhari. n.d. *Sahih Al-Bukhari* (vols 1–9) (M.M. Khan, Trans. 1996). New Delhi, India: Dar us Salam. "bullionism." *Encyclopædia Britannica Online.* 2004. 18 Oct. 2004. Available: http://www.search.eb.com/eb/article?tocId=9018053.

Bulloch, John. n.d. "King Hussein: The Arab Century." *Arab Trends Magazine.*

Bullough, V. L. 1996. "Medieval Scholasticism and Averroism: The Implication of the Writings of Ibn Rushd to Western Science." In M. Wahba and M. Abousenna, eds. *Averroes and the Enlightenment.* Amherst, NY: Prometheus Books.

Burton, J. 1979. "Institutional Values and Human Needs." In *Deviance, Terrorism & War.* New York: St. Martin's Press.

Burton, J. 1993. "Conflict Resolution as a Political Philosophy." In D. Sandole and H. van der Merwe, eds. *Conflict Resolution Theory and Practice.* New York: Manchester University Press.

Byrne, Gerry. 2004, *Bolsheviks and Islam part 3: Islamic Communism, worker's liberty.* Available: www.workersliberty.org.

Cain, P. J., A. G. Hopkins. 1980. "The Political Economy of British Expansion Overseas, 1750–1914." *The Economic History Review* 33, 4.

Canadian Broadcasting Corporation. *Saudi Arabia's peace plan.* Available: http:// www.cbc.ca/printablestory.jsp. Center of Emerging Arabian Heritage. 1998. *Alfutuhat Almakiyah.* Beirut, Lebanon.

Capitalism.org. 2003. *Poverty* [Frequently Asked Questions]. Available: http://www.Capitalism.org.

Chaqueri, Cosroe. 2001. *Origins of Social Democracy in Modern Iran.* Seattle, WA: University of Washington Press.

Chejne, Anwar G. 1974. *Muslim Spain: Its History and Culture.* Minneapolis, MN: University of Minnesota Press.

Chengappa, Bidanda M. 2002. *Pakistan: Impact of Islamic Socialism,* Strategic Analysis, IDSA, Jannuary–March, xxvi, 1.

Chittick, William C. 2000. *Sufism: A Short Introduction.* Boston, MA: Oneworld Publications.

Chittick, William C. *Ibn al-'Arabi.* New York: State University of New York. Available: http://www.arches.uga.edu/~godlas/ibnarab.html.

Christman, H. M. 1988. *Qaddafi's Green Book: An Unauthorized Edition.* Buffalo, NY: Prometheus Books.

CIA World Fact Book: http://www.cia.gov/cia/publications/factbook.

Clark,Steve. 1992. *The Final Speeches of Malcolm X.* New York: Pathfinder Press.

Clough, Shepard B. 1968. *European Economic Histroy: the Economic Development of Western Civilization.* New York: McGraw Hill.

Coleman, D. C. 1980. "Mercantilism Revisited." *The Historical Journal.* 23, 4:781.

Collopy Michael et al. 2000. *Architects of Peace: Visions of Hope in Words and Images.* Novato, California: New World Library Press.

Comprehensive Development Framework of the Kyrgyz Republic to 2010. Akaev, A. (President of The Kyrgyz Republic). (2003–2005). *National Poverty Reduction Strategy (NPRS).* Available: (http://poverty.worldbank.org/files/Kyrgyz_PRSP.pdf). The Kyrgyz Republic: World Bank. Retrieved December 23, 2004, from World Bank.org Web site: http://poverty.worldbank.org/files/Kyrgyz_PRSP.pdf.

Constraints and Challenges in a Global Environment. The World Bank Group. Washington, DC: World Bank Publications.

Dallas, Roland. (1999). *King Hussein: A Life on the Edge.* New York: Fromm International.

Danow, M. (1999). A political survivor and a gentle champion of peace. Jewish Telegraphic Agency, 1. Retrieved March 4, 2003 from the World Wide Web: http://www.jewishsf.com/bk990212/idoakjtapolitical.htm.

Davis, Ralph. 1956. "Merchant Shipping in the Economy of the Late Seventeenth Century." *The Economic History Review* 9, 1:60.

Dawood, N. J., ed. and trans. 1983. *The Koran*. London, England: Penguin.

DeBlij, H. J. 1997. *Geography Realms, Regions and Concepts*. New York: John Wiley & Sons.

DeCaro, Louis. 1996. *On the Side of My People: A Religious Life of Malcolm X*. New York & London, England: New York University Press.

Djavadov, M. 2004. *Islamic State in Central Asia* [Article: 2 June 2003]. Available from Geocities.com Available: http://www.geocities.com/WestHollywood/Park/6443/CentralAsia/state.html.

Dominguez, R. 2001. *History of Islam: Islam Religious and Political Organization* from http://www.biblia.com/islam/history.

Doran, M. S. 2004. The Saudi Paradox. *Foreign Affairs 83,* 1:35–51.

Dougan, D. ed. 2004. *Arab and Muslim Countries Profiles In Contrast,* 2nd ed. Washington, DC: Brookings Institute Press.

Durant,Will. 1935. "The Story of Civilization. "New York: Simon and Schuster. East. *International Affairs.* 32.1.

Easwaran, E. 2002. *Nonviolent Soldier of Islam: Badshah Khan, A Man to Match His Mountains*. Tomales, CA: Nilgiri Press.

Eatwell, John. 1987. *The New Palgrave Dictionary of Economics*. New York: Stockton Press.

Egyptian Ministry of Foreign Affairs. n.d. President Sadat's Address to the Knesset, 20 November 1977. Accessed online at: http://www.mfa.gov.eg/getdoc.asp?id=47&cat=030103.

El-Khawas, M. A. 1986. *Qaddafi: His Ideology in Theory and Practice*. Brattleboro, VT: Amana.

El-Sadat, Anwar. 1978. *In Search of Identity: An Autobiography*. New York: Harper & Row.

El-Sadat, Anwar. 1984. *Those I Have Known*. New York: Continuum.

El-Soufi, Denise. Spring, 1996. Abbasids. *The Islamic Timeline*. Available: http://www.princeton.edu/~batke/itl/denise/abbasids.htm.

Elias, Robert and Jennifer Turpin, eds. 1994. *Rethinking Peace*. Boulder, CO: Lynne Rienner Publishers.

Emerson, R. W. 1841. Self-Reliance. In *Essays and English Traits*. Cambridge, MA: The Harvard Classics.

Encarta Encyclopedia, "Sir Allama Muhammad Iqbal."

Encyclopedia Britannica. 2004.

Entelis, John P. 1997. *Islam, Democracy, and the State in North Africa*. Indianapolis, IN: Indiana University Press.

Ernst, Carl W. 1997. *The Shambhala Guide to Sufism*. Boston, MA: Shambhala.

Fadiman, James and Frager Robert. 1997. *Essential Sufism*. New York: HarperCollins Publishers.

Fakhry, Majid. 2002. *Al-Farabi Founder of Islamic Neoplatonism*. Oxford, England: Oneworld Publications.

Fakhry, Majid. 1997. *A Short Introduction to Islamic Philosophy, Theology and Mysticism*. Oxford, England: Oneworld Publications.

Findly, Ellison B. April-June 1988. "The Capture of Maryam-uz-Zamani's Ship: Mughal Women and European Traders." *Journal of American Oriental Society* 108, 2:233.

Foreign Policy's Globalization Index: http://www.foreignpolicy.com/story/files/story2493.php.

Frederick, William H. and Robert L. Worden. 1993. *Indonesia: A Country Study*. Wahington, DC: Library of Congress.

Frederick, William H. and Robert Worden. 1993. "Indonesia: A Country Study." Washington, DC: Library of Congress.

Friedmann, J. 1986. "Regional Development in Industrialized Countries: Endogenous or Self-reliant?" In *Self-Reliant Development in Europe*. Hampshire, England: Gower Publishing Company Ltd.

Fukuyama, Francis. 1992. *The End of History and the Last Man*. New York: Free Press, Frank Cass and Co. Ltd.

Gallen, David. 1994. *A Malcolm X Reader: Perspectives on the Man and the Myths*. New York: Carroll & Graf Publishers, Inc.

Galston, Miriam. 1990. *Politics and Excellence. The Political Philosophy of Al-Farabi*. Princeton, NJ: Princeton University Press.

Galtung, Johan. 1980. "Self-Reliance: Concepts, Practice and Rationale." In *Self-Reliance: A Strategy for Development*. London, England: Villiers Publications Ltd.

Glyn, Andrew. 2001. *Social Democracy in Neoliberal Times.* New York: Oxford University Press.

Goldstone, Jack. January 1988. "East and West in the Seventeenth Century: Political Crises in Stuart England, Ottoman Turkey, and Ming China." *Comparative Studies in Society and History* 30, 1:112.

Goodwin, J. 1994. *Price of Honor.* New York: Penguin Group Publishing.

Gowers, Andrew. 1991. *Behind The Myth.* New York: Olive Branch Press.

Greaves, Richard L. 1990. *Civilizations of the World: The Human Adventure.* New York: Harper and Row Publishing.

Green, J. and C. Voyageur. 1999. "Globalization and Development at the Bottom." In *Feminists Doing Development.* New York: Zed Books Ltd.

Guichard, Pierre. 1994. "The Social History of Muslim Spain." In Salma Khadra Jayyusi, ed. *The Legacy of Muslim Spain.* Leiden, The Netherlands: E.J. Brill.

Gurnah, Abu. Abu Al-Hasan Al-Mawardi (Alboacen). Available: http://www.geocities.com/abu_gurnah/abualhasanalmawardi.html.

Habib, Ifran. March 1969. "Potentialities of Capitalistic Development in the Economy of Mughal India." *The Journal of Economic History* 29, 1:35.

Habib, O. 2004. "IMF Calls for Regulation to Help Develop Islamic Banking Sector." *The Daily Star.*

Haeri, S. 2002. "Religion: Reinterpreting the Text, Reinventing the Self." In *No Shame for the Sun.* Syracuse, NY: Syracuse University Press.

Halman, Talat. 1981. *Yunus Emre and His Mystical Poetry.* Bloomington, IN: Tulip Tree Publications.

Hamarneh, Sami Khalaf. c1983-c1984. *Health Sciences in Early Islam: Collected Papers*–2 vol. San Antonio, TX: Zahra Publications.

Hamarneh, Sami Khalaf and Glenn Sonnedecker. 1963. *A Pharmaceutical View of Abulcasis al-Zahrawi in Moorish Spain.* Leiden, The Netherlands: E. J. Brill.

Hamarneh, Dr. Sami Khalaf and Mrs. Nazha Tawfiq Hamarneh n.d. *The Physician-Surgeon Al-Zahrawi and the Natural Origins and Manufacture of Drugs.* http://www.islamset.com/isc/zahrawi/hamarneh.html.

Hammon, Robert. 1947. *The Philosophy of Al-Farabi And Its Influence on Medieval Thought.* New York. The Hobson Book Press.

Harder, R. J. 2000. *The Culture of Capitalism*. Available from Future Connections: http://www.futureconnections.com/capitaltext.htm.

Heckscher, Eli F. November 1936. "Revisions in Economic History: V. Mercantilism." *The Economic History Review* 7, 1:53.

Heikal, M. 1983. *Autumn of Fury: The Assassination of Sadat*. London, England: Andre Deutsch.

Heydemann, Steven. 1999. *Authoritarianism in Syria: Institutions and Social Conflict 1946–1970*. Ithaca, NY: Cornell University Press.

Hilal, Kashan. May 1977. "The New World Order and the Tempo of Militant Islam." *British Journal of Middle Eastern Studies* 24,1:15–24.

Hillenbrand, Robert. 1994. The Ornament of the World@ Medieval Córdoba as a cultural centre. In Salma Khadra Jayyusi, ed. *The Legacy of Muslim Spain*. Leiden, The Netherlands: E.J. Brill.

Hilton, Boyd. September 1979. "Peel: A Reappraisal." *The Historical Journal* 22, 3:591.

Hirtenstein, Stephan. 1990. *Muhyiddin Ibn 'Arabi: The Treasure of Compassion*. Available: http://www.ibnarabisociety.orgTreasureofCompassion.html. This article first appeared in *Beshara Magazine*, Issue 12, Autumn 1990, in celebration of the 750th anniversary of the Shaikh's death.

Hitti, P. 1970. *The Arabs: A Short History*. South Bend, IN: Regency/Gateway.

Hooker, M. B. 2003. *Indonesian Islam*. Honolulu, HI: University of Hawaii Press.

Hooker, R. 2003. *The Qur'an* from http://wsu.edu/~dee/ISLAM/QURAN.HTM.

Hosseinzadeh, Esmail. 1989. *Soviet Non-Capitalist Development. The Case of Nasser's Egypt*. New York: Praeger Publishers.

Hourani, G. F. 1987. Ibn Rushd. In Mircea Eliade, ed. *The Encyclopedia of Religion*. New York: MacMillan Publishing.

Hourani, G. F. 1976. *Averroes' On the Harmony of Religion and Philosophy*. London, England: Luzac.

Hoyt, Charles Alva. 1970. The Five Faces of Malcolm X. *Negro American Literature Forum*,4 107–112.

http://www.birthpsychology.com/messages/lithotomy/lithotomy.html.

http//www.hemophiliagalaxy.com/l_PATIENTS/topics/hist/hist05.html.

http://www.polybiblio.com/watbooks/2353.html.

http://www.eia.doe.gov/emeu/cabs/iran.html August 2004. *Iran.* Country Analysis Brief. Department of Energy.

http://www.eia.doe.gov/emeu/cabs/libya.html August 2004. *Libya.* Country Analysis Brief. Department of Energy.

http://www.mapquest.com/atlas/?region=libya *Libya.* World Atlas. MapQuest.

http://www.worldbank.org/cgibin/sendoff.cgi?page=%2Fdata%2Fcountrydata%2Faag%2Firnaag.pdf

http://www.worldbank.org/cgi-bin/sendoff.cgi?page=%2Fdata%2Fcountrydata%2Faag%2Flbyaag.pdf

http://www.worldbank.org/cgi-bin/sendoff.cgi?page=%2Fdata%2Fcountrydata%2Faag%2Ftzaaag.pdf

http://www.nationmaster.com

http://www.parstimes.com

Hudson, M. 1980. "Islam and Political Development." In J. Esposito, ed. *Islam and Development: Religion and Sociopolitical Change.* New York: Syracuse University Press.

Human Governance for Human Security and Sustainable Human Development. *On the PARAGON (Participatory Action Research to Advance Governance Options and Networks) section of the United Nations Development Program website.* http://www.undp-paragon.org.

Human Rights Watch. 2004. Turkey: Progress on Human Rights Key to EU Bid [Published Article: Brussels, October 4]. Available from Human Rights Watch: http://hrw.org/english/docs/2004/10/04/turkey9434_txt.htm.

Human Rights Watch. July 2004. *Bad Dreams: Exploitation and Abuse of Migrant Workers in Saudi Arabia* 16, 5E:1–54). New York: Human Rights Watch.

Huntington, Samuel. 1996. *Clash of Civilizations.* New York: Simon and Schuster.

Huntington, Samuel. 1994. *The Clash of Civilizations and the Remaking of World Order.* New York: Touchstone.

Huntington, Samuel. 1993. "The Clash of Civilizations?" *Foreign Affairs* 72, 3:22–50.

Hussain, A. 1983. *The Islamic Movement in Iran, Islamic Movement in Egypt, Pakistan and Iran.* New York: Mansell Publishing Limited.

Hussain, Arif. 1966. *Pakistan its ideology and foreign Policy.* London: Frank Cass Ltd.

Hussain, F. 1984. *Muslim Women.* Sydney, Australia: Croom Helm Australia Pty. Ltd.

I Doi, A. R. 1984. *Shariah: The Islamic Law.* Zaria, Nigeria: Ahmado Bello University.

Ibn Kathir. 2000. *Tafsir Ibn Kathir:Tafseer Ibn Katheer*. Houston, Texas: Darussalam Publications.

Ibn Rushd. Available: http://www.muslimphilosophy.com/ei/ei-ir.html.

Ibrahim, Ayman Adel. Abu Al-Hasan Al-Mawardi. Available: http://ahram.org/islamic/almawardi.htm.

Imad-ad-Dean, A. May 1996. Islam, Market Economy and the Rule of Law [Lecture Transcript]. Available from Islam For Today: http://www.islamfortoday.com/imad01.htm.

Imad-al-Dean, A. 1993. Riba and Interest: Definitions and Implications [Lecture Transcript]. Available from Minaret of Freedom: http://www.minaret.org/*riba*.htm.

Inalcik, Halil. March 1969. "Capital Formation in the Ottoman Empire." *The Journal of Economic History* 29, 1:97–101.

Inayatullah, Sohail. 2002. "Pedagogy, Culture and Future Studies." In J. A. Dator, ed. *Advancing Futures: future studies in higher education*. Westport, CT: Prager, and Indiana: Indiana University Press.

India: A Country Study. 1995. Washington, D.C.: Library of Congress.

International Crisis Group. June 30, 2003. *Radical Islam in Central Asia: Responding to Hizb Ut-Tahrir* (ICG Asia Report No 58 Osh/Brussels, p. 37). Brussels, Belgium: International Crisis Group.

Iqbal, Javid, ed. 1961. *Stray Reflections: A Note-Book of Allama Iqbal.* Lahore, Pakistan: Sh. Ghulam Ali & Sons.

Irwin, Douglas A. 1991. "Mercantilism as Strategic Trade Policy: The Anglo-Dutch Rivalry for the East India Trade." *Journal of Political Economy* 99,6:1296.

Islamic Philosophy Online, *Al-Farabi*. hhttp://www.muslimphilosophy.com/ip/rep/H021.htm.

Ismael, Tareq and El-Sa'id, Rifa'at. 1990. *The Communist Movement in Egypt 1920–1988.* Syracuse, NY: Syracuse University Press.

Issawi, Charles. 1987. *An Arab Philosopher of History: Ibn Khaldun*. Princeton, NJ: Darwin Press.

Issawi, Charles. October 1980. "Europe, the Middle East and the Shift in Power: Reflections on a Theme by Marshall Hodgson." *Comparative Studies in Society and History* 22, 4:503.

Issawi, Charles. 1956. *Economic and Social Foundations of Democracy in the Middle East.* New York: Columbia University Press.

Jawed, Nasim A. 1999. *Islam's Political Culture Religion and Politics in Predivided Pakistan*. Austin, TX: University of Texas Press.

Jewish Virtual Library. King Hussein bin Talal (1935–1999). Retrieved March 4, 2003 from the World Wide Web: http://www.usisrael.org/jsource/biography/Hussein.html.

Kahf, M. 2001. *Live Fatwa* [Financial Fatwa Session]. Available from Islam Online, http://www.islamonline.net/livefatwa/english/Browse.asp?hGuestID=006037.

Kalim Bahadur. 1977. *Jama'at-i-Islami of Pakistan,* New Delhi, India: Chetna Publications.

Kaplan, Mehmet. 1981. Humanism and Yunus Emre. In *Yunus Emre and His Mystical Poetry.* Bloomington, IN: Tulip Tree Publications.

Kaplan, Robert D. 2001. *Soldiers of God.* New York: Vintage Books.

Kaplan, Robert. February 1994. "The Coming Anarchy." *The Atlantic Monthly* 44–76.

Kateb, G. 1995. *Emerson and Self-Reliance.* New York: Rowman & Littlefield Publishers, Inc.

Kesselman, M. 1982. *Prospects for Democratic Socialism in Advanced Capitalism: Class.* New York: Houghton Mifflin.

Kessler, P. L. 1999. Middle East Kingdoms. *Kessler Associates.* Available: http://homepages.tesco.net/~plk33/plk33/HistoryFiles.htm.

Khan, Hazrat Inayat.1999. *The Heart of Sufism.* Boston, MA: Shambhala Publications.

Khan, Quamaruddin. 1983. *Al-Mawardi's Theory of the State.* Lahore, Pakistan: Islamic Book Foundation.

Kienle, Eberhard. 1995. *Arab Unity Schemes Revisited: Interest, Identity, and Policy in the Middle East.* London: I.B. Tauris.

Kiernan, V. G., trans. 1947. *Poems from Iqbal.* Bombay, India: Commercial Printing Press.

Kirchheimer, Otto and Franz Neumann. 1987. *Social Democracy and the Rule of Law.* New York: Routledge.

Kogan, B. 1985. *Averroes and the Metaphysics of Causation.* Albany, NY: State University of New York.

Komba, D. 1995. "Contribution to Rural Development: Ujamaa and Villagisation." In C. Legum and G. Mmari, eds. *Mwalimu: The Influence of Nyerere.* Trenton, NJ: Africa World Press.

Kostas, Ahmed. 2000. *Nibras Almureed Ila Tareeq Altawhedd.* Casablanca, Morocco: Casablanca Press.

Kuran, Timur. June 2003. "The Islamic Commercial Crisis: Institutional Roots of Economic Underdevelopment in the Middle East." *The Journal of Economic History* 63, 2:414.

Kurtz, P. 1996. Intellectual freedom, rationality and Enlightenment: The contribution of Averroes. In M. Wahba and M. Abousenna, eds. *Averroes and the Enlightenment.* Amherst, NY: Promethens Books.

Labib, Subhi Y. March 1969. "Capitalism in Medieval Islam." *The Journal of Economic History* 29, 1:86.

Lacoste, Yves. 1984. *Ibn Khaldun: The Birth of History and The Past of the Third World.* London, England: Verso.

LaHaye, Laura. 2004. "Mercantilism." *The Concise Encyclopedia of Economics.* Liberty Fund. Available: http://www.econlib.org/library/Enc/Mercantilism.html.

Leaman, O. 1996. Averroes and the West. In M. Wahba and M. Abousenna, eds. *Averroes and the Enlightenment.* Amherst, NY: Promethens Book.

Leon Hadar. Spring 1993. "What Green Peril?" *Foreign Affairs* 27.

Lerner, G. 1986. The Creation of Patriarchy. In *The Creation of Patriarchy.* Oxford: Oxford University Press.

Lewis, Bernard. 2003. *The Crisis of Islam.* New York: Modern Library.

Lewis, Bernard. September 1990. "The Roots of Muslim Rage." *The Atlantic Monthly* 266, 3:47–60.

Lewis, Bernard. 1988. *The Political Language of Islam.* Chicago: University of Chicago Press.

Lewis, Franklin D. 2000.*Rumi. Past and Present, East and West: The Life, Teaching and Poetry of Jalal al-Din Rumi.* Boston, Massachusetts: Oneworld Publications.

Library of Congress, Federal Research Division Country Studies. Accessed December 19, 2004. Available: http://lcweb2.loc.gov/frd/cs.

Library of Congress: country studies: http://lcweb2.loc.gov/frd/cs.

Lippman, T. W. 1989. *Egypt After Nasser: Sadat, Peace, and the Mirage of Prosperity.* New York: Paragon.

Lipset, Seymour Martin. 1995. *Encyclopedia of Democracy.* Washington, DC: Congressional Quarterly Press.

Lipson, E. 1959. *Economic History of England.* New York: Barnes.

MacClintock, S. 1976. Averroes In P. Edwards, ed. *The Encyclopedia of Philosophy.* New York: The Macmillan Company & The Free Press.

Mackey, S. 1992. *Passion and Politics: The Turbulent World of the Arabs.* New York: Dutton.

Madigan, T. J. 1996. "Averroes and the Inquiry: The Need for Enlightened Community." In M. Wahba and M. Abousenna, eds. *Averroes and the Enlightenment.* Amherst, NY: Prometheus Books.

Mahdi, Muhsin S. 2001. *Al-Farabi and The Foundation of Islamic Political Philosophy.* Chicago, IL: The University of Chicago Press.

Malcolm X and Alex Haley. 1964. *The Autobiography of Malcolm X.* New York: Grove Press, Inc.

Malek, M.A. 2000. *Implications for the Study of a Hadith.* Retrieved March 4, 2003 from http://members.aol.com/MAmalek2/qbook10.htm.

Malhauf, M.F. 1987. "The Jamahriya Model in Planning, with Some Indications of Social and Economic Development and Change in Libyan Arab Society." In B. Khader and B. El-Wifati, eds. *The Economic Development of Libya.* London, UK: Croom Helm.

Malkawi, M. March 28, 2002. *Economic Justice: Islam Versus Capitalism* [Lecture Transcript]. Available: http://www.internetmuslim.com/economic, http://www.internet-muslim.com/?economic.

Mannan, M. A. 1987. *Islamic Economics: Theory and Practice* (Rev. ed.). Boulder, CO: Westview Press.

Mansfield, Peter. 1992. *A History of the Middle East.* New York: Penguin.

Mardin, Serif. June 1969. "Power, Civil Society and Culture in the Ottoman Empire." *Comparative Studies in Society and History* 11, 3:262.

Marín, Manuela. 1994. Muslim religious practices in Al-Andalus (2nd/8th-4th/10th Centuries). In Salma Khadra Jayyusi, ed. *The Legacy of Muslim Spain.* Leiden, The Netherlands: E.J. Brill.

Marks, Harry J. 1939. *The Sources of Reformism in the Social Democratic of Germany.* New York: Cambridge University Press.

Martell, Luke. 2001. *Social Democracy: Global and National Perspectives.* New York: Palgrave Macmillan.

Marvin, Chris. 1995–2000. Abu Al-Hasan Al-Mawardi: Iranian, Muslim Scholar. *The Window: Philosophy on the Internet*. Available: http://www.trincoll.edu/depts/phil/philo/phils/muslim/mawardi.html.

Marx, Karl and Friedrich Engels. 1992. *Communist Manifesto: a Modern Edition*. Oxford; New York: Oxford University Press.

Mawardi (Al-), Abu Al-Hasan. Excerpt from *Al-Ahkam as-Sultaniyyah* (Dr. Asadullah Yate, translator). Available: http://www.bysiness.co.uk/excerpts/excerptahkam.htm.

Mazrui, Ali. 1972. *Cultural Engineering and National Building in East Africa*. Evanston, IL: Northwestern University Press.

McDonald, D. and E. N. Sahle, eds. 2002. *The Legacies of Julius Nyerere: Influences of Development Discourse and Practice in Africa*. Trenton, NJ: Africa World Press.

Merriman, John M. 1996. *A History of Modern Europe: from the Renaissance to the Present*. New York: W.W. Norton.

Metz, Helen Chapin. 1989. *Iran: A Country Study*. Washington, DC: Government Printing Office.

Meyer, A. E. 1995. *Islam & Human Rights: Traditions and Politics*. Boulder, CO: Westview Press.

More information about Ibn Khaldun can be found at the Web site for Ibn Khaldun: http://www.witness-pioneer.org.

Muller, A., ed. 1999. *Global Capitalism, Liberation Theology and the Social Sciences*. Huntington, NY: Nova Science Publishers.

Muslim (n.d/Circa 1000 AD). *Sahih Muslim*, vol 1. (A.H Siddiqi, Trans.1989). Lahore, Pakistan: Muhammad Ashraf Publishers and Booksellers.

Naimi, A. 2004. "Saudi Arabia: Economic, Oil, And Mineral Restructuring and Reforms" (Saudi-U.S. Relations Information Service, Trans.). *Middle East Economic Survey, December*.

Naples Daily News. *Analysis: Is Sharon's goal peace?* Available: http://www.naplesnews.com/03/02/perspectives.

Naqvi, S. 1994. *Islam, Economics, and Society*. New York, NY: Kegan Paul International. New York: Palgrave Publishers Ltd.

Nasser, Seyyed Husein. 1968. *Three Muslim Sages*. New York: Caravan Press.

Nicholson, Reynold A. 1950. *Rumi: Poet and Mystic*. London: Bradford and Dickens.

Nicholson, Reynold A. 1923. "A Literary History of the Arabs." In Siddiqui, A. H. *Life of Muhammad (PBUH).* London: Kazi Publications Incorporated.

Nijib, Ghadbian. 1997. *Democratization and the Islamist Challenge in the Arab World.* Boulder, CO: Westview.

Nimtz, A. H. 1980. *Islam and Politics in East Africa: The Sufi Order in Tanzania.* Minneapolis, MN: University of Minnesota Press.

Nobel, 2002 http://nobelprize.org/nobel_prizes/peace/laureates/1994/arafat-lecture.html

Noble Qur'an, the. Translation by Dr. Muhammad Taqi-ud-Din al-Hilali and Dr. Muhammad Muhsin Khan. Medina, Saudi Arabia: King Fahd Complex for the Printing of the Holy Qur'an.

Norberg, J. 2004. *In Defense of Global Capitalism* [Online PDF]. Available from Johan Norberg.net: http.//johannorberg.net/pdfs/chapter1.pdf.

Obituary: Mahbub ul-Haq. *The Economist.* London: 7-25-98, *On the Proquest Electronic Database*. Available: http://www.proquest.umi.com.

Objectives. *On the Mahbub ul-Haq Human Development Center Web Site.* http://undp.un.org.pk/hdc/Objectives.

O'Brien, Patrick. 1966. *The Revolution in Egypt's Economic System. From Private Enterprise to Socialism 1952–1965.* London: Oxford University Press.

Official Website of Her Majesty Queen Noor. Available: http://www.kinghusseinfoundation.org/index.php?pager=end&task=view&type=content&pageid=61.

Official Website of His Majesty King Abdullah II. Available: http://www.kingabdullah.jo/homepage.php.

Olson, Robert. 1982. *The Ba'th and Syria, 1947 to 1982: The Evolution of Ideology, Party, and State.* Princeton, New Jersey: The Kingston Press Inc.

Omori, C.K. 1995. "The Management of Tribal and Religious Diversity." *In C.* Legum and G. Mmari, eds. *Mwalimu: The Influence of Nyerere.* Trenton, NJ: Africa World Press.

Packard, Laurence Bradford. May 1923. "International Rivalry and Free Trade Origins, 1660–78." *The Quarterly Journal of Economics* 37, 3:423.

Pakistan-Background to Partition. *On the Encyclopedia Britannica Online website. Updated 2003, http://search.eb.com/ article?eu=115031.*

Palmer, R. R. 1984. *A History of the Modern World.* 6th Edition. New York:Knopf.

Parmar, S. L. 1975. "Self-Reliant Development in an 'Interdependent' World." In *Beyond Dependency*. Washington, DC: Overseas Development Council.

Personalities in Islam, *Abu Nasr Muhammad Al-Farabi.* Available: http://www.islamic-paths.org/Home/English/Personalities/Content/Farabi.htm.

Phillips, D. 2004. "Turkey's Dreams of Accession." *Foreign Affairs 83,* 5:86–98.

Pierson, Christopher. 2001. *Hard Choices Social Democracy in the 21st Century*. New York: Malden.

Pratt, C. 1976. *The critical phase in Tanzania 1945–1968: Nyerere and the Emergence of a Socialist Strategy*. New York: Cambridge University Press.

Queen Noor of Jordan: Biography. Available: http://www.biography.com/articles/Queen-Noor-of-Jordan-9542217.

Rafi Raza. 1997. *Zulfikar Ai Bhutto and Pakistan, 1967–77*. Karachi, Pakistan: Oxford University Press.

Rahnema, Ali. 2000, *An Islamic Utopia.* New York and London: I.B. Tauris & Co Ltd.

Raslon, Y. F. 1997. Ibn Rushd. Philosopher and Theologian. Available: http://www.aljadid.com/classics/0320raslan.html.

Razavi, H. and F. Vakil. 1984. *The Political Environment of Economic Planning in Iran, 1971–1983: From Monarchy to Islamic Republic.* Boulder, CO: Westview Press, Inc.

Republic of Turkey. Ministry of Foreign Affairs. (2003, March). *Yunus Emre's Humanism.* Retrieved March 15, 2003, from http://www.mfa.gov.tr/grupe/eg/eg23/default.htm.

Reuters AlterNet country profile. Available: http://www.alertnet.org/thefacts/country-profiles/220758.htm?v=details#cp_poli_profile.

Rich, Paul. Spring 2003. "Mercantilism and the Future: The Future Lives of an Old Philosophy." *International Journal of Theory and Behavior.* 6, 1:131.

Richards, J.F. April 1981. "Mughal State Finance and the Premodern World Economy." *Comparative Studies in Society and History* 23, 2:292.

Roberts, David. 1987. *The Ba'th and the Creation of Modern Syria*. London: Croom Helm.

Rodinson, Maxim. 1981, *Marxism and the Muslim World*, New York, New York. Monthly Review Press.

Rosser, J. Barkley and V. Marina. 1999. "The New traditional Ecnomy: A New Perspective for Comparative Economics." *International Journal of Social Economics* 26, 6.

Rourke, John T. and Mark A. Boyer. 1988. *World Politics: International Politics on the World Stage.* Brief. 2nd ed. New York: Dushkin/McGraw-Hill.

Rubinstein, Danny. 1995. *The Mystery of Arafat.* South Royalton, VT: Steerforth Press.

Ruthven, Malise. 2000. *Islam in the World.* New York: Oxford University Press.

Ryan, Curtis R. 2002. *Jordan in Transition: From Hussein to Abdullah.* London, England: Lynne Riener Publishers.

Sabbagh, Isa Khalil. 1985. *"As the Arabs Say..." Volume II: Arabic Quotations Recalled and Interpreted.* Washington, DC: Sabbagh Management Corporation.

Sadat, C. 1985. *My Father and I.* New York, New York: Macmillan.

Sadowski, Yahya. 1998. *The Myth of Global Chaos.* Washington DC: Brookings Institution Press.

Saeed, J. 1994. Islam and Modernization. In *Islam and Modernization.* Westport, CT: Praeger.

Sagiv, David. 1995. *Fundamentalism and Intellectuals in Egypt.* Portland, OR: Portland State University Press.

Said, Abdul Aziz, ed. 2003. *Cultural Diversity and Islam.* Lanham, MD: University Press of America.

Said, Abdul Aziz and Abdul Karim Bangura. 2004. *The World of Islam: Country by Country Profiles.* Boston, MA: Pearson Publishing.

Said, Abdul Aziz. 2000. "Memorandum: To the Next President." *Middle East Insight* November-December Issue, p. 58.

Said, Abdul Aziz et al., eds. 2001. Peace *and Conflict Resolution in Islam: Precept and Practice.* Lanham, MD: University Press of America.

Said, Abdul Aziz, and Charles O. Lerch, Jr. 1970. *Concepts of International Politics.* Englewood Cliffs, N J: Prentice-Hall Press.

Said, Abdul Aziz. 1978. *Human Rights and World Order.* New York: Praeger Publishers.

Said, Abdul Aziz, and Collier, Daniel. 1971. *Revolutionism.* Boston, MA: Allyn and Bacon, Inc.

Salibi, Kamal. 1993. *The Modern History of Jordan.* New York: St. Martin's Press.

Salloum, H. Averroes-The Great Muslim Philosopher: Who planted the seeds of the European Renaissance. Available: http://www.alhewar.org/september%2011/habib_sa-loum-averroes.htm.

Salloum, H. 1997. Ibn Rushd. The Great Muslim Philosopher who planted the seeds of the European Renaissence. Available: http://www.aljadid.com/classics/0422salloum.html.

Salmi, Ralph H., Cesar Adib Majul, and George K. Tanham. 1998. *Islam and Conflict Resolution: Theories and Practices*. Lanham, MD: University Press of America.

Sawers, Larry. May 1992. "The Navigation Acts Revisited." *Economic History Review* xl, 2:263.

Sayigh, Y. A. 1991. "What is Self-reliant Development?" In *Elusive Development: From Dependence to Self-Reliance in the Arab Region*. New York: Routledge.

Schimmel, Anne Marie. 1992. *I am Wind, You are Fire: The Life and Work of Rumi*. Boston, MA: Shambhala Publications.

Schimmel, Anne Marie. 1975. *Mystical Dimensions of Islam*. Chapel Hill, NC: University of North Carolina Press.

Schneider, Howard. June 19, 1999. Queen Noor, Standing Alone. *Washington Post Foreign Service*; p.C01.

Schuyler, Robert Livingston. September 1922. "The Rise of Anti-Imperialism in England." *Political Science Quarterly* 37, 3.

Schwedler, Jillian. 2001. "Islamic Identity: Myth, Menace, or Mobilizer?" *SAIS Review* 21, 2.

Sedgwick, Mark J. 2000. *Sufism: The Essentials*. Cairo, Egypt: American University in Cairo Press.

Sen, G. and C. Grown. 1987. "Gender and Class in Development Experience." In *Development Crisis, and Alternative Visions*. New York: Monthly Review Press.

Seyyid Hossein Nasr. 1997. *Metaphysical Roots of Tolerance and Intolerance: An Islamic Interpretation*. Albany, NY: State University of New York Press.

Shadid, Anthony. 1997. *Marxism makes way for Islam*, Broadcasted on BIC. Available: News, http://www.iol.ie/afifi/BICNews/Islam.

Shanti Nair. 1997. *Islam in Malaysian Foreign Policy*. London: Routledge.

Sharif, M. M. 1983. Foreword to *Al-Mawardi's Theory of the State*, by Quamaruddin Khan. Lahore, Pakistan: Islamic Book Foundation.

Sherbaz, Khan Mazari. 1999. *Journey to Disillusionment*. Karachi, Pakistan: Oxford University Press.

Sherbiny, Naiem. Obituary: Mahbub ul-Haq: Champion of the Poor. *Civil Society: Democratization in the Arab World. Accessed on the Ibn Khaldun Center website: December 1998*. Available: http://www.ibnkhaldun.org.

Simons, G. 1993. *Libya: The Struggle for Survival.* New York: St. Martin's Press.

Singh, Iqbal. 1997. *The Ardent Pilgrim: The Life and Work of Mohammed Iqbal.* Delhi, India: Oxford University Press.

Sisk, Timothy D. 1992. *Islam and Democracy, Religion, Politics, and Power in the Middle East.* Washington, DC: United States Institute of Peace Press.

Smith, Grace Martin. 1993. *The Poetry of Yunus Emre, A Turkish Sufi Poet.* Los Angeles, CA: University of California Press.

Smith, Margaret. 1954. *The Sufi Path of Love.* London, England: Luzac & Company.

Smock, David R. 1995. *Perspectives on Pacifism.* Washington, DC: United States Institute of Peace Press.

Social Entrepreneurs and Globalization.2003. Muhammad Yunus, Banker to the Poor. Available: http://www.aworldconnected.org/article.php/378.html.

Sonar Bangla. What is Sonar Bangla? Retrieved April 28, 2003. Available: http://www.qmw.ac.uk/~surfwave/projects/amena/p9.html

South Asia Regional Office. *On The United Nations Development Fund for Women website.* http://www.unifem.org.in.

Sparrow, Gerald. 1960. *Hussein of Jordan.* London, England: George G. Harrap & Co. Ltd.

Spink M. S. and G. L. Lewis. 1973. *On Surgery and Instruments,* A Definitive Edition of the Arabic text with English Translation and Commentary. Los Angeles, CA: University of California Press.

Stearns, Peter N. 2001. *The Encyclopedia of European Social History from 1350–2000.* New York: Scribner.

Stein, K. 1999. *Heroic Diplomacy: Sadat, Kissinger, Carter, Begin, and the Quest for Arab-Israeli Peace.* New York: Routledge.

Stephen, C. 2000. [Interview with Founder of Grameen Bank, Muhammad Yunus]. *State of World Forum,* 12–16.

Stokes, B. 1978. *Local Responses to Global Problems: A Key to Meeting Basic Human Needs.* Washington, DC: Worldwatch Institute.

Subrahmanyam, Sanjay. October 1995. "Of *Imarat* and *Tijarat*: Asian Merchants and State Power in the Western Indian Ocean, 1400 to 1750." *Comparative Studies in Society and History* 37, 4:754.

Taylor, Keith, ed. 1975. *Henri Saint-Simon (1760–1825): Selected Writings on Science, Industry and Social Organization*, London: Croom Helm.

The Holy *Qur'an.*

The Islamic Development Bank. 2004. *Islamic Economics Cooperation and Development Division (IECD).* Available from The Islamic Development Bank–English Home Page: http://www.irti.org/?IECD_ma.htm.

The Islamic Development Bank. 2004. *The IDB in brief* [Purpose, Function, and Membership]. Available from Islamic Development Bank. English Homepage: http:// www.isdb.org/english_docs/ idb_home/backgrnd.htm.

The Journal of Modern History. 1890–1914. 11, 3.

"The Letter of Br. Malik Shabazz to the Director of Islamic Center in Geneva, Switzerland" Dr. Said Ramadan. (January 11, 1965).Beyond Malcolm. The Message International. Available: http://www.messageonline.org/malcolmx/cover6.htm.

Trimingham, John Spencer. 1964. *Islam in East Africa.* Aberdeen, Great Britain: Oxford University Press.

United States Department of State. *Middle East Quartet Statements.* Available: http:// www.state.gov/p/nea.

Urvoy, D. 1991. *Ibn Rushd.* London, England: Routledge.

Usmani, M. T. 2004. *Islamic Finance* [Musharakah & Mudarabah]. Available from Islamic Finance: http://www.darululoomkhi.edu.pk/?fiqh/?islamicfinance/?limitedliability.html.

Viotti, Paul R. and Mark Kauppi. 1997. "International Relations and World Politics: Security, Economy and Identity." Upper Saddle River, NJ: Prentice-Hall, Inc.

Voll, John Obert. 1994. *Islam Continuity and Change in the Modern World.* Seattle, WA: University of Washington Press.

Washington Times. "Crown Prince Abdullah: A Leader of Global Vision." Available: http://www.washtimes.com

Waterbury, John. 1983. *The Egypt of Nasser and Sadat: The Political Economy of Two Regimes.* Princeton, NJ: Princeton University.

Weaver, G. 2000. "Contrasting and Comparing Cultures." In G. Weaver, ed. *Culture, Communication and Conflict.* Rev. ed., Vol. 2. Boston, MA: Pearson Publishing.

Weiss, A. M. 1998. "The Slow Yet Steady Path to Women's Empowerment in Pakistan." *Islam, Gender & Social Change.* Oxford: Oxford University Press.

Weiss, H., ed. 2002. *Social Welfare In Muslim Societies In Africa.* Stockholm, Sweden: Elanders Gotab.

Wines, Leslie. 2000. *Rumi: A Spiritual Biography.* New York: The Crossroad Publishing Company.

Wright, Robin. 1996. "Two Visions of Reformation." *Journal of Democracy* 7, 2:64–75.

Yom, Sean L. 2002. *Islam and Globalization: Secularism, Religion and Radicalism. Essays on the Formation of the Human Character (1816).* Available: http://www.marxists.org/reference/ subject/economics/owen.

Zaharna, R. S. Bridging Cultural Differences: *American Public Relations Practices & Arab Communication Patterns.* Available: http://academic2.american.edu/~zaharna/arab-comm.htm.

Zahoor, A. Abul-Waleed Muhammad Ibn Rushd Averroes: The Great Commentator Available: http://www.cyberistan.org/islamic/rushd.html.

ABOUT THE AUTHOR

Abdul Karim Bangura is Professor of Research Methodology and Political Science at Howard University and Researcher-In-Residence on Abrahamic Connections and Peace Studies at the Center for Global Peace at American University in Washington, DC. He holds a PhD in Political Science, a PhD in Development Economics, a PhD in Linguistics, and a PhD in Computer Science. He is the author of 61 books and approximately 500 scholarly articles. He is the winner of numerous teaching and other scholarly and community service awards. He is a member of many scholarly organizations and a former President and then United Nations Ambassador of the Association of Third World Studies. He is fluent in a dozen African and six European languages, and is studying to strengthen his proficiency in Arabic, Hebrew, and Hieroglyphics.

9 781609 278588

Printed by Libri Plureos GmbH in Hamburg,
Germany